AF817304

"Our Jewish risen Lord and Savior Jesus Christ, in John 8:32 (KJV) said, 'And ye shall know the truth, and the truth shall make you free.' This great, amazing, and outstanding book will 'make you free.' Free to comprehend and heal what the great Swedish economist Gunnar Myrdal called an 'American dilemma.' Free to learn why former President Donald Trump and others are given white American affirmative action and President Barack Obama was criticized for wearing a tan suit. When you open this book, you will not be able to put it down. This book is a major contribution to the fact that there is One Race and that is the Human Race. It is a reminder that all people on this planet have a right to 'Life, Liberty, and the pursuit of Happiness.' This book will set new and old generations free."—*Rev. Prof. JH Scott III, Founding Pastor, JSFLJ Ministries, Inc., Prof. of Business/Business Pre-Law Advisor, New Haven, Connecticut*

"One of the barriers to overcoming the racial divide that persists in contemporary times is the pervasive belief among many in society that yes, there was racial injustice in the past, but that was long ago, and therefore they have no responsibility for, or role in, any remedies for that injustice today. This kind of thinking fuels much of the resentment toward affirmative action by whites who feel they are being unfairly targeted by 'reverse discrimination,' or who see no need for society to address inequities of the past. One of the major accomplishments of this book is that by providing the historical thread that binds many of the legal barriers imposed by society to give advantage to some and deny advantage to others, we find a continuing trail that leads to current societal outcomes."—*The Late Oliver Hill Jr. (from the Preface)*

"This study offers a splendid exposition of the muddles of white American affirmative action—as Professor Hill notes in his arresting Preface, the book is constructive, and instructive, cultivating 'the sense that in this long history of racial (and gender) discrimination in this country, we are all inextricably bound together, and that we all have a part to play in coming up with solutions'—this for South Africans, no less than for Americans."—*Edwin Cameron, Chancellor of Stellenbosch University and Retired Justice South African Constitutional Court*

"The book is a comprehensive documentation of the true history and practices of one of the worst forms of wicked and unfair treatment of human beings by fellow human beings for economic power and domination under the guise of the color of the human race that has ever occurred in the history the world, which lasted for about 400 years. For the proper understanding of the structure of the American society, from economic to social order and the governance system, this book is a must read for all."—*Professor Kwame Frimpong, Founding Dean of GIMPA Law School (Accra, Ghana); Founding Dean of UPSA Faculty of Law (Accra, Ghana)*

"*No Clue*, by Jonathan Stubbs and Oliver Hill, is an ambitious, comprehensive, yet compact book that demonstrates clearly the huge economic, social, and educational advantages white people have created for themselves through the law throughout American history. As the authors show, these advantages continue into the present, despite some small progress in small areas. From the colonies to the Constitution to the present, American law has been written almost entirely by white men mostly for their own benefit. Slave codes legalized the forced, unpaid labor of enslaved persons, and violence against them if they sought escape into freedom. Law facilitated the theft of native lands and their redistribution to white people. Racist administration of New Deal–era law resulted in much of today's racial wealth gap.

“The authors make excellent use of legal history to demonstrate these and many more examples of legal preferences for whites that have built the racial disparities that we observe today. Despite all the evidence, most white Americans have no clue about how law and power have been used to create their well-being at the expense of others. For these reasons, the authors have written this excellent book. We need this book to correct the record and to provide an evidentiary basis for why affirmative action is as necessary today as it has ever been. The authors write with hope and optimism that the story they tell will help others understand the need for remedial action in response to white racism.”—*Juan F. Perea, Curt and Linda Rodin Professor of Law and Social Justice, Loyola University Chicago School of Law*

“Dr. Stubbs’ work is a masterpiece exposing the bias in our laws and Constitution in favor of privileged white males. He gives a detailed account of the formation of our laws and the biased interpretation throughout the centuries.

“Most importantly, Dr. Stubbs lays out the corrective action needed to create a free and just society for all people by retelling history from all perspectives and uniting our society in love.”—*Rev. Dr. Emanuel C. Harris*

# Jonathan Kenneth Stubbs

JONATHAN K. STUBBS was born in Gloucester, Virginia, two years before *Brown v. Board of Education* heralding the death knell of legalized apartheid in America. The son of the late Deacon Calvin K. Stubbs and the late Mrs. Edith H. Stubbs, Stubbs graduated from the public schools of Gloucester, Virginia, and then Haverford College in Haverford, Pennsylvania. He earned law degrees from Oxford University (England), Yale Law School, and Harvard Law School. He is licensed to practice law in Pennsylvania and Virginia.

Stubbs also received a Master of Theological Studies Degree from Harvard Divinity School. Since 1984, Stubbs has served as an associate minister at Bethel Baptist Church, Sassafras, Virginia. He edited *The Big Bang,* Brown v. Board of Education *and Beyond: The autobiography of Oliver W. Hill, Sr.* published originally in 2000 by 4-G Publishers, and edited the 100th Birthday Edition of Oliver Hill's Autobiography published in 2007 by Granthouse Publishers.

Stubbs is a prostate cancer overcomer and shares his experiences in a book entitled *Out of the Boat: Trusting God in the Midst of Life's Storms* (Granthouse and Empire

Publishers 2013). Stubbs served as co-editor (with Danielle Wingfield-Smith) of *The Memoirs of Henry L. Marsh, III: Civil Rights Champion, Public Servant and Lawyer* by Henry L. Marsh III (Granthouse Publishers 2018).

Stubbs has published articles on human rights, jurisprudence, lawyers' professional ethics, constitutional law, criminal procedure, and on the interrelationships between race, religion, and the law. He is also a contributor to an electronic book by Pamela Hamilton-Stubbs, M.D., entitled *Teen Drug Abuse How to Spot the Early Warning Signs: A Parent Resource Guide.*

Since 1988, Stubbs has taught law at the University of Richmond. He has served as a visiting law professor at the law schools of Howard University, the University of Seattle, and the Marshall-Wythe Law School of the College of William and Mary. Stubbs serves on the Board of Directors and is a Past President of the Oliver White Hill Foundation. Stubbs is married to Dr. Pamela E. Hamilton-Stubbs, M.D., who is the President and CEO of Dr. Hamilton-Stubbs' Sleep and Total Wellness Institute LLC, a Christian-based conventional and alternative medicine practice. They are very proud parents and grandparents.

# Oliver W. Hill

Oliver W. Hill was born in Richmond, Virginia, May 1, 1907. He completed elementary school in Roanoke and high school in Washington, D.C. He was a graduate of Howard University, where he received the degrees of A.B. from the College of Liberal Arts and J.D. from the School of Law. He was married to the late Beresenia A. Walker, and they had one son, the late Oliver W. Hill Jr.; a daughter in law, Renee Hill; a granddaughter, Jananda Hill; a step granddaughter, Maia King; and a step grandson, Ja'maa Beckley-King.

Until his retirement in July 1998, Mr. Hill was a partner in the law firm of Hill, Tucker and Marsh. He became a member of the Virginia Bar in 1934 and, except for time out in the service of the United States government, practiced law in Richmond, Virginia, beginning in 1939. He served in the Armed Forces from June 1943 through November 1945; and from May 1961 to September 1966, was with the Federal Housing Administration, first as Assistant to the Federal Housing Commissioner and later, as Assistant to the Assistant Secretary for Mortgage Credit and Federal Housing

Commissioner in the Department of Housing and Urban Development.

Mr. Hill entered Howard Law School in 1930 with the express intention of challenging America's segregation laws. Mr. Hill and other dedicated lawyer/activists (including his law school classmate and special life-long friend, Thurgood Marshall) worked assiduously under the tutelage of Dean Charles Hamilton Houston to secure all rights incident to first-class citizenship for African Americans. At great personal risk, these courageous individuals educated the general public and the courts as they pursued civil rights litigation on the behalf of their clients.

In 1935, Mr. Hill was one of the founders of the Virginia State Conference of NAACP Branches. This was the first of such organizational tools, which played a pivotal role in fulfilling the mission of the NAACP.

In 1940, Thurgood Marshall succeeded Charles Houston as special counsel to the NAACP and founded the NAACP Legal Defense and Educational Fund (LDF) to offer some limited protection to both civil rights litigants and the NAACP from an angry public and hostile institutions. From the inception of the LDF until his death, Oliver White Hill remained closely associated with the legal and policy work of the LDF. During his career, Mr. Hill litigated many cases on its behalf.

Some of the landmark cases in which Mr. Hill participated involved such diverse matters as equalization of salaries for public school personnel; the right to serve on grand and petit juries; inclusion in the program of free bus transportation for public school children; equalization of public school facilities; protection of firemen and other railway workers in rights to employment and to fair and impartial representation by the statutory bargaining agent; the right of participation in primary elections; the elimination of segregation on common carriers in both intrastate and interstate travel; the use of public places in a nondiscriminatory and unsegregated fashion, including public schools and places of public assembly and recreation; the securing of housing of their choice; and the right, through an organization such as the NAACP, to assert their constitutional rights and seek redress of their grievances in courts and otherwise, free from harassment by legislative investigatory committees.

He encouraged and helped develop the use of the ballot among minorities and sought to stimulate their participation in organized political party activities. He was a former member of the Richmond City Council, of the Richmond City Democratic Committee and of the first President's Committee on Government Contracts Compliance, known later as the President's Committee on Equal Employment Opportunity. His initial national recognition was in 1948 when he won a seat on the Richmond City Council in a city-wide election, becoming the first African American so elected since Reconstruction Days.

Mr. Hill received numerous awards and honorary degrees, including the NAACP's Spingarn Medal, the Presidential Medal of Freedom (the highest civilian award of the United States of America), and the highest award of the American Bar Association.

Oliver White Hill, the consummate lawyer, legal trailblazer, and social activist died at his home in Richmond, Virginia, on August 5, 2007, at the age of 100 years.

# No Clue

## White American Affirmative Action Exists and Demands a Moral Revival Now!

# No Clue

## White American Affirmative Action Exists and Demands a Moral Revival Now!

Jonathan K. Stubbs

*with* the late Oliver W. Hill, Esq.

Twelve Tables Press

Copyright © 2025 Enlightened Ethos Global Publishers LLC

ISBN: 978-1-946074-43-0

All rights reserved. No part of this work may be used or reproduced in any manner whatsoever or transmitted in any form or by any means, electronic or mechanical, including photocopying, recording, or any information storage and retrieval system, without written permission from the copyright owner. Permission may be obtained through contacting the publisher at the following address:

Twelve Tables Press
P.O. Box 568
Northport, New York 11768
www.twelvetablespress.com

All rights reserved. Printed in the United States of America.

This book is dedicated to Oliver W. Hill, Esq.,
activist, freedom fighter, fearless attorney,
and champion of the despised, rejected, and abused.

Affirmative action, as currently understood and promoted, is also ahistorical. For more than 200 years, white males benefited from their own program of affirmative action, through unjustified preferences in jobs and education resulting from old-boy networks and official laws that lessened the competition. Today's affirmative action critics never characterize that scheme as affirmative action, which of course it was. By labeling problematic, troublesome, and ethically agonizing a paltry system that helps a few of us get ahead, critics neatly take our eyes off the system of arrangements that brought and maintained them in power, and enabled them to develop the rules and standards of quality and merit that now exclude us, make us appear unworthy, dependent (naturally) on affirmative action.[1]

—Professor Richard Delgado

# Contents

# Author's Note

OLIVER W. HILL, ESQ., was sitting in his reclining chair late one afternoon shortly after the dawn of the twenty-first century. I had just read to him an excerpt from a law review article that I had drafted involving race and human rights. Mr. Hill commented that academicians often used long and complicated sentences (I could not help but wonder who he might have meant!). He said to me, "We need to write a book. Something for the man in the street."

Mr. Hill explained that "we have a whole lot of denial in this country." Specifically, he singled out the general public's lack of knowledge regarding history, race, and the law in America. From his perspective, many people in the United States had no clue that from colonial times to the present day, the law has been used to create and maintain advantages for White persons. In other words, legalized White American affirmative action exists and is nothing new. Mr. Hill was keenly aware of that reality.

In these circumstances, Mr. Hill was convinced that we could perform a valuable public service by producing a short book for the everyday reader. He suggested that such a book use uncomplicated language, with the goal of providing facts for thoughtful discussion. He also stated that such facts as opposed to myths could be helpful in the context of hot debates regarding issues like "confederate heritage" and affirmative action for people of color.

I readily agreed with Mr. Hill and began to research material for the book. He was approaching 100 years of age, was blind, and hard of hearing. Accordingly, I felt some urgency in getting the book done.

We ran into some obstacles. Mr. Hill was hospitalized with a serious medical condition and not long afterward I was diagnosed with early stage prostate cancer. Nevertheless, we both remained committed to the project. Mr. Hill steadily recovered and God gave me a healing touch.[1]

On August 5, 2007, we had a nearly complete draft done when Mr. Hill died suddenly at age 100. Having known him for over 15 years and having worked with him on his autobiography, Mr. Hill had become more to me than just the most senior human rights lawyer in America, he was also my friend. The shock of losing a dear friend has been great; nevertheless, I have worked hard to make this document that we began together a fitting expression of some of his and my beliefs. Any errors, omissions, or shortcomings in this work are mine alone.

The goal of this book is not to provide a quick and easy fix to a centuries-long American problem: how to create a society committed to "liberty and justice for all." The book has more modest goals. It discusses selected historical facts. Such facts can prod us to effect constructive societal change and create opportunities so that individuals can reach their maximum potentials.

How could we reach this goal?

So kind of you to ask.

In his autobiography, Mr. Hill pointed the way. He argued that we should start at the bottom of the social ladder and work our way up:

> [W]e should seek new and unique ways of helping human earthlings starting with those below the poverty level and moving upward, at least through the lower middle class. In an evolutionary fashion, we must find ways through economic development—for example labor, industry and discovery—to help those at the bottom to receive a larger share of the economic wealth derived from labor, technology and natural resources.
>
> Business is no more important than technology, health services, or recreation. We need all these things. Consequently, people ought to be trained to do whatever their talents enable them to do; and then work cooperatively to utilize these talents for the benefit of all people.[2]

In concluding these comments, I offer a few additional observations. First, Mr. Hill firmly believed that change was inevitable, and that humans must guide change for the good of all. His approach was consistent with Charles Hamilton Houston's view that lawyers should be "social engineers."[3]

Second, Mr. Hill's worldview was broad. He was concerned not just with human rights in the United States, but also globally. Third, Mr. Hill recognized that humans are part of the vast expanse of the universe. We are living beings on earth: in other words, we are earthlings. In fact, because we are humans living on earth, he referred to us as "human earthlings." He recognized that at this crossroads in human history, we—human earthlings—are poised to leave our earthly home and explore other parts of the universe.

Accordingly, we must be broad minded. For instance, we need to abandon pedestrian and destructive earthly distractions like engaging in violent conflicts based on skin color as well as material wealth. Instead, we should embrace a more cosmic consciousness.[4]

Indeed, Mr. Hill asked, "Why do we look up when we speak of heaven?" He suggested that it might be more accurate to "look out and over." Look out from our earthly home, and over the breadth of creation.[5]

As we look out and over the physical universe, we need also to look into the mirror. Let's each ask a personal question: What can I do to make myself and the world better? How can I help to "childproof the world"? In other words, what can I contribute to make earth a safe place for all children to live and reach their potential? To be bold and blunt: What can I do to treat others as I want to be treated? What can I do and who do I need to be to exemplify "love your neighbor as yourself"? In sum, who do I need to be and what do I need to do to nurture the change that I wish to see?

# Foreword[1]

Oliver Hill Sr. is one of my heroes of the civil rights generation. Born in Richmond, Virginia, on May 1, 1907, Hill lived beyond his centennial anniversary (May 1, 2007) and died shortly thereafter. I met him on several occasions and all of our meetings were incredibly memorable.

When I first met Oliver Hill, he was still actively practicing law in Virginia even though he was in his nineties. I remember being involved in a death penalty case early in the twenty-first century, and went to Virginia to plead with the governor to give this person, who was on death row, an opportunity to serve a life sentence rather than the death penalty. I was more than surprised when Hill joined me in my plea with the governor. When I asked him why he was there, he responded, "Professor Ogletree, I have been meeting with the last eight governors of Virginia about the death penalty, and I certainly wouldn't miss this one." The idea that someone would have been involved for many decades against the death penalty and persistently meeting with governors from Virginia only reinforced my respect for this great man.

When Oliver Hill went to Howard University School of Law, his classmate and best friend was none other than Thurgood Marshall.[2] Born in Baltimore, Maryland, Marshall had earned his undergraduate degree from Lincoln University, a historically Black university in Oxford, Pennsylvania.

At the inception of their careers, Hill and Marshall received expert tutelage from Charles Hamilton Houston, a Howard University School of Law graduate who served as the vice dean at Howard University School of Law.[3] Houston was born in Washington, DC, in 1895 and died in 1950. In his 54 years, Houston contributed immensely to the preparation of people like Thurgood Marshall and Oliver Hill so that they could become effective civil rights lawyers and social engineers.[4] When you compare Hill and Marshall with their White contemporaries who had abundant financial resources and the privilege of knowing that the White man's word would be taken as gospel, it is amazing what Houston was able to achieve. He expertly trained people at Howard University School of Law to do excellent civil rights work.[5]

For instance, upon their graduation from law school, Houston took Hill and Marshall to the national convention of the National Bar Association, a voluntary organization comprised mostly of African Americans because the American Bar Association limited its membership to Whites only. Houston introduced them to more seasoned members of the Bar and personally strategized with Marshall and Hill on a range of cases, including teacher salary equalization, criminal defense litigation, and transportation desegregation.

Early in Marshall's career, Houston served as the NAACP's Special Counsel. Houston groomed Marshall to take over Houston's responsibilities by hiring Marshall as Assistant Counsel.[6] In that capacity, Marshall gained valuable experience trying civil rights cases around the country. Furthermore, when Houston stepped down as Special Counsel, Marshall led efforts to create the NAACP Legal Defense Fund (LDF), which carried forward much of the work that Houston and Marshall had been doing. In fact, before and after the incorporation of the LDF, Houston, Marshall, and Hill collaborated on a wide range of human rights activities involving education, transportation, and labor relations.[7] Marshall would later become the chief lawyer who argued *Brown v. Board of Education*.

In 1967, President Lyndon Baines Johnson appointed Marshall as the first African American to ascend to the United States Supreme Court. Marshall served with distinction. Indeed, in the late 1960s, Marshall was in the majority in some of the most important Warren-era cases. He stayed on the Court until he retired in 1991, having had a tremendous impact as a Justice who concentrated on ensuring that the rights of all people were respected and that the general public understood the role of lawyers.

Oliver Hill was not far behind. Hill spent most of his career in practice. Working with Houston, Marshall, and a team of other superb human rights lawyers, Hill won landmark cases in teacher salary equalization[8] and transportation desegregation.[9] In addition, Hill was lead trial counsel in the Prince Edward school case, which was consolidated in *Brown*.[10] His many decades of social activism, effective advocacy, and committed leadership earned him the prestigious Spingarn Medal from the NAACP[11] and the Presidential Medal of Freedom from President Bill Clinton.[12]

I was personally amazed to see his enthusiasm even in his later years. His commitment to justice never abated. In fact, Hill was one of the *Brown* lawyers who I honored at Harvard Law School in the fall of 2000.[13] At that time, we recognized all of the plaintiffs' lawyers who were living (and their descendants if they had passed away)

Not long thereafter, on the fiftieth anniversary of *Brown v. Board of Education* in 2004, Hill came to Harvard again even though he was afflicted not only with the need for a wheelchair but also was legally blind. That did not stop him from being very aggressive. For example, during a session to celebrate the fiftieth anniversary of *Brown*, Hill became agitated when one of my young colleagues from Harvard Law

School talked about the role of Black lawyers. My colleague didn't seem to either know the real firsthand history that Hill and others experienced or fully appreciate their accomplishments. Hill not only interrupted the lawyer and made it clear that the *Brown* lawyers had done something unparalleled and unprecedented in history, but he also went on to write an important essay that became a part of his remarkable legacy.[14] I salute him and honor him—the Renaissance man of the Civil Rights Movement: Oliver Hill.

Charles J. Ogletree Jr.
Late Jesse Climenko Professor of Law Emeritus
Harvard Law School

# Preface

MY FATHER, OLIVER W. HILL SR., lived to be 100 years old. Born a mere 11 years after the infamous *Plessy v. Ferguson*[1] decision of the Supreme Court, which established the legal basis of American apartheid, most of his adult life was spent living under, and fighting against, laws that relegated Blacks in this country to the status of second-class citizens. In this book, he and his long-time collaborator and friend, Jonathan Stubbs, attempt to give some historical context to the notion of "White privilege," particularly "White male privilege," which was overtly manifested in restrictive laws more than a century before *Plessy*, and which has covertly formed the basis for much more subtle continuing race, class, and gender discrimination in this country, even beyond the lingering effects of slavery and "Jim Crow."

One of the barriers to overcoming the racial divide that persists in contemporary times is the pervasive belief among many in society that, yes, there was racial injustice in the past, but that was long ago, and therefore they have no responsibility for, or role in, any remedies for that injustice today. This kind of thinking fuels much of the resentment toward affirmative action by Whites who feel they are being unfairly targeted by "reverse discrimination," or who see no need for society to address inequities of the past. One of the major accomplishments of this book is that by providing the historical thread that binds many of the legal barriers imposed by society to give advantage to some and deny advantage to others, we find a continuing trail that leads to current societal outcomes. If my great-grandfather was denied access to a job that would have led to the elevation of his family to the middle class, and someone else's great-grandfather who was less well qualified was given that job because he didn't have to compete against my great-grandfather, the ramifications of that set of circumstances could reverberate for generations.

However, I don't think the point of this book is just to increase the level of "White guilt" in readers. Rather, I think the purpose is to give the sense that in this long history of racial (and gender) discrimination in this country, we are all inextricably bound together, and that we all have a part to play in coming up with solutions.

One of the most well-known cases my father was involved with was the 1954 *Brown v. Board of Education*[2] decision that ended the doctrine of "separate but equal" in schools, and for all practical purposes, served as the death knell for segregation in the larger U.S. society. Yet over 60 years after that decision, glaring inequities continue to exist between predominantly minority and predominantly White school districts. What started out as strictly racial (and legally mandated) disparities, has been confounded over the years by issues of class.

For example, with the fall of segregation, many Whites fled the cities in droves. As more opportunities opened up in society, often middle- and upper-class Blacks joined their White counterparts in moving to the suburbs, leaving cities and their schools bereft of an adequate tax base.

Ironically, the quality of education also suffered as women began to be given more career opportunities at the same time. It used to be that the best and brightest women who wanted a career would often choose education, and now that there are more options, society has not put sufficient incentives in place to continue to attract the "best and brightest."

The crisis in education is but one of the examples of major societal problems whose roots are in the racial politics of our past. Only as we come to be more aware of that story, and embrace our complete history as a nation, can we hope to effectively address these major issues. This book will make a valuable contribution to that process.

Oliver W. Hill Jr.
Late Professor of Experimental Psychology
Virginia State University

# Acknowledgments

IT HAS TAKEN TWENTY YEARS TO WRITE THIS BOOK.

Accordingly, I thank God for allowing me to make this work the best that I presently can. I also am deeply grateful for my Dear Bride, Dr. Pamela Hamilton-Stubbs, who is a life partner, medical missionary, and powerful woman of God. She sacrificed herself in innumerable ways to help me.

Thanks to my daughter, son in love, and many other family members (biological, legal, and most of all spiritual) for their encouragement and support. My spiritual family has made a decisive and positive difference: they have interceded with the Spirit . . .

Thanks to colleagues and friends at the University of Richmond. Each member of that special community has made a positive contribution by helping to foster an environment where work like this can move forward. I especially note the support of the University of Richmond School of Law Library staff, including the invaluable research help of Sylvia Yanes, Esq., and her proficient team of law student assistants.

I extend additional thanks to friends and colleagues at many other educational institutions, legal advocacy organizations (particularly the NAACP LDF), and the Oliver White Hill Foundation who have provided encouragement.

Moreover, I wish to extend my deepest appreciation to the families of Oliver W. Hill, Esq. and Professor Charles J. Ogletree Jr. Their support has had an immeasurable positive impact.

My sincere appreciation to the publisher, Steve Errick, and the production editor, Sharon Ray, for their professionalism as well as their infinite patience.

*I simply wish to thank each person who contributed constructively in any way.*

Finally, thanks to you, Gentle Reader, who thought it not robbery—a waste of your time—to read this book.

# No Clue

## White American Affirmative Action Exists and Demands a Moral Revival Now!

# Prologue

Living things on earth are earthlings. Human beings are earthlings: or as Oliver Hill Sr. said, "human earthlings." Human earthlings have done something historic and relatively rare: we have lived through the end of a century and into a new millennium. And, as human earthlings, we are just beginning to appreciate that we are a tiny part of something much bigger than ourselves or our planet. Scientific discovery has provided us with a glimpse of the huge expanse of the universe. Based on data collected through the Hubble Space Telescope, evidence exists that there may be over 2 trillion galaxies in the universe.[1] While no one can know for sure, it is also possible that each of the 2 trillion galaxies may have over 100 billion stars. The launch of the James Webb Space Telescope is illuminating *this mind-boggling vastness.*[2]

We are standing on the edge of unlimited possibilities.

At this busy and challenging intersection of human history, we are reminded of the perceptive warning of a remarkable philosopher, George Santayana: "[T]hose who cannot remember the past are condemned to repeat it."[3] We take Santayana's warning seriously, and ask: What negative experiences should we remember so that we do not repeat them?

## The Color Line

In *The Souls of Black Folk*, published in 1903, W.E.B. Du Bois, a prolific scholar and committed social activist, stated that in the twentieth century, the paramount human challenge was "*the problem of the color line.*"[4] Today in the United States, huge gaps in education resources, material wealth, and health care persist. Often disparities fall along the color line.[5] These differences are indefensible.

Over 120 years after Du Bois' prophecy, why is the color line problem still a problem? Stated another way, why does race still matter? For at least three reasons. First, many human earthlings (in the United States and elsewhere) live in denial: "No color line problem exists." For example, some persons claim that in America we live in a post-racial society. One example of this is expressed by persons who claim, "I don't see color." And if they do happen to see color, then "it really does not matter to me." In other words, "I am not a racist because I do not think about race." This line of thought has undergirded much of United States Supreme Court race-related jurisprudence. The Court frequently requires that a person who has suffered race discrimination prove what was in the mind of the person who acted in a racist manner. So, for instance, it is not enough to show that a municipal police or fire department chose a written test that disproportionately affects African Americans in a negative way. Rather, an unsuccessful job applicant must show that public officials adopted the test with discrimination in mind.[6] Proving what a person is thinking is extraordinarily difficult. In deciding whether race discrimination exists, why not give greater weight to what the person actually does: actions often speak louder than words!

Frankly speaking, when decisions are made along the color line, a double standard seems to exist. For instance, periodically efforts have been made to help persons who have historically been oppressed because of their skin color. Some such initiatives focus upon assisting unprivileged persons to achieve their maximum potential. In making amends for the legacy and practical effects of color discrimination, on occasion policy makers have considered how remedies would likely impact persons of various skin colors. Using a color-conscious approach to remedy color-conscious harms upsets some judges as well as other policy makers. Objectors to color-conscious remedies claim that the courts must be consistent in rejecting all consideration of race in policy decisions. Such judges and decision makers presume that if a policy helps disadvantaged persons catch up with the privileged ones, the privileged have suffered race discrimination. As this work explains in more detail later, in a prescient dissent, in *Adarand Constructors v. Pena*, Justice John Paul Stevens spotlighted the Court's deeply flawed analysis.

> The consistency that the Court espouses would disregard the difference between a "No Trespassing" sign and a welcome mat. It would treat a Dixiecrat Senator's decision to vote against Thurgood Marshall's confirmation in order to keep African Americans off the Supreme Court as on a par with President Lyndon Johnson's evaluation of his nominee's race as a positive factor. It would equate a law that made Black citizens ineligible for military service with a program aimed at recruiting Black soldiers. An attempt by the majority to exclude members of a minority race from a regulated market is fundamentally different from a subsidy that enables a relatively small group of newcomers to enter that market.[7]

In other words, fair opportunities frequently mean that persons of privilege will actually have to earn rather than inherit their place at the front of the line.

What's a practical example of such double standards? Kind of you (again) to ask. Good illustrations are the two recent Supreme Court of the United States decisions that, in nearly all circumstances, struck down the use of race to promote equal opportunity for members of disadvantaged groups seeking admission to institutions of higher education.

In *Students for Fair Admissions v. President and Fellows of Harvard College*[8] and *Students for Fair Admissions v. University of North Carolina*,[9] Students for Fair Admissions (SFFA), a nonprofit organization, sued Harvard University and the University of North Carolina. In these cases, SFFA claimed that both institutions had established admissions programs that discriminated against Asian American and White students on the basis of race in violation of the Constitution of the United States. The trial courts in both cases held that in a holistic way, each of the universities' admissions programs evaluated each individual applicant on her own merits. During the admissions process, the educational institutions considered a host of factors, including but not limited to applicant grades, standardized test scores, extracurricular activities, letters of recommendations, the applicant's personal statement, whether the applicant was a relative of a university alumnus or major donor, and the race of the applicant.

The Court reversed the lower court decisions and ruled in favor of SFFA. The gist of the Court's decision was that in the higher-education context, educational institutions are prohibited from considering the race of an applicant in almost all circumstances other than "an applicant's discussion of how race affected his or her life, be it through discrimination, inspiration, or otherwise."[10] In such circumstances, the Court said that "[a] benefit to a student who overcame racial discrimination, for example, must be tied to *that student's* courage and determination. Or a benefit to a student whose heritage or culture motivated him or her to assume a leadership role or attain a particular goal must be tied to *that student's* unique ability to contribute to the university."[11]

The Court's decision exemplifies a form of White American affirmative action. The principal reason is that the Court, acting as a national policy maker, created additional barriers for persons seeking admission whose families are not materially wealthy and White. The Court let stand admissions preferences for university alums or large financial donors. Most of such individuals are both wealthy White folks and are often admitted at disproportionately higher rates. By legalizing as well as fortifying the tremendous head start of privileged white persons, the Supreme Court deprives less privileged persons of a fair chance to succeed.[12]

Stated differently, by taking away a possible benefit from some persons of color and leaving benefits in place for persons who are overwhelmingly affluent White people, the Court reinforces the ladder to success for privileged White persons.

Moreover, one might ask: Why of the many factors that contribute to a university admission decision—grades, test scores, reference letters, overcoming adversity, extracurricular activities, geographic residence, relationship to alums—the Court fixates on race alone? It is especially troubling that the Court chose to limit the opportunities of persons from groups that Harvard and the University of North Carolina have historically excluded solely because of their skin color. For over 200 years, both Harvard and the University of North Carolina practiced race discrimination in their admissions policies. In the past few decades those institutions have attempted to address their institutional misdeeds along the color line through efforts to integrate their academic communities. To make their admissions process more fair, both institutions decided to broaden the factors that can be considered for admission. In doing so these institutions made it easier for persons other than materially wealthy and well-connected applicants to be admitted. Stated differently, Harvard and the University of North Carolina recognized that they needed "institutional repentance." The Court made it harder for them to redeem themselves.

Remarkable! As the old saying goes, "No good deed goes unpunished . . ."

Similar examples of White American affirmative action are considered in subsequent chapters.

Returning to the discussion about why we still have such difficulty with dealing with the color line, many human earthlings try to cover the problem up. One method of camouflaging the color line problem is to say that "it's natural." For instance, there are folks who assert that "it's natural" that Whites are more cerebral, thoughtful, and rational. On the other hand, some people perceive persons of color as inherently more impulsive, thoughtless, sensual, and temperamental.[13]

And third, regarding the color line, we have been taught more mythology than fact about the history of human relations. You know about "the good old days" when everybody knew and stayed in their place (making no waves). In fact, across the United States many individuals are demanding that historical facts not be taught in public schools. Truth killers often want to spread historical fairy tales—the precise problem that Mr. Hill suggested we address. For instance, many well-intentioned individuals have been misled to believe that public kindergarten, elementary, and high school students are being taught something called "critical race theory."[14]

An illuminating *Washington Post* article describes the primary purpose of persons attacking critical race theory in the following terms:

> We have successfully frozen their brand—"critical race theory"—into the public conversation and are steadily driving up negative perceptions . . . We will eventually turn it toxic, as we put all of the various cultural insanities under that brand category. The goal is to have the public read something crazy in the newspaper and immediately think "critical race theory."[15]

In reality, as Professor Kimberlé Williams Crenshaw, one of the founders of critical race theory, has perceptively stated, critical race theory is not a subject offered in many (if any) public primary or secondary schools in America.[16] Critical race theory is principally a way of analyzing, and explaining, long-standing socio-economic as well as political inequity within the United States. Critical race theorists often provide information and insight regarding how law contributes to widespread inequity along color lines. In this context, courses on critical race theory are offered in some law school and graduate programs.[17]

So, what's all the fuss about? It seems that many opponents of teaching critical race theory simply fear teaching historical facts. Teaching facts can cause thoughtful students and other concerned persons to ask uncomfortable questions about American history as well as contemporary society. Some parents and other authority figures do not want to respond to questions that challenge their perception of the United States as a near perfect society. This book will consider facts that show areas where the United States has progressed, regressed, and needs to improve. Accordingly, reading this book is not recommended for the faint of heart: you may need a bit of "emotional inoculation" because you might find some facts troubling.

We invite you to consider information this book presents, use the selected bibliography provided, and do your own research. *Think for yourself.* Reach your own conclusions. And then act to make your own constructive contribution to creating a better society based on liberty and justice for all. Such positive societal change is especially vital because in the United States and abroad, governments based on the respect for human rights are under attack by neo-Nazi sympathizers. Followers of an unsuccessful presidential candidate recently attempted to overthrow the government of the United States by force and fraud.[18]

The opposition to truth telling in public schools helps to explain a broader problem. In the United States, members of the general public have often not been taught sufficient historical facts to help us understand and address current challenges regarding "race." *Many of us simply have no clue.*

To make matters worse, *critics of critical race theory advocate an approach designed to result in continuing cluelessness.* For example, many high school students have learned little more about Dr. Martin Luther King Jr. than that he gave a speech ("I Have a Dream") in which he stated that he looked forward to an America in which a person "will not be judged by the color of their skin but by the content of their character." Such students are often encouraged to believe that King's words mean that it is wrong to address present-day inequities like underrepresentation of students of color in many institutions of higher education. Increasing the small populations of students of color could require policy makers to first recognize that a problem exists. In other words, they need to take off their blinders and see the low numbers of students of color. Next, they must make a reasonable interpretation of what they see: the low numbers are unnatural. Perceiving that such underrepresentation was unnatural would also compel decision makers to do something constructive to alleviate the situation. For instance, persons in positions of authority could consciously try to recruit, admit, and retain qualified students of color. However, doing something constructive about the underrepresentation problem means taking color or race into account. For some persons, even opening our eyes and acknowledging that a problem exists is a no-no.

King was a strong advocate of opening our eyes to the effects of racism. He demanded creation of programs to promote equal opportunities for those who have been shut out—especially persons of color and, more broadly speaking, impoverished persons. In fact, in his "I Have a Dream" speech, King explicitly stated:

> When the architects of our republic wrote the magnificent words of the Constitution and the Declaration of Independence, they were signing a

> promissory note to which every American was to fall heir. This note was a promise that all men—yes, Black men as well as white men—would be guaranteed the unalienable rights of life, liberty and the pursuit of happiness.
>
> It is obvious today that America has defaulted on this promissory note insofar as her citizens of color are concerned. Instead of honoring this sacred obligation, America has given the Negro people a bad check, a check which has come back marked insufficient funds.
>
> But we refuse to believe that the bank of justice is bankrupt.
>
> We refuse to believe that there are insufficient funds in the great vaults of opportunity of this nation. And so we've come to cash this check, a check that will give us upon demand the riches of freedom and the security of justice.[19]

King's speech was a clarion call to recognize injustice along America's color divide: "America has given the Negro people a bad check, a check which has come back marked insufficient funds." King demanded that America address this societal inequity, and to address it by opening "the great vaults of opportunity of this nation" not just to White persons but to everyone.

Unfortunately, in America, many persons avoid our unfinished work of healing our battered, bruised, and broken national community. Failure to come to terms with the past—good, bad, and in between—will result in continued conflict and misunderstanding. We need the courage to look at ourselves and our society in the mirror of both our past and present. Otherwise, we will (unintentionally?) assist persons both at home and abroad who seek the undoing of the *United* States of America. To put it in everyday language: America needs to come clean about its past and present. Only then can we work effectively as a united people to secure America's future.

In contrast, other societies like South Africa have much more forthrightly dealt with the reality of racial injustices. As the late, much beloved, Bishop Desmond Tutu pointed out in his path-breaking book, *No Future Without Forgiveness,*[20] South African society rejected national amnesia.[21] South Africans consciously turned away from the temptation to pretend that past atrocities never happened, and that all is now well. South Africa's Truth and Reconciliation Commission seems to have been a constructive tool to address some of that country's ills. Nevertheless, the work of reconciliation in South Africa remains unfinished. South Africa's persisting struggle continues with the deeply entrenched legacy of apartheid. For instance, some recent widespread social unrest in South Africa has been closely linked with pervasive material wealth inequality established during the era of apartheid.[22]

In short, Du Bois' prophesy regarding the color line spotlights today's uncomfortable reality. For better or worse, the color line (race!) will affect whether human earthlings can successfully meet the greatest human challenge of the twenty-first century: *human survival.* Stated differently, and in Mr. Hill's words, we must "promote in the twenty-first century a renaissance in human relations."[23]

The renaissance includes a spiritual component. On an individual basis we need to see our neighbors as part of our extended human family—whether they live down the street or look very different and live on the other side of the globe. In other words, such a global movement needs to reimagine race: we are one family and one race—the human race. We are not and must not continue to act like hostile competing tribes. To avoid human extinction in this century, real family values are essential. We need a paradigm or worldview shift. We are all kin. We kin shall be free together or else . . .

In this context, this book's conclusions are likely to be considered controversial. Furthermore, to thoroughly discuss the facts that support our conclusions would require many volumes. Mr. Hill and I consciously decided not to undertake that arduous task. To do so would have diverted us from our central mission: a short, readable, fact-based book. Consistent with our primary objective, *we have outlined only the tip of the iceberg of facts that support our conclusions*. In addition, we have provided some end notes and a selected bibliography so that if you so choose, you may have an easier time conducting your own further research.

Decide for yourself the extent to which people you know have *no clue*. Then consider this question: Dare we each look intently into our own mirror?

It is said that knowing the truth will set you free.[24] That said, *while the truth may set you free, it will not necessarily make you happy*. With that word of caution, we begin with a confession of some important facts.

## Confession: Medicine to Heal the Soul of a Stressed Society

Confession of past errors helps to establish and strengthen bonds of human friendship, cooperation, and community. Confessions of sins of the American legal system in dealings with people of darker color, especially African Americans, begins with the colonial period. We outline America's long-standing preference programs for privileged individuals and groups—especially White males. As Richard Delgado perceptively pointed out, such racial preference programs reflected an abuse of affirmative action.[25]

The term "affirmative action" is loaded. Because this book is, as Mr. Hill mandated, "for the [person] in the street," we give a brief, non-technical explanation of what is meant here by affirmative action. When is it appropriate? Why affirmative action should be used? And how?

## Affirmative Action: What, When, Why, and How

### *What?*

So, what is the core of affirmative action? What does it boil down to? To put it in everyday language, at its best, affirmative action refers to programs, policies, practices, and laws that create equal opportunity for all. Sometimes this is referred to as establishing a level playing field.

### *When and Why?*

Affirmative action programs are required primarily for situations where members of a privileged group have received and benefited from unfair preferences. Preferences are unfair when based on criteria that lack merit. For instance, examples of unmerited favoritism include superficial factors like the color of a person's skin, his biological sex, or his material wealth. Benefits for privileged persons often result in individuals in relatively unprivileged groups being harmed. Unprivileged persons often suffer harm when privileged persons receive various rewards like money, high social status, and significant decision-making authority based on bogus criteria. Such fake qualifications encompass accidents of birth like the color of an individual's skin, their biological sex, the family into which they are born, or their material wealth.

A fair-minded person might ask: Specifically, what do you mean? Here's some historical background followed by a concrete modern example.

### *A Historical Note*

This book outlines how beginning during the colonial period in English colonies like Virginia, and continuing for over 300 years, in many parts of the United States, the laws discriminated along the skin color line. As a direct consequence, White persons had widespread access to education, jobs, housing, health care, and political office. The law denied persons of color such opportunities. Enhanced opportunities for White persons, especially materially affluent White men, gave individuals from such social groups a tremendous head start in obtaining positions of authority and power.

Among White persons, affirmative action created favored classes, such as male over female, materially wealthy over impoverished, Christian over Jew and Muslim. The chief beneficiaries of this affirmative action pyramid were (and are) materially affluent White males. The abuse of affirmative action—meritless privileges and benefits—severely curtailed opportunities for the majority of Americans.

One outrageous example of mistreatment of the majority by the privileged few is the law's treatment of women. Even during the colonial era, such treatment did not go unnoticed. For example, while her husband, John Adams, was feverishly working with other colonists to sever ties with Great Britain, Abigail Adams decided to write him a letter. A few months before the colonists promulgated the Declaration of Independence, Abigail Adams said:

> [A]nd by the way in the new Code of Laws which I suppose it will be necessary for you to make I desire you would Remember the Ladies, and be more generous and favourable to them than your ancestors. Do not put such unlimited power into the hands of the Husbands. Remember all Men would be tyrants if they could. If perticuliar care and attention is not paid to the Laidies we are determined to foment a Rebelion, and will not hold ourselves bound by any Laws in which we have no voice, or Representation.
>
> That your Sex are Naturally Tyrannical is a Truth so thoroughly established as to admit of no dispute, but such of you as wish to be happy willingly give up the harsh title of Master for the more tender and endearing one of Friend. Why then, not put it out of the power of the vicious and the Lawless to use us with cruelty and indignity with impunity. Men of Sense in all Ages abhor those customs which treat us only as the vassals of your Sex. Regard us then as Beings placed by providence under your

> protection and in immitation of the Supreem Being make use of that power only for our happiness.[26]

In everyday language, Abigail Adams simply asked that her husband respect her as an equal—as a friend.

In his reply letter, John Adams tried to brush off Abigail's serious request by saying:

> As to your extraordinary Code of Laws, I cannot but laugh. We have been told that our Struggle has loosened the bands of Government every where. That Children and Apprentices were disobedient—that schools and Colledges were grown turbulent—that Indians slighted their Guardians and Negroes grew insolent to their Masters. But your Letter was the first Intimation that another Tribe more numerous and powerfull than all the rest were grown discontented.—This is rather too coarse a Compliment but you are so saucy, I wont blot it out.
>
> Depend upon it, We know better than to repeal our Masculine systems. Altho they are in full Force, you know they are little more than Theory. We dare not exert our Power in its full Latitude. We are obliged to go fair, and softly, and in Practice you know We are the subjects. We have only the Name of Masters, and rather than give up this, which would compleatly subject Us to the Despotism of the Peticoat, I hope General Washington, and all our brave Heroes would fight.[27]

Beneath John Adams' dismissive response to Abigail's request lurked a genuine fear that the colonists' talk about freedom, taxation without representation, equality, and other revolutionary ideals would be embraced by the majority of colonists. Thus, a few weeks later, in a letter to James Sullivan, Adams shared his concerns about emphasizing freedom and justice for all. In a letter dated May 26, 1776, Adams said:

> Depend upon it, sir, it is dangerous to open So fruitfull a Source of Controversy and Altercation, as would be opened by attempting to alter the Qualifications of Voters. There will be no End of it. New Claims will arise. Women will demand a Vote. Lads from 12 to 21 will think their Rights not enough attended to, and every Man, who has not a Farthing, will demand an equal Voice with any other in all Acts of State. It tends to confound and destroy all Distinctions, and prostrate all Ranks, to one common Levell.[28]

Adams' letter to Sullivan indicates that Adams was adamantly opposed to recognizing equality of rights for women, materially impoverished men, and other persons near the bottom of the societal order. In Adams' own words, equality would "confound and destroy all Distinctions, and prostrate all Ranks, to one common Levell." The tone of Adams' letter suggests that only the rights of materially wealthy White males mattered. In this context, less than two months later the colonists would declare their own freedom from and equality with Great Britain.

Perhaps, not surprisingly, when the Constitution of 1787 went into effect, only one state, New Jersey, allowed women to vote.[29] Women of color were particularly vulnerable to abuse. Such women were frequently enslaved and legally defenseless against rape, torture, and even murder. To a lesser extent, men of color lived under a similar regime of intimidation intended to engender fear. For instance, the comprehensive Virginia Slave Codes of 1705 permitted a slaveholder to petition the county court to punish a runaway slave "by dismembering, or in any other way, not touching his life, as they in their discretion shall think fit, for the reclaiming any such an incorrigible slave and *terrifying* others from the like practices."[30] Thus, to maintain control of enslaved workers, colonists sometimes established a system of legal terrorism, including spectacles of public torture in which local law enforcement officers cut off the limbs of escaped slaves in front of community members.

History matters. Genuine affirmative action programs targeted to create equal opportunities for unprivileged groups and individuals can alleviate the deleterious effect of a particularly pernicious form of White American affirmative action: unmerited privileges for materially wealthy White males.

We now turn to the question of how do we deal with the effects of traditional White affirmative action?

### *How?*

To create equal opportunity for all, affirmative action programs will often need to consider the same factors that caused inequities. For example, color prejudice as well as bias based on sex and economic class create and perpetuate gross disparities in many areas like education, housing, employment, access to health care, and leadership positions. To remedy effects of race, sex, and economic class discrimination requires seeing the individuals and groups negatively affected. In the Preface to this book, the late Oliver Hill Jr. said that we must recognize:

> [the] continuing trail that leads to current societal outcomes. If my great-grandfather was denied access to a job that would have led to the elevation of his family to the middle class, and someone else's great-grandfather who was less well qualified was given that job because he didn't have to compete against my great-grandfather, the ramifications of that set of circumstances could reverberate for generations.[31]

In this context, we come to a practical present-day example of why affirmative action is still necessary.

## A Contemporary Example of the Need for Affirmative Action

In the United States, the belief that White persons are inherently better than other persons is a long-standing societal fairy tale. For instance, white supremacy was the cultural myth supporting the establishment of the federal judiciary of the United States that, for the first 145 years (1789-1934), was comprised solely of White males.[32] This historical pattern and practice of race and sex discrimination is evident in the composition of today's federal courts. Today, in the United States, men are a minority group constituting approximately 49% of the national population.[33] Nevertheless, as this book goes to press, only 33% of sitting federal judges are women—67% are men.[34] Indeed, White men, who comprise a little over 30% of the general population,[35] constitute approximately 52% of the federal judiciary.[36] Academic studies provide evidence that over 80% of federal appellate judges appointed to the bench in recent years have a net wealth of over a half million dollars.[37] The reason for this inequitable imbalance in the federal judiciary stems from long entrenched sex, race, and economic class discrimination. The present composition of the federal judiciary reflects enduring, practical effects of fictional tales about white supremacy—particularly "rich" white male supremacy.

To redress the gross imbalance in the federal judiciary, an appropriate affirmative action program would do several things.

First, decision makers would need to acknowledge that an inequitable distribution of judges based on sex, race, and material wealth exists. An effective affirmative action program cannot be blind to the real-world impact of prejudice based on race, sex, and material wealth. Such negative bias, whether conscious or unconscious, results in some individuals progressing primarily because they "look the part." Regardless of their qualifications, they at least fit the (White male) mold of many who have preceded them and attained elevated status. This "identity qualification" (looking the part) is true of judges, legislators, civic, and religious leaders.

Second, to accelerate the race, gender, and class desegregation of the federal judiciary, decision makers should appoint more qualified women, men of color, and less materially affluent White men to the federal bench. Such an appointment process should last as long as disproportionate imbalances exist. Doors for public service as federal judges must open to a broader swath of America's population. A more diverse federal judiciary, including women, men of color, LGBTQ+ persons, and materially less affluent White males would allow federal courts to view facts from perspectives drawn from a wider range of life experiences than now exists.

This background frames the focus of this book. We highlight the United States' long-standing race and to a lesser extent sex-based preference practices and laws. Beginning in colonial America, the laws and social practices were oriented to benefit a relatively small group of White persons—materially well-to-do White men. Stated bluntly, the Founders of the 1700s sought to protect the privileges of their own social group. The patterns and practices of discrimination of the 1700s have subsided somewhat: but nonetheless continue to impact the United States today.

To create equal opportunity, laws and public policy programs must be specifically designed to ensure a more equitable distribution of social, political, and economic resources. In short, we cannot afford the luxury of burying our collective heads in the twenty-first century sands and pretending that we live in a "post-racial" society or one in which your sex does not impact your life's chances. In this context, the critical race theory uproar provides opportunities to ask why are some persons afraid of learning facts about the United

States—past and present? Only by confronting rather than whitewashing historical facts can we have a nation that is more secure, just, and free.

Repeating for emphasis: this book is not trying to write the definitive social, political, or legal history of the United States. *This book seeks to give individuals a fact-based foundation—an overview, not an encyclopedia.* These facts can facilitate intelligent discussion, further research, and better-informed decision making. We hope to help create a genuine, respectful community in which all persons can excel not only in America but also globally.

Furthermore, to create a more civilized society we need to deal with controversial historic events and figures. As an example, the book includes a short chapter that addresses attempts to honor Confederate leaders.

Mr. Hill suggested that we attempt to do our part to nourish a renaissance in human relationships so that human earthlings (people living on the planet earth) can live through this century in a more peaceful and joyous manner. This book seeks to contribute to fulfilling Mr. Hill's vision.

Putting things in a broader context, we need to recognize another significant reality: as human earthlings embark on interplanetary travels, outer space will become a significant area in which we work and play. This is both exciting and challenging. Hopefully this book will contribute to broadening our collective horizons. As we learn more about situations confronting us, we need to accept this reality: *the struggle for liberty and justice always continues.*

Chapter I

# Justice Denied: Examples from the Colonial American Legal System

IN THE EARLY 1600S, some of the founding English great-grandfathers came to this country with visions of finding huge amounts of mineral resources, especially gold. They had heard of Spain's fabulous discoveries in Latin America, and had witnessed the bountiful treasures (like silver and gold) the Spanish had seized from the Indians. All too often, many of the founding great-grandfathers were determined to follow the Spanish example. Historians Peter N. Carroll and David Noble put it like this:

> The first permanent English colony began in May 1607 when three vessels dropped anchor several miles up the James River in Virginia at a site they named Jamestown. Financed by the Virginia Company of London, a joint-stock corporation, and settled by ambitious young men employed by the company, the colony was expected to produce lucrative profits by locating gold mines and a water route through the continent to the fabulous markets of Asia. The vision of duplicating Spanish

> success, however, blinded the adventurers to realities of colonization.[1]

These invaders were intent on finding gold and often had no problem with taking the land from the native people (Indians) by any available means (including hook or crook).

Like their Spanish competitors, many English founding great-grandfathers argued that God had authorized them to conquer the New World and spread Christianity to the savage inhabitants. Upon arriving, the colonial great-grandfathers asserted that the British monarch had the only true title to land. They claimed that the natives' property rights, along with the rights of other European nations, were inferior to the English settlers. By asserting that the land belonged to them, the great-grandfathers expected to quickly obtain vast estates and personal fiefdoms. They soon discovered, however, that they were ill-prepared for the rigor of life in the New World.

Fortunately, for these colonists, the native peoples in Virginia and in the Massachusetts Bay Colony often befriended them. Indeed, the natives helped the colonists to survive the early years in an unfamiliar, hostile, and sometimes deadly environment. For instance, in Virginia, following the founding of Jamestown, the colonists and Indians lived in relative peace for most of the first 15 years. Recent archaeological research shows that Indian women lived in the Jamestown settlement during its early years.[2] Such evidence suggests that the native people attempted to create alliances with the English by encouraging the settlers to intermarry with Indian women.

Controversy exists regarding when Blacks first arrived at Jamestown, Virginia—the first permanent English-speaking settlement in North America. According to John Rolfe, 20 Blacks arrived in Jamestown on a Dutch sailing vessel in August 1619.[3] Rolfe's account is widely accepted as an accurate record of the arrival of the first Blacks.

However, evidence exists that these might not have been the first Blacks to come to Jamestown. In March 1619, *five months before the Dutch ship arrived*, the Virginia Company of London conducted a census of the Jamestown colony, which revealed *that there were already 32 Africans in Jamestown.*[4] How long these 15 Black men and 17 Black women had been in Virginia is not clear. It is reasonable to believe that they arrived much earlier with other English settlers. The March 1619 census lists 4 Indians as servants as well. The Blacks and Indians were referred to as "non-Christians." If this evidence is accurate, then contrary to widespread belief, Blacks arrived in Jamestown before August 1619.

In addition, it is nearly certain that the 20 Blacks who landed in August 1619 did not arrive in Jamestown as slaves.[5] For instance, Cassandra Newby-Alexander, a highly respected scholar and Dean of Norfolk State University, has cogently argued that Africans arrived at Jamestown as servants, not as enslaved persons.[6]

As the British colonies along the Atlantic Coast grew, tensions between the Native Americans and English colonists increased. For example, in Virginia the Native Americans complained repeatedly regarding the colonists' invasions of Native Americans' land. Following the discovery that tobacco could be profitably grown on a large scale as the colony's cash crop, the settlers' accelerated their squatting on Native American lands. The steady stream of settlers started to become a river of humanity: homeless children, Irish indentured servants, convicted criminals, and poor English persons came to America seeking "a howse [sic], orchard and garden ... and a possession of lands ... one hundred acres for every man's person that hath a trade, or a body able to endure day labor."[7] Many migrants seeking a new life felt entitled to take the land however they could get it even if someone else (specifically, Native Americans) had been living on the land since time immemorial.

Feeling threatened, in 1622, the Native Americans launched a military attack designed to destroy the Jamestown colony before the colonists destroyed the Native Americans. The preemptive attack killed nearly one-third of the settlers. The English colonists asked the Mother Country for reinforcements and eventually subjugated the native people.

At gunpoint, the colonial great-grandfathers soon established a "to the victor goes the spoils" system. In practice this system was based on skin color. In implementing this racial preference program, English settlers gave Native Americans three options: (1) keep moving further west, (2) give up most (if not all) of their valuable land, or (3) die.[8]

The migrants' approach to the native people was an early example of a glaring abuse of affirmative action. The English colonists obtained other persons' material assets based largely on race. The English often used physical violence to seize Native American land. The English settlers persuaded themselves that because the Native Americans looked different, spoke a different language, and lived different lifestyles, the settlers were superior to the Native Americans. To some English people, their supposed natural superiority supported their policies of oppression. Put another way, the English law, practice, and policy were not designed to create equal opportunity for all. The settlers intended to establish social, economic, political, and military domination along the color line. The settlers' behavior constituted an abuse of affirmative action.

When practices, policies, and laws are devised, implemented, and interpreted to maintain White people's domination over others, these essays refer to that fact situation as *White affirmative action*. For instance, the English—new uninvited, undocumented, foreign immigrants to Indian Country—used force and fraud to implement a "by any means necessary" program to exploit the Native Americans. Those practices and policies exemplify White affirmative action.

John Woolman, a remarkable eighteenth-century Quaker thinker and activist, critiqued such White affirmative action. Woolman vividly described how settlers schemed to entice Native Americans to consume alcohol, which inevitably led to fights among the Native Americans:

> I perceived that many white people often sell rum to the Indians, which I believe is a great evil. In the first place, they are thereby deprived of the use of reason, and, their spirits being violently agitated, quarrels often arise which end in mischief, and the bitterness and resentment occasioned hereby are frequently of long continuance. Again, their skins and furs, gotten through much fatigue and hard travels in hunting, with which they intend to buy clothing, they often sell at a low rate for more rum, when they become intoxicated; and afterward, when they suffer for want of the necessities of life, are angry with those who, for the sake of gain, took advantage of their weakness.
>
> Their chiefs have often complained of this in their treaties with the English. Where cunning people pass counterfeits and impose on others that which is good for nothing, it is considered as wickedness; but for the sake of gain to sell that which we know does people harm, and which often works their ruin, manifests a hardened and corrupt heart, and is an evil which demands the care of all true lovers of virtue to suppress.[9]

Woolman recognized and deplored the cold, calculated plans of some colonists to destroy Indian communities through promoting alcoholism.

Furthermore, English settlers sometimes included germ warfare to intentionally spread deadly plagues like smallpox among the Native Americans. In 1763, Indians in the Great Lakes defended their lands from an invading British force by besieging Fort Pitt. In response, members of the British contingent allegedly infected blankets with smallpox and supplied the blankets to unsuspecting native people. Large numbers of the Delaware tribes were wiped out.[10]

In addition, as they sought to conquer the Native Americans, the colonists had a gratuitous ally. During the course of ordinary human contacts like trading, the British introduced a variety of new diseases. A conversation between a settler infected with the flu and a Native American could lead to an epidemic (or even a pandemic), wiping out many Native Americans over a large area. Foreign diseases decimated native populations, which had not developed natural immunity to such illnesses. Some scholars estimate that in the first hundred years after Columbus arrived in the New World, the native population fell by 90%.[11]

Why did English colonists resort to such ruthless violent methods in dealing with native peoples? One reason seems that the English had recently used merciless, scorched-earth, genocidal tactics against another ethnic group who shared similarities with Native Americans. These recipients of English oppression practiced a nomadic lifestyle, spoke a different language, engaged in different religious practices, and established family as well as property laws that diverged from the English legal system. About whom do we speak? *The Irish.*

As the English were colonizing the Atlantic coastline of the New World, England was also closing another chapter in a fierce struggle lasting hundreds of years with the Irish. In 1603, English forces defeated Irish clans, ending a long, bloody conflict known as Tyrone's Rebellion. Many Irish combatants and civilians were captured and forcibly removed from Ireland. At gunpoint, thousands of Irish persons were transported to the Caribbean and Atlantic Coast colonies.[12] These Irish captives were held in conditions that resembled slavery. Irish indentured servants could be bought, sold, and inherited. An important distinction between indentured servitude and slavery was that indentured servitude was for a fixed term of years usually ranging between four and seven years. In contrast, slavery was for life.[13]

Frequently, English colonial authorities abused Irish indentured laborers, referring to them as "savages."[14] Moreover, English employers made Irish servants work longer than English indentured servants and subjected them to severe beatings, poor food, and cruel working conditions. Many indentured servants (in colonies like Virginia) died within the first few years of their employment because of deplorable working conditions, disease, and related circumstances.[15]

In addition, English persons, often from the criminal or impoverished classes, suffered under similar harsh labor conditions. Between 1607 and 1682, it was not uncommon that homeless people ("vagabond" men, women, and children) were rounded up, kidnapped, and shipped to the New World colonies to provide workers to produce a major cash crop—namely, tobacco.[16]

In essence, this egregious treatment of Irish and poor English workers helped to create a model for the English elite to use in dealing with Native Americans and Africans. English colonial leaders imposed indentured servitude upon all four groups: the Irish, poor English persons, Africans, and Native Americans. Indentured workers were treated more like things than persons.[17]

Unlike their English and Irish counterparts, African indentured servants were easily identifiable. In addition, some Africans were especially valued workers because they had greater familiarity with organized farming in a warm climate. For instance, a specialized slave trade developed that brought skilled African rice farmers from parts of the "Rice Coast" of West Africa (Senegal and Gambia) to the low country of South Carolina. Some African captives were crafts persons, too.[18]

To control the colonial labor force, laws in colonies like Virginia evolved to discourage and penalize alliances between Europeans, Native Americans, and African indentured servants. An illustrative case is *In Re Negro John Punch*, decided in 1640. *Punch* involved a Negro servant who ran away from Virginia to Maryland with two White servants. All three of the servants, when captured, were sentenced to be whipped. The two White servants, one of whom was Dutch and the other a Scot, were sentenced to serve four additional years of indentured servitude. The Negro, John Punch, was sentenced to lifetime servitude. In essence, the colonial court made him a slave.

In the *Punch* case, all three of the servants committed the same crime. They all tried to attain their freedom from the brutality of indentured servitude by running away. Nevertheless, only Punch was punished by being made a slave for life. John Punch's case illustrates how colonial courts were sometimes biased based on a person's skin color. The colonial elites were prone to pervert the laws to oppress Africans and to divide the servant class along the color line.[19]

In addition to color bias in some court decisions, Virginia's legislature enshrined skin color prejudice into colonial statutes. For instance, in the usual case involving a runaway worker, the legislature imposed multiple punishments. The law compelled the runaway to work a longer employment term, and endure a severe whipping. Moreover, such escapees often were subjected to a large fine, which sometimes could be paid in tobacco.

Occasionally, however, an English servant ran away with a Negro. If the runaway Negro had been enslaved, a unique problem arose. When the fugitive English servant and his enslaved Negro coworker absconded and were later captured, one of the usual punishments was not an option. The Black slave could not be forced to work any longer than the law already required; that is, until the day she died.

In contrast, if you were English and ran off with a Black, once captured you could expect the ordinary punishment for runaways. You would be required to work for a longer time for your employer. You would also probably suffer a beating and pay a fine.

In these circumstances, the colonial legislature enacted legislation specifically crafted to teach English servants to not form alliances with Black enslaved persons. Specifically, in 1661-62, Virginia's colonial legislature passed a law that presumed that the escape of indentured servants and slaves caused economic loss to slaveholders. While the slave and English servant had escaped and were seeking freedom, the slaveholder did not have the economic benefit of the slave's free labor. To compensate the slaveholder, the law forced the English servant to work for the slaveholder long enough to compensate the slaveholder for the slave's absence. Thus, if you were an English servant, the law punished you for your Black compatriot's escape as well as for your own attempt to free yourself from exploitation. The Virginia statute said:

> [I]n case any English servant shall run away in company of any negroes who are incapable of making satisfaction by addition of a time, *it is enacted* that the English soe running away in the company with them shall at the time of service to their owne masters expired, serve the masters of the said negroes for their absence soe long as they should have done by this act if they had not beene slaves, every christian in company serving his proportion.[20]

The law purposely drove a legal wedge between working people (indentured or enslaved). Even though indentured and enslaved workers experienced similar harsh conditions, colonial law attempted to create malice and distrust (along the color line) among the workforce.

In summary, in employment relations, the Virginia colonial legislature did not use the law as a servant of justice. The legislature employed the law as an engine of oppression.[21] Instead of relieving employees working under brutal conditions, the colonial legislature punished them more harshly for seeking freedom by running away. In addition, the law aggressively attempted to sabotage alliances between European and African laborers through making European runaways work longer if they fled with enslaved Africans.

Similar blatant efforts to divide working people continue. For instance, in the twentieth century, some White employers in the United States colluded with White workers to exclude Blacks and other persons of color from employment.[22] In the early 1940s, the Supreme Court decided the cases of *Steele v. Louisiana and Nashville Railroads* and *Tunstall v. Brotherhood of Locomotive Firemen and Enginemen.*[23] These cases involved the White railroad unions which called themselves Brotherhoods and which (in an unbrotherly manner) denied membership to Negroes. Under the relevant railroad labor legislation, the Brotherhoods were allowed to be the bargaining agent for the railway workers. *Steele* and *Tunstall* held that the Brotherhoods had to fairly represent non-member Negroes.

Moreover, by excluding persons of color, government entities like police and fire departments actively participated in race-based employment discrimination. As a result, in large metropolitan areas White persons, particularly White males, are overrepresented especially in leadership positions.[24] In sum, such pervasive, entrenched unrelenting patterns and practices of White (often male) preferences persist. Such long-standing "baked-in" institutional bias exemplifies White American affirmative action.

Another example of legalized oppression in colonial Virginia involved a law enacted in 1667 that said that a slave's conversion to Christianity did not result in freedom.[25] Thus, Virginia's 1667 colonial legislation legally enslaved Black Christians. Stated another way, one's freedom in Christ could not be allowed to interfere with the slaveholder's pursuit of material riches. The colonial law reflected a cynical use of the Christian gospel. The law turned the Good News on its head. Instead of reflecting the love of God and love for other human beings, the law promoted idolatry: love of material wealth. The law failed its fundamental duty—to act as a servant of justice.

Virginia's 1667 Christian enslavement law represented an unfortunate departure from a 1641 colonial court decision that provided protection for the human rights of a Negro indentured servant, John Graweere. Graweere sought to purchase the freedom of his child who had been born to an enslaved woman. In 1641, Virginia's colonial court had granted Graweere's petition to raise his child so that the child "should be made a Christian and be brought up in the fear of God and in the knowledge of religion taught and exercised by the church of England."[26] Thus, the *Graweere* case recognized that Negro indentured workers possessed and were entitled to exercise some human rights. A little more than a quarter century later, Virginia's 1667 statute entrenched Christian enslavement. The 1667 statute was a colossal retreat from Graweere's more compassionate attempt to protect the best interests of the child.

*While change is inevitable, all change is not for the better.*

In further contrast to Graweere's more humane approach, in 1680, the Virginia legislature passed a statute making it a crime for a Negro to defend himself from punishment by a slaveholder. A Negro who "lift[ed] up his hand against any Christian ... shall receive thirty lashes." If he chose flight rather than fight, that same Negro if captured could be lawfully killed.[27]

The statute of 1680 may well have been a partial response to the rebellion led by Nathaniel Bacon that had erupted in Virginia four years earlier (1676). A member of the colonial elite, Bacon had married a cousin of Virginia's governor, and been given a lucrative fur trading license. Despite his privileged position, Bacon spearheaded an uprising against Virginia's colonial government. Among other things, Bacon and other planters living on Virginia's western frontier wanted a more aggressive White American affirmative action plan to seize Native American land by any means—fair or foul. Bacon and his followers forced the colonial government to authorize a military attack against Native Americans.[28]

The rebellion disintegrated following Bacon's relatively quick and unanticipated death. Why did European and African indentured servants as well as enslaved Africans join Bacon? Some scholars contend that all of these workers sought to improve their economic condition. Moreover, the slaves also supported Bacon because he declared them to be free.[29] The uprising served notice on the colonial elite that workers of all colors were prone to unite and attempt to redistribute the economic pie.

As far as interpersonal relations were concerned, the colonial legislators provided great opportunities for English males to exploit women. The law described male employers as "masters," and punished women (regardless of color) who had children by their employers. According to a 1662 Virginia colonial law, if a master impregnated an unmarried indentured servant woman and she gave birth to his child, the law did not free the unmarried mother. Instead the law forced her to continue working for the father of her child until her original employment contract with the father ended. Afterward the law mandated that she be sold by the Churchwardens to work two more years for the financial benefit of the local vestry.

Moreover, in 1662 the colonial legislature in Virginia also enacted a law providing that if an English male conceived a child with a Negro female, the child would be free or enslaved depending on the legal status of the mother.[30] This was the opposite of English common law, which made the status of a child born out of wedlock dependent on the legal status of the father.[31] The English common law favored freedom for the children of "illicit" unions of English men and women.

In the colonies, however, the law mandated slavery for the children of English men and enslaved African women. In effect, the law encouraged English men to have sexual relations with enslaved Negro women because their children would be slaves—a financial asset to their slaveholding fathers. In addition, an enslaved child could not inherit her father's material wealth unless the father freed her or took other appropriate legal steps. The enslaved population increased through importation and procreation among slaves. In addition, the law facilitated growth of the enslaved population by encouraging and protecting White males who practiced sexual immorality and exploitation.

On the other hand, in 1691, the colonial Virginia legislature mandated that if an English woman had a child with a Negro, the English woman must suffer much harsher punishment than her English brother. If she was a free woman, the law required her to pay a fine of £15 because she had a Black child. If she failed to pay the fine, she would lose her freedom. If she were too poor to pay the fine, the law required that she serve five years as an indentured servant for the wardens of the church. The law further mandated that her child work as a servant for the church wardens until the child became 30.[32]

Similarly, if the English woman was already an indentured servant, she would be sold to the church wardens to labor as an indentured servant for five additional years. This was two and a half times longer than she would have been forced to work had she given birth (out of wedlock) to an English master's child. As to her child, "bastard children" were compelled to work for the colony as well.[33]

The practical effect of the law gave males comprising the colonial elites the material benefits from increasing the size of their labor force through sexual oppression. In this manner, the law further encouraged (White) male employers to abuse their power to fulfill their personal lust.[34]

Furthermore, the colonial statutes made it a crime if couples of different complexions ("races") sought to create families through marrying one another. The law criminalized marriage between "Negroes, mulattoes and Indians [and] English or other white [men] or [women]."[35] White persons who sought to uphold family values through marrying persons of color were banished from the colony forever.

We note in passing that the legal heritage passed down from the colonial great-grandfathers involving "miscegenation" stubbornly persisted in Virginia for nearly 300 years. In 1959, in *Loving v. Virginia*, a Virginia Circuit Court upheld early colonial legal precedent and banished a married couple from Virginia for 25 years because the wife was a woman of color and the husband was White.[36] Indeed, the trial court based its rationale for upholding Virginia's ban on marriage between people of different skin complexions (races) in part because the court claimed that God was a segregationist! Virginia State Circuit Judge Leon Bazile proclaimed:

> Almighty God created races white, black, yellow, malay and red, and he placed them on separate continents. And but for the interference with his arrangement there would be no cause for such marriages. The fact that he separated the races shows that he did not intend for the races to mix.[37]

The married couple appealed, and the Virginia Supreme Court upheld the state trial court. Fortunately, in 1967, the United States Supreme Court overturned the Virginia state courts' decisions in *Loving*.[38]

While we could list many more examples, we will conclude this section by mentioning once more a particularly egregious piece of colonial legislation: the comprehensive Virginia Slave Codes of 1705. As noted earlier, this Virginia statute allowed a slaveholder to petition the county court to punish a runaway slave "by dismembering, or in any other way, not touching his life, as they in their discretion shall think fit, for the reclaiming any such an incorrigible slave and *terrifying* others from the like practices."[39] The colonists clearly authorized law enforcement personnel to cut off slaves' hands, feet, arms, and legs to achieve the colonists' goal of "terrifying" slaves. But the Codes of 1705 went even further. If an enslaved person had escaped from bondage and was thought to be "lurking" in a community, the colonial legislature mandated that two justices of the peace issue a proclamation:

> Which proclamation shall be published on a Sabbath day, at the door of every church and chapel,

> in the said county, by the parish clerk, or reader, of the church, immediately after divine worship: And in case any slave, against whom proclamation hath been thus issued, and once published at any church or chapel, as aforesaid, stay out, and do not immediately return home, it shall be lawful for any person or persons whatsoever, to kill and destroy such slaves by such ways and means as he, she, or they shall think fit, without accusation or impeachment of any crime for the same . . .[40]

Virginia colonists deliberately used the law as a tool of terror and torture to control slaves. In essence, any English colonist could be judge, jury, and executioner of any enslaved person who ran away.

As might be expected, to protect the slaveholder's pocketbook, the statute also provided that if an enslaved person were killed, the slaveholder would receive financial compensation. The statute stated:

> [F]or every slave killed, in pursuance of this act, or put to death by law, the master or owner of such slave shall be paid by the public.[41]

A few years before the American Revolution, Virginia's colonists repealed the Slave Code of 1705's amputation provision but included another statute that allowed authorities to castrate Black men who tried to "ravish" a White woman.[42] The legislature did not pass a law mandating castration of White men who attempted to or actually succeeded in ravishing enslaved women.

In effect, colonial law and custom, particularly in slaveholding colonies, made slaveholders absolute rulers. Such persons could torture, rape, and kill enslaved persons without fear of legal punishment. After all, how can you commit a crime against your own property? In English slaveholding colonies like Virginia, it was neither a crime to break the legs of one's dining room table nor to fracture the legs of one's enslaved workers.

The law enforced an extreme form of color and sex-based preference system favoring White males—particularly materially wealthy ones. Rich White males wrote the law to confer benefits primarily upon themselves—often at the expense of others. *Slavery was a radical form of White American affirmative action.*

Nevertheless, while many English colonists sought to exploit other humans to obtain economic wealth, social status, and sexual gratification, some courageous, principled individuals did not yield to the lures and temptations of colonial society. For instance, in his journal, John Woolman shares this story:

> About this time, a person at some distance lying sick, his brother came to me to write his will. I knew he had slaves, and, asking his brother, was told he intended to leave them as slaves to his children. As writing is a profitable employ, and as offending sober people was disagreeable to my inclination, I was straitened in my mind; but as I looked to the Lord, he inclined my heart to His testimony. I told the man that I believed the practice of continuing slavery to this people was not right, and that I had a scruple in my mind against doing writings of that kind; that though many in our Society kept them as slaves, still I was not easy to be concerned in it, and desired to be excused from going to write the will. I spake to him in the fear of the Lord, and he made no reply to what I said, but went away; he also had some concerns in the practice, and I thought he was displeased with me. In this case I had fresh confirmation that acting contrary to present outward interest, from a motive of divine love and in regard to truth and righteousness, and thereby incurring the resentments of people, opens the way

to a treasure better than silver, and to a friendship exceeding the friendship of men.[43]

In fact, Thomas Jefferson, himself a deeply ambivalent Virginia slaveholder, recognized the moral impossibility of justifying the slaveholders' position:

> There must doubtless be an unhappy influence on the manners of our people produced by the existence of slavery among us. The whole commerce between master and slave is a perpetual exercise of the most boisterous passions, the most unremitting despotism on the one part, and degrading submissions on the other. Our children see this, and learn to imitate it; for man is an imitative animal ... If a parent could find no motive either in his philanthropy or his self-love, for restraining the intemperance of passion towards his slave, it should always be a sufficient one that his child is present. But generally it is not sufficient. The parent storms, the child looks on, catches the lineaments of wrath, puts on the same airs in the circle of smaller slaves, gives a loose to his worst of passions, and thus nursed, educated, and daily exercised in tyranny, cannot but be stamped by it with odious peculiarities. The man must be a prodigy who can retain his manners and morals undepraved by such circumstances. And with what execration should the statesman be loaded, who permitting one half the citizens thus to trample on the rights of the other, transforms those into despots, and these into enemies, destroys the morals of the one part, and the amor patriae of the other. For if a slave can have a country in this world, it must be any other in preference to that in which he is born to love and labour for another; in which he must lock up the faculties of his nature, contribute as far as depends on his

> individual endeavours to the evanishment of the human race, or entail his own miserable condition on the endless generations proceeding from him . . .

Jefferson concluded his perceptive analysis with these haunting words:

> Indeed I tremble for my country when I reflect that God is just: that his justice cannot sleep for ever: that considering numbers, nature and natural means only, a revolution of the wheel of fortune, an exchange of situation, is among possible events: that it may become probable by supernatural interference! The Almighty has no attribute which can take side with us in such a contest.[44]

This brief recitation of the legal legacy of the colonial great-grandfathers is neither exhaustive nor is it intended to be. We simply wish to give a flavor of the heritage of legal discrimination (institutional racism), which the great-granddads passed on to the founding fathers at the time of the American Revolution.

Chapter II

# The American Revolution and the United States Constitution: Liberty and Justice for Some

THE DECLARATION OF INDEPENDENCE reflected the influence of European Enlightenment thinkers like John Locke and Jean Jacques Rousseau. In his writings about the social contract, Rousseau had emphasized human freedom and equality. Rousseau argued that no natural right existed to own slaves because freedom is the birthright of every human.[1] The Declaration of Independence echoed that theme: "[A]ll men are created equal [and] they are endowed by their creator with certain unalienable rights, that among these are life, liberty and the pursuit of happiness."

As compared to the king of England and his supporters, the colonists viewed themselves as progressive thinkers on human rights. For example, an early draft of the Declaration of Independence bluntly said that the English king had

> [w]aged cruel war against human nature itself, violating its most sacred rights of life and liberty in the persons of a distant people who never offended him, captivating and carrying them into slavery in another hemisphere, or to incur miserable death

> in their transportation thither. This piratical warfare . . . is the warfare of the Christian king of Great Britain.[2]

The Declaration's language condemning slavery and the slave trade proved politically too hot to handle. After all, a number of leading American revolutionaries held Africans in bondage. Prominent slaveholders included four future presidents, George Washington, Thomas Jefferson, James Madison, and James Monroe, as well as future Chief Justice John Marshall, all of Virginia. Indeed, Patrick Henry, who uttered the unforgettable words, "give me liberty, or give me death!" held Black slaves. In this vein, Robert Pleasants, a Quaker, sent Henry a copy of a book condemning the slave trade. In his letter replying to Pleasants, Henry admitted his hypocrisy.

> I cannot but wish well to a people whose System imitates the Example of him whose Life was perfect, and believe me I shall honor the Quakers for their noble Effort to abolish Slavery. It is equally calculated to promote moral and political Good. Would any one believe that I am Master of Slaves of my own purchase? *I am drawn along by the general Inconvenience of living without them. I will not, I cannot justify it.*
>
> However culpable my Conduct, I will so far pay my Devoir to Virtue as to own the Excellence and Rectitude of her precepts, and to lament my want of Conformity to them.
>
> I believe a time will come when an Opportunity will be offered to abolish this lamentable Evil, every thing we can do is to improve it, if it happens in our Day, if not let us transmit to our Descendants together with our Slaves, a pity for their unhappy Lot and an abhorrence for Slavery—If we cannot

> reduce this wished for Reformation to practice let us treat the unhappy Victims with Lenity . . .[3]

On the eve of the American War for Independence from Great Britain, a deep gulf existed between many of the leading Framers' words and their deeds. The Declaration proclaimed that "all men are created equal." In 1776, the term "men" could have referred to all humans. Thus, the *Oxford English Dictionary* states that a man is "[a] human being (irrespective of sex or age)."[4] A contemporaneous example of how "man" could be used to include males and females, is found in Scots philosopher, David Hume's 1753 book entitled *Essays and Treatises on Several Subjects*. Hume states "[T]here is in all men, both male and female, a desire and power of generation more active than is ever universally exerted . . ."[5]

On the other hand, in practical terms, the Declaration most likely meant "men" to include all property-owning White men. While some exceptions existed, many of the Founding Fathers did not believe that Black men (or poor White men) were entitled to the protections that the Declaration trumpeted. Nor did the Declaration seem to contemplate women as equals.

*Again: the truth will set us free; but the truth might not make us happy*. More to the point, it may not be flattering, but strong evidence exists that many American revolutionary leaders had an impoverished version (and vision) of freedom: life, liberty, and the pursuit of happiness was reserved primarily for White males with property. *In other words: the Founders behaved like they fervently believed in White American (male) affirmative action for themselves and their peers*.

Accordingly, one should not be surprised that when the Revolutionary War began, one of George Washington's first acts was to exclude Blacks, whether enslaved or free, from military service. In contrast, the British promised to liberate slaves who fought with the king. Understandably, the enslaved African captives found the choice between these options easy. Slaves initially flocked to the British army. In fact, in Virginia, the English established a Black regiment of troops loyal to the king. Some scholars of the American Revolution believed that as many as 800 Virginia Blacks joined the regiment, and thousands more were encouraged to support those they viewed as British Liberators.[6]

Influential Virginia leaders noted and complained about King George III's (the English king) promise to free enslaved Africans. For example, in the Virginia Constitution of June 29, 1776, leading Virginians justified repudiating the authority of King George because the king had in numerous ways "endeavored to pervert" his "kingly office." The colonists especially objected to the king, "prompting our negroes to rise in arms against us."[7]

The Virginia Constitution influenced the Declaration of Independence, which was promulgated less than a week later. For example, the Virginia Constitution said:

> SECTION 1. That all men are by nature equally free and independent, and have certain inherent rights, of which, when they enter into a state of society, they cannot, by any compact, deprive or divest their posterity; namely, the enjoyment of life and liberty, with the means of acquiring and possessing property, and pursuing and obtaining happiness and safety.

The Declaration of Independence echoed these words when the Declaration proclaimed:

> We hold these truths to be self-evident:
>
> That all men are created equal; that they are endowed by their Creator with certain unalienable rights; that among these are life, liberty, and the pursuit of happiness.

While colonial Virginia leaders were bellowing words of freedom, in practice, Virginia's charter of freedom was written in part to protect the material wealth of property-owning (White) males who were the only ones who could vote and hold elective office.[8] The majority of Virginians—women of all backgrounds (free, indentured, and enslaved), men who owned no real estate, and men of color—were all excluded from participating in governmental elections. Even Thomas Jefferson objected to limiting the franchise to property-owning males. Jefferson also wanted persons who were in the colonial militia to be able to vote as well.[9]

Thus, the majority of English colonists were excluded from voting for persons to represent themselves. However, many English males at least had the possibility of becoming landowners and improving their general standard of living. For enslaved Africans, their prospects mainly revolved around permanent degradation. Accordingly, it is not surprising that many enslaved Africans had limited loyalty and incentive to support the cause of the colonists. During the Revolutionary War, in three southern states alone, more than 60,000 African Americans ran away from slavery. The escapees hoped to gain freedom with the British. Thomas Jefferson estimated that over 30,000 slaves fled Virginia; South Carolina historian David Ramsay claimed that at least 25,000 Blacks left South Carolina, and it is estimated that over 10,000 of the 15,000 slaves in Georgia escaped to freedom during the war.[10]

Even in northern colonies many Blacks left their slaveholders, hoping to secure freedom by supporting the British. For example, when the British occupied Philadelphia in 1778, large numbers of Blacks crossed over to join the king's supporters. The British later evacuated the city and many Blacks left with the British for New York.[11]

From a military perspective the British tactics were understandable. On the eve of the American Revolution, of the approximately two and a half million British colonists about a half million, one out of every five, were enslaved.[12] Depending on how they behaved (or not!), a half million enslaved people could greatly influence the outcome of the war.

According to noted historian Benjamin Quarles:

> The Negro's role in the Revolution can best be understood by realizing that his major loyalty was not to a place nor to a people, but to a principle. Insofar as he had freedom of choice, he was likely to join the side that made him the quickest and best offer in terms of those "unalienable rights" of which Mr. Jefferson had spoken. Whoever invoked the image of liberty, be he American or British, could count on a ready response from the blacks.[13]

The Declaration of Independence is America's bell of freedom. It could have and should have rung resoundingly: LIBERTY AND JUSTICE FOR ALL! Sad to say, the Founders exhibited a stingy idea of liberty. Their narrow-mindedness muffled that bell.

Some of the American revolutionaries' narrow vision had practical implications. For instance, Washington's initial order segregating the colonial armies seriously handicapped the colonists' war efforts. Washington's short-sighted thinking compelled him later to take a desperate military measure: George Washington reluctantly reversed part of his racial segregationist stand and decided to allow free Negro troops to fight in the American Revolutionary armies. As a result, less than six months after the Declaration of Independence was proclaimed, several Blacks crossed the Delaware with Washington on Christmas Day.[14]

In addition, many colonial legislators changed their positions and allowed enslaved persons and free Blacks to fight against the British Crown. Eventually, over 5,000 Negroes fought with the American armies.[15] In some cases (Rhode Island, for instance), slaves were freed when they enlisted in the Continental Army. Sometimes slaveholders were exempted from having to fight for freedom because their slaves served as substitutes fighting and dying in the place of the slaveholders. A number of colonies formally adopted laws or informal policies that allowed the substitution of Black bodies for White ones during the Revolutionary War. According to noted historian Professor Benjamin Quarles, Connecticut and Maryland passed laws sanctioning schemes to send enslaved persons to war in place of their enslavers. In practice, other colonies like New Jersey, New York, North Carolina, and Virginia also permitted such substitutions.[16] Blacks were not always welcomed by their colonial comrades in arms. Nevertheless, the Africans' heroism contributed to the military defeat of the British.

Regarding Africans who joined the British, some Africans' expectations of freedom were fulfilled while others were disappointed. The British sometimes failed to keep promises made during the tumult of war, especially to those who were sick and aged.[17] After the war, along with other colonists loyal to the king, some scholars estimate that at least several thousand Blacks fled to Canada and the Caribbean islands. These free Blacks began new lives as British subjects in places like Halifax (Nova Scotia) and Jamaica.

George Liele was such an immigrant. Born in Virginia before the Revolutionary War began and held in slavery in Georgia, Liele converted to Christianity. After Liele's conversion, Liele's slaveholder, Henry Sharp (who was a church officer), freed Liele. During the War, while fighting for the king's forces, Sharp was killed. Following the War, Liele joined other former Tories who left America. Liele established a church in Kingston, Jamaica, which in the late 1790s had over 300 members, a free school, and several acres of real property.[18]

With the War of Independence over, the new nation confronted significant challenges. The United States had obtained its freedom: What would America's freedom mean for people of African descent?

The Articles of Confederation (America's first constitution) created a new government. The Articles guaranteed that individual states could determine their own social and political institutions. For many African Americans, in practice, "states rights" meant the perpetuation of slavery. Blacks suffered grievous injuries and even death as they fought for freedom alongside other American colonists. The colonists won the war: but victory did not result in liberty for all. The Declaration's words of freedom—"all men ... [have] certain unalienable rights"—failed to translate into freedom for all persons living in the United States. Notwithstanding strident protests from notable political and religious leaders, slavery persisted and even grew.[19]

In practice, the Articles of Confederation furnished a grossly inadequate governmental structure for the new nation. For example, the Articles failed to authorize Congress to tax citizens. And state legislatures did not honor requests from Congress for funds to pay for national governmental expenses. In 1786, to pay the financial obligations of the United States, Congress "requisitioned" $3.8 million from the states. In fact, Congress only collected from the states a total of $663.[20]

In this context, to form a more perfect union and implement the ideals of the Declaration of Independence, the founding great-grandfathers decided to amend the Articles of Confederation. They wound up drafting a new constitution.[21] In so doing, the founders had another historic opportunity to ensure that the compelling ideals of the Declaration—life, liberty, and the pursuit of happiness—would be extended to all.

Indeed, during the Constitutional Convention, Gouverneur Morris, a lawyer and businessman, argued strenuously for the nationwide abolition of slavery. Morris had helped to lead the abolition movement in the state of New York, and accurately predicted that the failure to abolish slavery would eventually result in a national catastrophe.

Morris suffered a severe physical disability—a leg amputation requiring that he use a wooden prosthesis (a "peg leg"). Perhaps his own different status from his able-bodied colleagues helped Morris to empathize with other marginalized persons. In any event, Morris captured the spirit of

America's founding document: the Declaration of Independence. Morris inserted into the Constitution an inspiring preamble: "We the people of the United States, in order to create a more perfect union . . ."[22]

The Preamble boldly proclaims that "the people"—that is, *everyone* in the United States of America—created this nation. Despite the valiant efforts of progressive, antislavery statesmen like Morris, the Framers crafted a Constitution that could be (and was) interpreted to preserve slavery.[23]

The pro-slavery provisions of the Constitution were in part a response to South Carolina's threat to secede. For instance, to ensure an adequate pool of slave labor from abroad, Article I, Section 9 of the Constitution prohibited Congress from making any law interfering with the importation of slaves for 20 years (until 1808). In other words, the Constitution created a wealth accumulation scheme to ensure slaveholders a 20-year safe harbor to maximize the financial benefits derived from an international criminal conspiracy to kidnap and exploit African men and women. In practice, the Constitution's protection of the African slave trade embodied a racial preference and wealth accumulation program targeted primarily to benefit upper-class White folks like George Washington, Thomas Jefferson, James Madison, James Monroe, John Marshall, and other Founders. The slave trade provision exemplifies constitutional safeguards for White American affirmative action.

To facilitate White American affirmative action, other provisions of the Constitution followed colonial American precedents. For example, in colonies like Virginia, runaway indentured servants (like John Punch) as well as slaves were captured, returned, and punished. Likewise, the Constitution provided for the return of workers, whether enslaved or free, who ran away. Under the Constitution, slaves and indentured servants who ran away seeking freedom from bondage were required to "be delivered up on Claim of the Party to whom such Service or Labour may be due."[24]

In practice, this constitutional provision became a fugitive slave clause—a permanent legal device engraved in the Constitution to re-imprison escaped slaves. The Constitution guaranteed slaveholders a nationwide dragnet, including U.S. marshals, other federal law enforcement personnel, and deputized members of the public.

The courts vigorously implemented the Constitution's affirmative action program to protect slavery. The U.S. Supreme Court's early approach in *Prigg v. Pennsylvania*[25] exemplifies judicial activism on behalf of slaveholders. In *Prigg*, Jerry Morgan, a free Black from Pennsylvania, married Margaret Morgan, an enslaved Black woman who had been living in Maryland. With the slaveholder's apparent consent, Jerry and Margaret moved from Maryland (a slaveholding state) a few miles across state boundaries into Pennsylvania (a free state).[26]

After the slaveholder died, his heir sent bounty hunters to Pennsylvania. Using force and trickery the bounty hunters removed Margaret Morgan (the formerly enslaved wife) and her children from their home, husband, and father.[27] The captured mother and children were returned to Maryland. According to historian Paul Finkelman, "Margaret and her children were sold, shipped south, and disappeared from the records. Her husband, Jerry, was killed as he was returning from a visit to the Pennsylvania governor, while trying to secure the return of his wife and children."[28]

The state of Pennsylvania convicted Edward Prigg under a Pennsylvania statute that sought to protect Blacks from being (re)enslaved arbitrarily. Prigg, a Maryland attorney and small farmer, appealed his conviction to the United States Supreme Court.[29] The Court held the Pennsylvania statute unconstitutional. The Court said that the Constitution authorized slaveholders to go anywhere in the United States and forcibly take slaves back into captivity. The Court limited this broad slaveholder power slightly: the Court stated that in recapturing the slave, the slave catchers could not breach the peace.[30]

A somewhat redeeming aspect of *Prigg* existed: the *Prigg* Court ruled that the states could not pass legislation regulating the capture and return of fugitive slaves. The Court said Congress had the exclusive right and duty to do so.[31]

Whether intended or not, *Prigg* exemplified a legal system that promoted White affirmative action. Specifically, *Prigg* provided bounty hunters (especially diabolic ones) with great power. Bounty hunters sometimes kidnapped free Blacks and delivered them to slaveholders.[32] Kidnapped free people of color were at a great disadvantage in attempting to prove their free status. Their documents could conveniently *disappear*.

Moreover, Blacks frequently not only had their hands tied literally but also the law forced them to remain silent during legal proceedings to decide their destiny. Often Blacks could not testify in court against Whites. In these circumstances, bounty hunters could seize and sell a Black person—any Black person! Such unfortunate individuals would have little legal protection, and unscrupulous bounty hunters could reenslave (or enslave) a Black person without going to court to prove that they had snatched a slave rather than a free person.[33]

To re-enforce the laws that muzzled the voices of captured African Americans, congressmen from slaveholding states argued that Congress could not even discuss the plight of free Blacks who had been kidnapped. In these slaveholders' view, such discussion—people talking about whether to limit or abolish slavery—could spark slave unrest and insurrections.[34]

State and local governments in many parts of the United States continue today to pass legislation attempting to censor speech that presents historical facts and interpretations highlighting skin color–based oppression. Legal censorship is reflected in bans on teaching critical race theory. The rationale for doing so boils down to fear that knowledge of historical fact will provoke societal transformation aimed at liberty and justice for all, not just for the privileged few.

Returning to the discussion of the Fugitive Slave Clause, as applied to enslaved persons, the Clause followed colonial legislation and practice. English colonists captured and punished enslaved persons so that they could work them until death. Slaveholders found the Clause invaluable in accumulating great material wealth.

Despite the legal shackles placed on their desire for freedom, enslaved Americans were constantly tempted to follow the example of the colonists and resort to arms to set themselves free. If slaves rebelled to free themselves, Article I, Section 15 of the Constitution said that the federal government could call forth the militia to "suppress insurrections." Further, Article IV, Section IV required the federal government to protect the states from "domestic violence."

During the debates regarding whether to ratify the Constitution, an attractive selling point for southern state conventions was the Constitution's guaranteed federal military protection against slave conspiracies and insurrections.[35] In light of several Jamaican slave revolts during the colonial period plus the bloody struggle of Blacks for freedom in Haiti against the French, the United States Constitution's militia and domestic violence provisions provided some comfort to jittery southern slaveholders. In short, slaveholders and others deriving material benefits flowing from slavery could count on the American military to maintain white supremacy.

This was not all. By counting some of the slaves, the Constitution increased slaveholders' representation in Congress. For example, to determine the number of representatives that a state would have in the House of Representatives, the Constitution mandated that three-fifths of the slaves in the state must be counted. Thus, a slaveholder with five slaves would have the same representation as four free citizens.

The "three-fifths clause" generated controversy during the constitutional debates in part because the clause was a great incentive to increase a state's slave population. The more slaves you held, the more political power you had in Congress. Of course, the increased political clout benefited slaveholders, not enslaved individuals. Enslaved persons could not vote to free themselves or defend themselves from crimes like kidnapping, torture, rape, or homicide.

Further, the number of electoral votes a state cast for president also depended on the number of the state's representatives in Congress. A state's total electoral vote was and is calculated by adding the number of members of the House of Representatives from the particular state to the state's two U.S. Senators. In practice, the more slaves who resided in a state, the more House members the state garnered. Increased numbers of House members translated into increased state electoral votes. Because the number of a state's electoral votes is primarily based on a state's population, in presidential elections slaveholders had a political advantage.[36]

In fact, some thoughtful observers attribute Thomas Jefferson's narrow win over John Adams in the 1800 election to Jefferson winning the inflated electoral vote of slaveholding states. Wilfred Codrington III incisively captured the impact of the race-based electoral advantage that the Constitution conferred upon slaveholders as follows:

> What's less known about the election of 1800 is the way the Electoral College succeeded ... based on its embrace of the three-fifths compromise. The South's baked-in advantages—the bonus electoral votes it received for maintaining slaves, all while not allowing those slaves to vote—made the difference in the election outcome. It gave the slaveholder Jefferson an edge over his opponent, the incumbent president and abolitionist John Adams. To quote Yale Law's Akhil Reed Amar, the third president "metaphorically rode into the executive mansion on the backs of slaves." That election continued an almost uninterrupted trend of southern slaveholders and their doughfaced sympathizers winning the White House that lasted until Abraham Lincoln's victory in 1860.[37]

Unlike the enslaving states, free states could not boost their electoral vote total by counting three-fifths of enslaved persons because there were no enslaved persons in those states to count. Free states missed out on enslavement's electoral affirmative action because in those states slavery was illegal.

In short, during the 1800 presidential election, the slave states' electoral vote advantage fueled Jefferson's narrow victory. Although slaves could not cast votes, in practical effect, enslaved persons constituted an invisible Black vote.

Interestingly, historical and genetic research strongly suggests that Jefferson had an enslaved mistress and several children who would have been numbered among the "three-fifths of all other persons" used to calculate Virginia's electoral vote total.[38] Be that as it may, the Constitution was structured to promote White affirmative action that in practice benefited large slaveholders. In this case, the Constitution's presidential electoral process helped to fuel festering resentments. The Jefferson/Adams presidential contest helped to accent them.[39] The tensions were particularly acute because the Constitution's electoral slaveholder affirmative action not only affected the outcome of presidential elections but also public policy making in the legislative and other arenas.

The Framers also knew that if slavery existed in new states, when those states were admitted to the Union, the power of slaveholders in Congress would increase. In contrast, if only free persons were counted, slaveholders would have less representation in the House of Representatives—and less political power. The three-fifths compromise papered over the divisions that would later threaten the new nation's very existence.

Moreover, the Constitution mandated both a racial and gender preference regarding the election of members of the House of Representatives. To vote for members of the House of Representatives, the Constitution required that you must be eligible to vote for your state representative in the largest house of your state legislature. For example, if you lived in Virginia and wanted to vote for a member of the United States House of Representatives, you were required to be qualified to vote for members of the Virginia House of Delegates. The House of Delegates is the larger house in the Virginia General Assembly, having 100 members compared to the Virginia State Senate, which has 40 members.

When the Constitution was drafted, in most slaveholding states, only White men could vote. Some states required that voters own property. In state elections, race and property ownership requirements ensured that a relatively small minority could vote. The small state voting population translated into a diminished federal voter pool. Another way of putting it is: in practice, the Constitution ensured that a small group of mostly real estate–owning White men would dominate political decision making. In this way, the Constitution furthered White male affirmative action in voting. In essence, the Constitution established race- and gender-based minority rule.

In this regard, the Constitution followed colonial law and custom. Colonial laws placed a straitjacket on women's political and economic rights. For example, as previously noted, at the time of the American Revolution and for about 20 years after independence was achieved, only New Jersey allowed women to vote. New Jersey's progressive position seems due to the more generous spirit associated with Quakers who were influential in that state. In its design and practice, the Constitution fell short of its primary objective: to practically secure and promote universal human freedom espoused by the Declaration of Independence. Specifically, the Constitution provided little support for recognizing that women also had human rights.[40]

Similarly, most men of color were denied the right to vote until the Fifteenth Amendment was ratified in 1870. After the Fifteenth Amendment came into force, it took 50 more years for the ratification of the Nineteenth Amendment securing the right of women to vote. At the national level, the bottom line was this: the Constitution of 1787 promoted disproportionate congressional representation of slaveholders and their special interests.

Today, the legacy of America's political history of White male affirmative action is still reflected in Congress, state legislatures, governorships, and the courts. All of those institutions are dominated by a racial and gender minority: White men. In the spirit of maintaining the power of the few over the many, the 2018 and 2022 midterm elections witnessed mushrooming voter suppression efforts, widespread voter purges, fewer polling sites, less early voting opportunities, and ruthless prosecution of prospective voters of color.[41] Given the Framers' determined effort to limit the vote to persons like themselves, modern-day vote elimination tactics seem almost as American as apple pie.

The Due Process Clause of the Fifth Amendment to the Constitution provided another bulwark for protecting slavery and promoting White affirmative action. The Due Process Clause prohibits the government from taking a person's property without compensation. Under many states' laws, slaves were classified as property. Accordingly, any attempt by governmental institutions to confiscate and free enslaved individuals would have been extremely difficult. Governmental emancipation efforts would have required substantial litigation and time resources. In addition, taxpayers would have had to foot the financial bill for the government to pay (substantial) financial reparations to slaveholders for their economic loss.

For example, in private correspondence with Jared Sparks (a historian, Unitarian minister, and editor of the *North American Review*), Thomas Jefferson outlined a plan to resettle Blacks in Haiti. One of Jefferson's foremost concerns was ensuring (federal) government payment of slaveholders for the economic loss of emancipating their captive workers.[42] To address slaveholder compensation concerns, Jefferson proposed that the federal government sell public lands to pay the slaveholders for the cost of setting the captives free. Here's what Jefferson recommended:

> There is, I think, a way in which it can be done; that is, by emancipating the after-born, leaving them, on due compensation, with their mothers, until their services are worth their maintenance, and then putting them to industrious occupations, until a proper age for deportation. This was the result of my reflections on the subject five and forty years ago, and I have never yet been able to conceive any other practicable plan. It was sketched in the Notes on Virginia, under the fourteenth query. The estimated value of the new-born infant is so low, (say twelve dollars and fifty cents,) that it would probably be yielded by the owner gratis, and would thus reduce the six hundred millions of dollars, the first head of expense, to thirty-seven millions and a half; leaving only the expense of nourishment while with the mother, and of transportation. And from what fund are these expenses to be furnished? Why not from that of the lands which have been ceded by the very States now needing this relief? And ceded on no consideration, for the most part, but that of the general good of the whole. These cessions already constitute one fourth of the States of the Union. It may be said that these lands have been sold; are now the property of the citizens composing those States; and the money long ago received and expended. But an equivalent of lands in the territories since acquired, may be appropriated to that object, or so much, at least, as may be sufficient; and the object, although more important to the slave States, is highly so to the others also, if they were serious in their arguments on the Missouri question. The slave States, too, if more interested, would also contribute more by their gratuitous liberation, thus taking

on themselves alone the first and heaviest item of expense.[43]

A long chain of legal shackles supported enslavement. But there's even more. If someone wanted to lessen the yoke of slavery's oppression, yet another formidable constitutional barrier existed. The Constitution requires that three-fourths of the states ratify any proposed amendment. As late as the eve of the Civil War (1861), 15 states allowed (and were unlikely to abolish) slavery. If the 15 slaveholding states had remained united, it would have taken 45 non-slaveholding states to purge slavery from the Constitution. In other words, the Union would have had to consist of 60 states, with 45 state legislatures voting to abolish slavery. In 1861, and even today, the United States does not have 60 states.

The upshot of this background is this: the original Constitution cuddled and nursed slavery upon its legal bosom. Had the slaveholders employed constitutional means to defend their barbaric institution, slavery would probably have extended into the twentieth century. This is particularly true when one considers the Supreme Court's subsequent rulings in cases like *Dred Scott*. Based on the historical context, text, and structure of the Constitution, it is probable that the Framers anticipated slavery today, slavery tomorrow, and slavery forever.

The majority of American political decision makers could have adopted strong counterarguments for freedom. As will be outlined in more detail later, abolitionists like Frederick Douglass presented powerful justifications for universal freedom. For the most part, decision makers in America's government—executive, legislative, and judicial branches—rejected antislavery laws and policies.

Suffice it to say, the founding fathers left their slaveholding offspring impressive legal weapons to safeguard their political and economic interests. The law provided race-based preferences for slaveholders who were overwhelmingly White males. Some of these racial preferences included:

1. increased congressional representation,
2. a 20-year window to import Black slaves into the United States,
3. armed militia and military forces to capture escaped slaves and repress slave revolts,
4. a vote advantage in the Electoral College,
5. a free national fugitive slave capture and return system,
6. guaranteed reparations if the government ever abolished slavery, and
7. a constitutional amendment process that virtually ensured that slavery would be perpetual.

Not satisfied with these sturdy constitutional protections, the slaveholding children and grandchildren of the founders decided later to use military violence to fight against the Union in an attempt to create a new nation: the Confederate States of America.

Chapter III

# A Bigger Nation: But Better?

FROM THE FOUNDING OF THE UNION, the United States Constitution was conflicted about human freedom. America's political leaders struck compromises to accommodate slaveholding elites and non-slaveholders. In practice, Congress passed legislation that maintained a nation that was half slave and half free.

For example, in 1820 the Missouri Compromise attempted to balance the interests of slaveholders who wanted to expand slavery into the western American territories versus some non-slaveholders who wanted to see those territories become exclusively (or "lily") White free states. Indeed, Illinois Senator Lyman Trumball was quoted as saying, "I wish to have nothing to do, either with the free negro or the slave negro we wish to settle the territories with free white men."[1] Historian John Dippel put it this way:

> Not politics or economic clout, but climate and soil were the key factors determining where the slave system would take hold and grow. Almost the entire West was geographically predestined to be "free";

> As a consequence, the more pressing racial question of the day was this: *would the rest of the West be reserved exclusively for whites?* Once it became clear that the chattel system was unlikely to spread beyond the Mississippi Valley and the Gulf coast, pioneers and prospective migrants began to worry more about the coming of an even more unwanted racial minority—free blacks.[2]

A major problem with legislation like the Missouri Compromise was that it disposed of hundreds of millions of acres of land that Native Americans had owned and occupied for centuries. The federal government claimed the right to give Native American lands to White settlers without paying the Native Americans. Giving Native American land away without their advice and consent or offering them adequate compensation did not promote good relations between the growing republic and its native neighbors.

In fact, the 1823 landmark case of *Johnson v. McIntosh* reflected some of the practical difficulties flowing from settlers' attempts to acquire Native American lands by any available means. In *Johnson*, one group of individuals led by Joshua Johnson acquired land directly from the Native Americans. Another individual (William McIntosh) bought part of the same land from the government of the United States. In these circumstances, the Court confronted a situation where two different parties claimed exclusive title to the same property. The Court had to decide which party had superior title to land that formerly belonged to Native Americans. Writing for the Court, Chief Justice John Marshall stated:

> On the discovery of this immense continent, the great nations of Europe were eager to appropriate to themselves so much of it as they could respectively acquire. Its vast extent offered and [sic] ample field to the ambition and enterprise of all; and the character and religion of its inhabitants afforded

> an apology for considering them as a people over whom the superior genius of Europe might claim an ascendency. The potentates of the old world found no difficulty in convincing themselves that they made ample compensation to the inhabitants of the new, by bestowing on them civilization and Christianity, in exchange for unlimited independence. But, as they were all in pursuit of nearly the same object, it was necessary, in order to avoid conflicting settlements, and consequent war with each other, to establish a principle ... that discovery gave title to the government by whose subjects, or by whose authority, it was made, against all other European governments, which title might be consummated by possession.[3]

Once Europeans "discovered" property and decided that their supposed discovery gave them ownership of the property, what about the rights of Native people? After all, the Native Americans had lived on the property since time immemorial. The Court addressed those concerns by saying that Native Americans merely had the right to occupy the land. According to the Court, Native Americans did not have authority to dispose of their land as they pleased:

> In the establishment of these relations, the rights of the original inhabitants were, in no instance, entirely disregarded; but were necessarily, to a considerable extent, impaired. They were admitted to be the rightful occupants of the soil, with a legal as well as just claim to retain possession of it, and to use it according to their own discretion; but their rights to complete sovereignty, as independent nations, were necessarily diminished, and their power to dispose of the soil at their own will, to whomsoever they pleased, was denied by the

> original fundamental principle, that discovery gave exclusive title to those who made it.[4]

As to the morality of taking someone else's property by any available means, the Court said:

> We will not enter into the controversy, whether agriculturists, merchants, and manufacturers, have a right, on abstract principles, to expel hunters from the territory they possess, or to contract their limits. Conquest gives a title which the Courts of the conqueror cannot deny, whatever the private and speculative opinions of individuals may be, respecting the original justice of the claim which has been successfully asserted ... These claims have been maintained and established as far west as the river Mississippi, by the sword. The title to a vast portion of the lands we now hold, originates in them. It is not for the Courts of this country to question the validity of this title, or to sustain one which is incompatible with it.[5]

In essence, the Court concluded that it was too late to question the title to property that many settlers had acquired without directly or indirectly paying the Native Americans a dime. The Court simply declined "to enter into the controversy, whether [European colonists] have a right, on abstract principles, to expel hunters from the territory they possess."[6] One wonders what might have been the abstract principles to which the Court closed its judicial eyes? Abstract principles like "Thou shall not lie, cheat, steal or kill"?

Whatever principles the Court might have meant, the Court simply refused to "question the validity of [such] title" even when the Native Americans' property had been seized "by the sword."

*Naked physical violence.* How could confiscating land by participating in a vast, violent criminal conspiracy—featuring aggravated assault, robbery, kidnapping, and murder—form the basis for lawful title? The Court stated:

> However extravagant the pretension of converting the discovery of an inhabited country into conquest may appear; if the principle has been asserted in the first instance, and afterwards sustained; if a country has been acquired and held under it; if the property of the great mass of the community originates in it, it becomes the law of the land, and cannot be questioned.[7]

If title could be created by the sword, how could title to such blood-soaked title be transferred? The Court's response to that haunting question is telling:

> So, too, with respect to the concomitant principle, that the Indian inhabitants are to be considered merely as occupants, to be protected, indeed, while in peace, in the possession of their lands, but to be deemed incapable of transferring the absolute title to others. However this restriction may be opposed to natural right, and to the usages of civilized nations, yet, if it be indispensable to that system under which the country has been settled, and be adapted to the actual condition of the two people, it may, perhaps, be supported by reason, and certainly cannot be rejected by Courts of justice.[8]

In plain terms, the *McIntosh* Court held that the discoverers could extinguish the Native Americans' title of occupancy either by "purchase or by conquest"—meaning by fair means or foul. Having been dispossessed of their property rights, the Native Americans could not transfer title.

In *McIntosh*, the Court had other grounds upon which it could have decided which purchaser(s) had the best claim to Native Americans' land. The Court had the option of ruling that Native Americans could grant a fee simple ("free and clear") title to whomever the Native Americans chose to convey the land. The *McIntosh* Court could have recognized the Native Americans' unfettered freedom to sell to (1) individuals like Johnson or (2) to the United States. In either case, the Native Americans' right to dispose of their land (just like Europeans) would have been respected. Purchasers from Native Americans could resell the property to others. Indeed, before the matter came before the Supreme Court, neither Johnson's group of purchasers nor McIntosh had contested Native Americans' rights to own their own land or sell it to others.

Nevertheless, the Court did not choose to uphold Native Americans' power to confer a full title to land. Instead, the *McIntosh* Court asserted that Native Americans did not possess absolute ownership rights.[9] "[T]he Indian inhabitants are to be considered merely as occupants, to be protected, indeed, while in peace, in the possession of their lands, but to be deemed incapable of transferring the absolute title to others."[10] The Court's decision meant that the Native Americans could not sell the land upon which they had lived for centuries to whomever the Native Americans selected.

Moreover, evidence exists that many Native Americans had a very different understanding of land ownership. For many Native people, the land could not be sold to individuals anymore than one could sell air, light, water, or other life-sustaining necessities. Accordingly, the land could be used in common but no one could claim it as exclusively his own.[11]

In contrast to a live and let live approach to land possession, the Court's idea of property law boiled down "to the victor (in war) goes the spoils." Such a jurisprudence grounded often enough in physical violence fit well with the worldview of many other high-ranking government officials. Such persons viewed violent conflict with Native Americans as necessary and proper to facilitate the goal of enriching landless Whites as well as large landholders. As noted previously, the

*McIntosh* Court said that title had been "established as far west as the river Mississippi, by the sword."[12] The Court in essence held that armed violence was an acceptable way to create legal title to land.

One example of the U.S. government's "by any means necessary" land-grabbing policy involved the Cherokee people, who in 1822 declared themselves to be an independent nation. Near the time that the Cherokees declared independence, gold was discovered on Cherokee lands in present-day Georgia. The Georgia legislature reacted and passed laws dividing the Cherokee lands (totaling 4 million acres) into state counties.[13]

Seeking a peaceful resolution to the state of Georgia's attempt to seize their lands, the Cherokees appealed to the Supreme Court of the United States. In 1831, in *Cherokee Nation v. Georgia*,[14] they asked the Court to uphold their rights under treaties that the Cherokees had made with the United States. The Supreme Court dismissed the case, saying that it did not have jurisdiction. The *Cherokee Nation* Court turned a blind judicial eye to what amounted to an armed invasion and conquest of Cherokee lands.

The Cherokees did not give up. Still seeking justice, the next year they returned to the Supreme Court. In *Worcester v. Georgia*,[15] the state of Georgia had imprisoned Samuel Worcester, a missionary, for living on Cherokee lands without obtaining permission from the state of Georgia. Worcester challenged the Georgia statute under which he was convicted. Worcester argued that the statute violated the United States treaty obligations to the Cherokees.

In *Worcester*, the Court acknowledged that Indians were not living on their lands "merely as occupants." The *Worcester* Court made some amends for its prior unfortunate ruling in *McIntosh*. The *Worcester* Court said: "The Indian nations had always been considered as distinct, independent political communities, retaining their original natural rights, as the undisputed possessors of the soil, from time immemorial . . ."[16]

Nevertheless, the Court claimed that native rights had a severe limitation "imposed by irresistible power, which excluded them from intercourse with any other European potentate than the first discoverer of the coast of the particular region claimed: and this was a restriction which those European potentates imposed on themselves, as well as on the Indians."[17] The Court reaffirmed its position stated in *McIntosh* that once a European colonial power claimed authority over native land, the Native Americans were not free to deal with any other nations. Such limits on Native American freedom were repeatedly enforced from the barrel of a gun. Colonists' use of warfare and other forms of physical coercion severely hampered Indians' ability to freely determine how they would live with their new (European) neighbors.

In *Worcester*, the heart of Samuel Worcester's claim was that Georgia did not have authority to convict and punish him for preaching the Christian gospel on Cherokee lands. The Court ruled:

> The Cherokee nation, then, is a distinct community occupying its own territory, with boundaries accurately described, in which the laws of Georgia can have no force, and which the citizens of Georgia have no right to enter, but with the assent of the Cherokees themselves, or in conformity with treaties, and with the acts of Congress. The whole intercourse between the United States and this nation is, by our constitution and laws, vested in the government of the United States.[18]

While federal courts can issue rulings, enforcement lies primarily with other branches of government, specifically the national executive. President Andrew Jackson neither enforced the Court's ruling nor recognized limited Cherokee rule. Instead, Jackson supported unlawful acts of the state of Georgia and demonstrated utter contempt for Indians' treaty rights. Jackson's behavior is not at all surprising. In his 1829 State of the Union address, made three years before the Court ruled in *Worcester*, Jackson told Congress:

> Our ancestors found [Native People] the uncontrolled possessors of these vast regions. *By persuasion and force they have been made to retire from river to river and from mountain to mountain, until some of the tribes have become extinct and others have left but remnants to preserve for awhile their once terrible names.* Surrounded by the whites with their arts of civilization ... destroying the resources of the savage doom him to weakness and decay ... if they remain within the limits of the States ...[19]

Jackson's message suggests this: successful implementation of his race-based government wealth development policy would inevitably subjugate and if necessary annihilate Native Americans.[20]

To implement this national White American affirmative action plan, President Jackson proposed the Indian Removal Act to relocate Native Americans living in the eastern United States to lands west of the Mississippi River. Congress passed the legislation in 1830 and authorized armed force to carry out its objectives.

Working with other government leaders, Jackson promoted the large-scale removal of Indians at gunpoint from Georgia and other southeastern states to Oklahoma. The federal government policies made thousands of Native Americans homeless refugees. This government racial preference program opened up millions of acres east of the Mississippi River to White settlers.

Tragically, the U.S. government's violent removal of Indigenous people during the 1830s became known as the "Trail of Tears."[21] Ann Byers writes:

> Road conditions, illness, and harsh winter weather made death a daily occurrence. As many as 8,000

> Indians are thought to have died during the entire removal process and its aftermath. Roughly 4,000 Cherokee died on the trail itself.[22]

Ironically, some persons who supported forcibly relocating the Native Americans under threat of death believed that such displacement was an enlightened policy: it was viewed as more humane than slaughtering the native people outright.[23]

*Slow genocide.*

President Andrew Jackson's Native American policy was part of a broader American westward movement that sought to colonize as much of North America as possible. This policy, "Manifest Destiny," was viewed as the will of God.[24] As they moved westward, with the military and political assistance of the American government, squatters, homesteaders, and others killed many Native Americans and seized their land.

As we noted previously, the allure for English settlers coming to the New World included reports that Spanish colonists had made large fortunes through discovering gold and silver as well as taking such treasures by hook or crook from indigenous peoples. At its creation, the new Republic of Mexico inherited and benefited from the Spanish colonialism and seizure of native land. In this context it is not surprising that native people perceived both Anglo settlers and Mexican settlers as unwelcome invaders and squatters engaged in property theft on a large scale. In a brilliant *Washington Post* article, Professor A.S. Dillingham of Arizona State University outlined the practical realities that native peoples confronted in their relations with the United States and with Mexico:

> The two young countries were not identical, but both pursued colonial strategies informed by anti-Indigenous racism. In this sense, Native peoples confronted two competing colonial projects aimed, at best, at their subordinated incorporation

> into these nations and, at worst, at their extermination. For centuries, and on whichever side of the U.S.-Mexico border they found themselves, Native peoples have fiercely and creatively defended their communities and lands. That defiance continues.[25]

In addition to conflicts with Native Americans, American settlers sometimes clashed with residents of the newly formed nation of Mexico. Mexico was an enormous country, bordering the Pacific Ocean on the west, present-day Colorado and Utah on the north, Louisiana on the east, and Guatemala on the south. In 1821, Mexico achieved its independence from Spain.

Political leaders, land speculators, and members of the general public in the United States viewed Mexico's vast and rich land as a place of boundless opportunity. The U.S. government encouraged Americans to establish settlements in eastern Mexico (present-day Texas). In 1835-36, American settlers revolted against the Mexican authorities and proclaimed themselves to be the independent country of Texas. Mexico refused to recognize Texas' independence. However, the United States and France did.[26]

President John Tyler, a Virginia slaveholder, maneuvered to have the Republic of Texas annexed as a state. Normally, international agreements between nations are made through a legally binding agreement, referred to as a treaty. In the United States, once the president submits a proposed treaty to the Senate, a two-thirds vote of the Senate is required for treaty ratification. Accordingly, President Tyler transmitted and recommended a proposed treaty to the Senate that would have made the independent nation of Texas a state within the United States. Many opponents of the treaty feared that Texas would enter the Union as a slave state. The United States Senate rejected Tyler's proposed Texas statehood treaty.[27]

After the 1844 presidential election, Tyler was a lame-duck president, preparing to leave office. Undeterred, he and other supporters of Texan statehood introduced a joint resolution in Congress to make Texas a state. The Texas statehood legislation passed with a simple majority. In this manner, they achieved their objective of having Texas recognized as a state. Respected constitutional scholars have argued that the Constitution required ratification of Texas statehood by treaty, rather than by a congressional statute or resolution. Nevertheless, slaveholders and their allies prevailed. Pro-slavery activists had no qualms about taking great liberties with the Constitution.[28]

*The ends seemed to justify the means.*

In 1845, newly elected President James Polk sent troops into the disputed border region between Texas and Mexico. Both sides viewed sending military forces into a contested area as a provocative act calculated to spark a military conflict. Shortly thereafter hostilities erupted, resulting in Mexico's military defeat.

Following peace negotiations, the United States signed the Treaty of Guadalupe Hidalgo with Mexico and acquired territories that later became the states of New Mexico, California, Nevada, and Arizona. The treaty also embraced parts of Utah and Colorado. The United States paid $15 million to Mexico for the vast new territory, covering roughly 525,000 square miles. In other words, Mexico received compensation equal to about $30 per square mile![29]

The practical fallout from the Mexican-American War included deciding what to do about Mexican American property rights in the former Mexican territories. For example, before the American conquest, Spanish and (later) Mexican authorities had given private individuals generous land grants. The Spanish and Mexican officials had also conferred large tracts of land upon towns. These public lands were to be used as common areas.

After the United States assumed authority over the former Mexican territory, questions arose like what were the property rights of individual Mexicans who were now American citizens? What about the legal status of common lands owned by the former Mexican towns? Such questions stemmed from the decision of many Mexicans to remain in America as citizens rather than become refugees and head further south into the remnants of Mexico.

Further complicating matters, in 1848, gold had been discovered in California. Tens of thousands of Anglo-American settlers poured into California, causing the population to increase by nearly fortyfold from roughly 6,900 persons in 1845 to approximately 224,000 by 1852.[30] In many cases Mexican Americans were literally overwhelmed by such settlers who came swarming in and then squatted on Mexican Americans' lands seeking to strike it rich.

To deal with this situation, in 1851, Congress created the California Land Claims Commission. Congress required all Mexican Americans who had Spanish or Mexican titles to property to present their claims before the Commission. The law placed the burden on the landowner to prove that his title was valid. The California Land Claims Commission gave Mexican Americans only two years to present claims or forfeit their land. Thus, the Land Claims Commission decided that claims not filed by 1853 would result in Mexican American–owned lands being designated as belonging to the United States. Such lands would be available for sale to members of the general public seeking their fortunes in the West.[31]

California Land Claims Commission procedures made it expensive and difficult for Mexican American citizens to prove their land ownership. Such American government policies subverted efforts of American citizens from Mexico to retain their property and contradicted the spirit of the Treaty of Guadalupe Hidalgo. Among other things, the treaty was supposed to help ensure that Mexican American property rights would be respected. Instead, Mexican American citizens with perfectly good titles under prior Spanish colonial law or Mexican law found themselves effectively disinherited.

Furthermore, under American jurisdiction, the political franchise was frequently limited to only White men. For example, Article II, Section I of the 1849 California Constitution provided that "every white male citizen of the United States, and every white male citizen of Mexico, who shall have elected to become citizens of the United States ... shall be entitled to vote in all elections."[32] The California Constitution treated Mexican Americans consistently with America's long-standing race and gender preference program: confer material wealth and political power along color and gender lines. The California Constitution provided that by a two-thirds vote of the legislature, individual Indians and their descendants could also be given the right to vote.[33]

Similarly, in *People v. Hall*,[34] the California Supreme Court upheld legal oppression of people of color by interpreting the California Constitution to bar Chinese persons from testifying in court against Whites. In *Hall*, a White man had been convicted of murder based on the testimony of Chinese witnesses. The California Supreme Court said that the term "Black person" included Chinese persons as well because the state legislature intended to prohibit any person who was not White from testifying against a White person:

> We are of the opinion that the words "white," "negro," "mullatto," "Indian," and "black person," wherever they occur in our Constitution and laws, must be taken in their generic sense, and that, even admitting the Indian of this continent is not of the Mongolian type, that the words "black person," in the 14th section, must be taken as contradistinguished from white, and necessarily excludes all races other than the Caucasian.[35]

Accordingly, the law prevented recent Chinese immigrants from having full access to the legal process to protect their human rights. Such miscarriages of justice helped to confine many Chinese newcomers who were laborers to the lower rungs of America's social ladder.

In contrast, to promote material wealth development among White Americans, in 1850, Congress passed legislation granting nearly 3 million acres of federal lands to White settlers. Regarding White persons who had previously lived for four years on the land that formed the new Oregon territory, the statute said:

> [T]here shall be . . . granted to *every white settler or occupant* of the public lands . . . [who is] a citizen of the United States . . . now residing in [the Oregon] Territory . . . who shall have resided upon and cultivated the same for four consecutive years . . . one half section, or three hundred and twenty acres of land, if a single man, and if a married man . . . one section of six hundred and forty acres, one half to himself and the other half to his wife, to be held by her in her own right.[36]

Similarly, for White persons willing to relocate to and live on lands in the Oregon Territory, Section Five of the Oregon Land Donation Act provided:

> That to *all white male citizens of the United States* . . . above the age of twenty-two years, emigrating to and settling in said Territory . . . who shall . . . comply with the foregoing section and . . . this law, there shall be . . . granted the quantity of one quarter section, or one hundred and sixty acres of land, if a single man; or if married . . . one half section, or three hundred and twenty acres, one half to the husband and the other half to the wife in her own right.[37]

The Oregon Land Donation Act made no provision for federal land grants to single women of any complexion . . . Congress later carved the Oregon Territory into three states: Oregon, Washington, and Idaho. The Oregon State Constitution of 1857 had a dubious distinction: Oregon banned Negroes and Mulattoes from coming to live in what many Oregonians hoped would become an all-White state.[38]

A few months before Oregon adopted its Whites-only state constitution, the Supreme Court in *Dred Scott v. Sanford*[39] struck a powerful legal blow supporting slavery and white supremacy. In *Dred Scott*, the Court held that Blacks were not citizens under the United States Constitution. Chief Justice Taney's majority opinion reflected the prevailing view of America's dominant groups; namely, that Blacks were not humans:

> They had for more than a century before been *regarded as beings of an inferior order*, and altogether unfit to associate with the white race, either in social or political relations; and so far inferior, that they had no rights which the white man was bound to respect; and that the Negro might justly and lawfully be reduced to slavery for his benefit. He was bought and sold, and treated as an ordinary article of merchandise and traffic, whenever a profit could be made by it. This opinion was at that time fixed and universal in the civilized portion of the white race. It was regarded as an axiom in morals as well as in politics, which no one thought of disputing, or supposed to be open to dispute; and men in every grade and position in society daily and habitually acted upon it in their private pursuits, as well as in matters of public concern, without doubting for a moment the correctness of this opinion.[40]

The Court proceeded to address a controversial issue the parties had not presented for the Court to decide. That issue was the validity of the Missouri Compromise. Even though the Court lacked a compelling legal reason to address the Compromise, the *Dred Scott* Court proceeded to strike it down:

> [T]he right of property in a slave is distinctly and expressly affirmed in the Constitution. The right to traffic in it, like an ordinary article of merchandise and property, was guarantied to the citizens of the

> United States, in every State that might desire it, for twenty years. *And the Government in express terms is pledged to protect it in all future time, if the slave escapes from his owner* ... And no word can be found in the Constitution which gives Congress a greater power over slave property, or which entitles property of that kind to less protection than property of any other description. The only power conferred is the power coupled with the duty of guarding and protecting the owner in his rights.
>
> Upon these considerations, it is the opinion of the court that the act of Congress which prohibited a citizen from holding and owning property of this kind in the territory of the United States north of the line therein mentioned, is not warranted by the Constitution, and is therefore void.[41]

The Court not only invalidated the Missouri Compromise but also opened all of America's territories to slavery. The Court opined "that neither Dred Scott himself, nor any of his family, were made free by being carried into this territory; even if they had been carried there by the owner, with the intention of becoming a permanent resident."[42]

Further, if Dred Scott's captor had taken Scott to a free state and intended to live there permanently, the Court's decision implies that Scott would still not have been free. The Court said that Scott was property, and if a property owner can take his table to another state and use it there, then why not his enslaved worker? In other words, the *Dred Scott* Court signaled that slaveholders could freely move across the United States and establish slavery anywhere. Slaveholders had this freedom and power since slaves were constitutionally protected property. In the Court's own words, "the Government in express terms is pledged to protect [slavery] in all future time."[43] Bottom line: the Court signaled strongly that the Constitution protected slavery forever.

By deciding an explosive constitutional matter not before the Court, the *Dred Scott* majority upset the Constitution's balance of power between the three governmental branches.

Specifically, the Court could have respected Congress' role as a co-equal branch of government that had passed legislation to effect a political compromise of a hotly disputed national issue: whether to allow slavery in territories of the United States. This national political controversy threatened to split the Union. Instead of limiting its opinion to whether Dred Scott's travel to and residence on free soil made Scott free, the Court invaded Congress' authority to govern American territories. In doing so, rather than demonstrating judicial restraint, the Court boldly sided with slaveholders and stirred a political hornet's nest.

In fact, Frederick Douglass, a leading human rights advocate and abolitionist, argued that the Constitution had deliberately not used the term slave or slavery. Accordingly, Douglass contended that the Constitution should be construed to favor freedom rather than oppression. In a memorable address delivered on March 26, 1860, in Glasgow, Scotland, Douglass stated:

> The Supreme Court of the United States lays down this rule, and it meets the case exactly—"Where rights are infringed—where the fundamental principles of the law are overthrown—where the general system of the law is departed from, the legislative intention must be expressed with irresistible clearness." The same court says that the language of the law must be construed strictly in favour of justice and liberty. Again, there is another rule of law. It is—Where a law is susceptible of two meanings, the one making it accomplish an innocent purpose, and the other making it accomplish a wicked purpose, we must in all cases adopt that which makes it accomplish an innocent purpose ...[44]

Douglass described persons who favored a pro-slavery interpretation of the Constitution in these words:

> They are in the habit of treating the Negro as an exception to general rules. When their own liberty is in question they will avail themselves of all rules of law which protect and defend their freedom; but when the black man's rights are in question they concede everything, admit everything for slavery, and put liberty to the proof. They reverse the common law usage, and presume the Negro a slave unless he can prove himself free. I, on the other hand, presume him free unless he is proved to be otherwise.[45]

Rather than follow Douglass' wise counsel, unwittingly (?) the *Dred Scott* Court helped to precipitate another great societal upheaval, indeed, a revolution: the American Civil War.

*Dred Scott* gave legal approval to prevailing social custom and practice: the law did not recognize Blacks as human. As Chief Justice Taney said, "they were *beings of an inferior order*"—not human beings. The legal significance of Blacks not being perceived as human led to the *Dred Scott* Court's conclusion that Blacks had "no rights that the white man was bound to respect." Again, *Dred Scott* said Blacks were "treated like ordinary articles of merchandise," basically like property—tables, chairs, plows. And who ever heard of a plow suing a farmer for assault and battery? In practical terms, the law acted as an insurance policy protecting slaveholders from criminal liability for any and all violent acts committed against enslaved individuals. In plain language, *Dred Scott* harkened back to and reaffirmed the law reflected in Virginia's 1705 Slave Codes: Blacks could be beaten, raped, dismembered, and even murdered with impunity.

The widespread legalized violence that slavery engendered was part of the heritage passed down from colonial times. That bloody legacy is still manifested in hate crimes, like mass shootings directed at people of color, Jews, and other societal scapegoats.

When we consider these facts of American history and confess past sins, troubling questions arise. Why did the America's Founders, who recognized human rights like freedom of speech, press, peaceful assembly, and religion, lack the moral courage to eliminate the legal barbarism of slavery? Could hundreds of thousands of deaths in the Civil War have been avoided? As we noted before, Thomas Jefferson had a premonition that eventually the violence and terror inherent in slavery would erupt and explode like a gigantic volcano devastating the young nation. In 1782, he penned the following words in his *Notes on Virginia*:

> I tremble for my country when I reflect that God is just: that his justice cannot sleep forever: that considering numbers, nature and natural means only, a revolution of the wheel of fortune and exchange [in] situation, is among possible events: that it may become probable by supernatural interference! The Almighty has no attribute that can side with us in such a contest.[46]

Jefferson's words indicate that he—and doubtless other Founders—saw but failed to seize historic opportunities to avoid a national catastrophe.

Chapter IV

# America's Second Revolutionary War and Its Aftermath

AS A NATIONAL CALAMITY APPROACHED, America's elite groups continued to vigorously orchestrate national class and race-based preference programs. Some pro-slavery advocates sought to reintroduce the African slave trade, others schemed to acquire Cuba, and yet others argued for the establishment of new slave colonies in Latin America.[1]

On November 6, 1860, Abraham Lincoln was elected President. Six weeks later, on December 20, 1860, South Carolina announced that "the union now subsisting between South Carolina and other states under the name of the 'United States of America' is hereby dissolved."[2] By February 1, 1861, six other states (Florida, Georgia, Mississippi, Texas, Louisiana, and Alabama) had declared they were also leaving the Union.[3] On February 8, 1861, these seven states held a convention and proclaimed themselves to be the "Confederate States of America." In addition, the rebels seized federal fortresses and property throughout the South.

Hoping to entice them to end their rebellion, President Lincoln promised to uphold slavery provided the southern states refrained from armed violence against the national government. Lincoln pledged that the national government would return fugitive slaves and protect slaveholders from rebellious slaves.[4]

On April 12, 1861, when the rebels attacked Fort Sumter in South Carolina, the Civil War began in earnest.[5]

To suppress the rebellion, on April 15, 1861, Lincoln called for 75,000 troops. Two days later, on April 17, 1861, Virginia cast its lot with the secessionists. An interesting historical note is this: Evidence exists that through an intermediary, President Lincoln offered newly promoted United States Colonel Robert E. Lee the opportunity to command the 75,000-man army that Lincoln requisitioned to restore law and order. Colonel Lee declined.[6] We will address the Lee situation later.

Even after the Civil War began, the federal government maintained its commitment to preserving slavery within the rebelling states. The national government promised to protect pro-Union slaveholders from slave revolts, to return runaway slaves to such slaveholders, and to otherwise uphold the legal powers of slaveholders.[7]

## The Point of No Return

As the war progressed, thousands of slaves fled slavery and joined the Union army as workers. In addition, as a military measure, Lincoln became convinced that it was imperative to emancipate the slaves in rebelling states. On September 22, 1862, Lincoln gave the rebels one last chance to end their war against the Union. If the rebels laid down their arms, Lincoln promised they could continue to hold slaves and that the Constitution would protect slavery. On the other hand, Lincoln's "preliminary emancipation proclamation" warned the rebels that if they continued to rebel, their slaves would be free beginning on January 1, 1863. The rebels continued their attempts to overthrow the government, and on January 1, 1863, the Emancipation Proclamation became effective.

In the wake of the Emancipation Proclamation, thousands of enslaved individuals left slavery. In so doing they followed the example of many of their ancestors who joined the British during the Revolutionary War. The former slaves joined the Union forces because the Union (belatedly?) promised freedom. The slaves' freedom exodus undercut the rebels who increasingly had to look elsewhere for persons to plant and harvest crops, make clothes, dig fortifications, nurse the sick and dying, as well as perform the manifold tasks associated with fighting a war. In addition, in the last two years of the war, nearly 200,000 Blacks joined the Union army and contributed substantially to the Union victory.

On January 1, 1863, the same day on which the Emancipation Proclamation freed many enslaved persons in the rebelling states, the Homestead Act of 1862 went into effect.[8] The Act allowed American citizens (or persons who had filed documentation to become citizens) to rob Native Americans by seizing their lands. If settlers deemed it necessary, they could use violence to commandeer Native American lands. Such settlers could point to the Homestead Act as a federal law that allowed settlers to increase their material wealth at the expense of Native Americans.

Thus, the Homestead Act involved massive theft of Native American land under the cloak of a legal process that excluded Native Americans from having an opportunity to defend their rights. In practice, the act barred most other persons of color from joining in the theft and pillage of Native American property. Blacks faced a legal bar because the *Dred Scott* Court[9] had held that Blacks were not U.S. citizens. Mexican Americans could only take limited advantage of the Act because their citizenship rights often depended on the color of their skin.[10] In the western United States, most Chinese workers were on short-term labor contracts.[11] Such individuals were not citizens and therefore could not participate in this wealth accumulation scheme.

Moreover, even though Native Americans had lived on their own land for centuries, they were treated as wards of the state with only a limited title to the land.[12] In that sense, the Homestead Act was consistent with the Supreme Court's decision in *Johnson v. McIntosh* in which the Court recognized that title to property could be established "by the sword" (or through the barrel of a gun).

Between Congress' passage of the Homestead Act and the end of the Civil War, one scholar estimates that approximately 25 million acres of land were given to American citizens.[13] The Library of Congress states that "[t]he Homestead Act led to the distribution of 80 million acres of public land by 1900."[14] The Homestead Act exemplified another virtually "Whites only" national wealth creation policy. In other words, the homestead legislation constituted a traditional White American affirmative action program.

## Starting Reconstruction

The Emancipation Proclamation heralded President Lincoln's attempt to reconstruct and reintegrate the rebel states.[15] To establish new state governments, on December 8, 1863, Lincoln issued a Proclamation of Amnesty and Reconstruction. Lincoln's plan required 10% of the individuals in each rebel state who were eligible to vote before the Civil War to swear allegiance both to the Union and to the new state government. In addition, such state governments had to adopt state constitutions abolishing slavery.[16]

This "10% plan" allowed individuals in rebel states to directly elect their own representatives to the House of Representatives. At that time, the Constitution did not allow individuals to directly elect U.S. Senators. Instead, individual voters voted for their state legislators. State lawmakers in turn elected U.S. Senators from the particular state. Lincoln's plan recognized that Congress retained the ultimate authority to decide its members' qualifications.[17]

Given the historical context, Lincoln's plan was a promising start. It reached out a generous hand of friendship and reconciliation to the rebels, who in plain language had committed treason. They had violated the Constitution by waging war against the United States.[18]

Nevertheless, Lincoln's Reconstruction plan had major limitations. For instance, as the war drew to a conclusion and some areas were undergoing Reconstruction, for political reasons, Lincoln did not publicly advocate Black suffrage. Behind the scenes, in 1864, Lincoln sought a limited franchise (in Louisiana) for Blacks who were "intelligent" or war veterans.[19] However, when he ran into opposition, Lincoln did not insist on voting rights for newly freed Blacks.

After Lee's surrender, Lincoln decided to publicly express support for the right to vote for intelligent Blacks and for Black Civil War veterans.[20] Lincoln's modest proposals reflected the prevailing societal bias against political participation by anyone except propertied White males. As mentioned before, many members of the ruling elite believed that women's suffrage was neither appropriate nor urgent.

Another shortcoming of Lincoln's Reconstruction plan involved its failure to clearly address the abolition of slavery in the states that had remained within the Union. Lincoln's plan affected rebel states, not slaveholding border states like Maryland. As a practical matter, thousands of slaves in the remaining Union states solved the problem. During the war, they left the plantations. Many (for example, in Kentucky) joined the Union army. The evolving, dynamic nature of the conflict changed many people's lives permanently. These circumstances made Lincoln's plan basically a work in progress providing positive baby steps toward a reunited nation.

## Old Wine in New Bottles

Before his plan for Reconstruction could be more fully implemented, on April 15, 1865, Lincoln was assassinated. His successor, Andrew Johnson, initially followed Lincoln's Reconstruction plan. For example, President Johnson supported the Thirteenth Amendment, which outlawed chattel slavery, and moved America a long way toward being a more civilized society.

In addition, at first, President Johnson refused to grant amnesty to former rebels who had been large landholders and prominent military leaders. However, Johnson soon retreated from his initial stand of excluding influential ex-rebels from positions of power. Instead, to form new state governments in the South, Johnson appointed persons who had supported the Union with lip service.[21]

Johnson's appointees in turn recruited former rebels. The newly reformed southern governments began to look and behave much like the old governments of the pre–Civil War South. For example, immediately after the war ended, at the state level, former Confederates passed laws commonly called "Black Codes." Among other things, such state laws prohibited Blacks from sitting on juries, owning or leasing land, making contracts, and working in lucrative trades.[22] These statutes demonstrated that the ex-rebels remained opposed to political and civil equality for the former slaves.

Another concrete example illuminating the ex-Confederates' lack of good faith involved their response to the Thirteenth Amendment. That Amendment said: "Neither slavery nor involuntary servitude, except as a punishment for crime whereof the party shall have been duly convicted, shall exist within the United States ..." In short, with only one exception, the Amendment abolished slavery and involuntary servitude in the United States. That exception was "as a punishment for crime whereof the party shall have been duly convicted." In practice, many southern state and local governments exploited the Amendment's criminal punishment exception to (virtually) re-enslave newly freed persons. For instance, during and after the Reconstruction period, a corrupt criminal legal system frequently convicted Black men of minor criminal offenses. Throughout the former Confederacy, governmental officials compelled such individuals to work on chain gangs under conditions barely distinguishable from slavery.[23]

Quickly, ex-Confederate-dominated state governments recognized that the Thirteenth Amendment, which sought to end slavery, could be manipulated to continue it. To achieve this and similar objectives southern legislatures used many legal devices. State vagrancy statutes were both broad and vague; they essentially made being unemployed a crime. A jobless ex-slave could be convicted, imprisoned, placed on a chain gang, and compelled to work for free on the local plantation at which he had been previously enslaved.

In addition, some southern lawmakers enacted legislation making it a crime to have no written employment contract at the beginning of each calendar year. These laws made criminals of many former Black male slaves who did not have a job or a work contract with a White person. Furthermore, such newly reconstituted criminal codes provided imprisonment for Blacks who engaged in a wide range of activities. Offenses included "impudence" (for example, failing to take off one's hat to a White person), petty larceny, and traveling without a pass.[24] African Americans confronted pervasive legal traps set to re-enslave them for real or imagined infractions—whether of social custom or law. The Thirteenth Amendment criminal labor exception frequently functioned like a legal wolf in sheep's clothing: it perpetuated slavery under a different name.

Moreover, armed bands of former rebels attacked, and in many parts of the South, terrorized former slaves.[25] In response, former slaves and their supporters protested the Black Codes and discriminatory treatment. Some newly freed persons wrote to elected officials, others refused to leave lands they claimed as their own, and yet others defended themselves with whatever resources they could muster.[26] Renowned historian Professor Eric Foner writes: "Farther South, although former Whigs controlled the elections, service to the Confederacy emerged as a virtual prerequisite for victory. The vast majority of the new Senators and Congressman had opposed secession yet nearly all had followed their states into the rebellion."

In this historical context, in 1865 many former Confederate military officers and other Confederate leaders were elected to Congress. For instance, the Georgia state legislature elected Alexander Stephens, former vice president of the Confederacy, to the U.S. Senate.[27] Such former rebels and many of their allies presented themselves as prospective members of the national Congress.

Not surprisingly, many Republicans who supported the Union did not believe that the former slaveholders and Confederate warriors had truly repented.[28] Only months before these individuals had been using all available means, including physical violence, to destroy the Union. Seeking to safeguard basic human rights, Congress refused to seat them.[29] Congress instead passed corrective legislation: the Civil Rights Act of 1866. The Act provided that American citizens

> of every race and color ... shall have the same right [throughout the United States] to make and enforce contracts, to sue, be parties, and give evidence, to inherit, purchase, lease, sell, hold and convey real and personal property, and to full and equal benefit of all laws ... for the security of person and property, as is enjoyed by white citizens.[30]

The Act basically said that all American citizens would have the same civil rights as White persons. Practically speaking, for many Whites, it was totally unacceptable that the law now protected African Americans equally with Whites. Less than a decade earlier, *Dred Scott* had affirmed that Blacks had no rights that Whites were bound to respect. Through the Civil Rights Act of 1866, Congress had repudiated legal white supremacy. From many White persons' perspectives, the Civil Rights Act put them on the same legal plain as Blacks—and that was a big step down!

In fact, President Johnson vetoed the bill, arguing that it constituted discrimination against Whites and centralized too much power in the federal government.[31] Johnson's view was consistent with a perception that equality under the law with African Americans would be a demotion for White folks. Congress overrode the presidential veto. However, enforcement of the Civil Rights Act was erratic and often inefficient.

## Land Ownership: Shaky Promises (for Some)

Regarding economic development, the idea of former slaves owning property was not novel. Several attempts had been made to initiate landowner programs. For example, during his march through Georgia and into South Carolina, Union General William T. Sherman issued a field order that allowed former slaves to farm and live on abandoned property. Sherman's order covered a significant area along the coast from Savannah to Charleston, and extended 30 miles inland. Sherman's order contemplated the subsequent division of the contraband properties into parcels that Blacks would own and farm themselves.

Following the end of the Civil War, Congress created the Freedmen's Bureau, a federal agency to help former slaves and disadvantaged Whites recover from the dislocation of the war. General Otis Howard headed the Bureau, and similar to General Sherman's approach, General Howard issued an order allocating abandoned slaveholder land to Blacks. Believing that they would be individual landowners, Blacks began farming the confiscated land on which they and their former slaveholders had lived. The former slaves also set up community institutions like churches and schools.

Consistent with his policy of pardoning wealthy rebels, virtually "lock, stock, and barrel," President Johnson overruled General Howard's directive providing land to former slaves. Instead, Johnson ordered the return of the land to the former rebels.[32] Former slaves who had worked the land for free were evicted (sometimes at gunpoint!) and often compelled to sign contracts that greatly favored their former slaveholders.[33]

President Johnson effectively pulled the economic rug from under the former slaves, leaving them the choice of working for their former slaveholders on terms favorable to the former slaveholders or possibly relocating elsewhere. Rather than supporting General Howard's initiative to help Blacks become self-sufficient, Johnson's actions curtailed land ownership—a cornerstone of the economic foundation for Blacks seeking a fresh start.

Despite some progress, a troubling contrast existed between the way Congress treated the still-impoverished former slaves and its approach to well-heeled businesses. For example, immediately following the Civil War, Congress readily embraced legislation granting over 100 million acres of property to the railroads. The grants made it possible to build a transcontinental railroad (a public highway) stretching more than a thousand miles from the Midwest to the Pacific.[34] To help effectuate this venture and promote home ownership particularly among Whites, Congress also authorized the continuing American racial preference plan: take Indian land by any available means. Historically, in *Johnson v. McIntosh*, the United States Supreme Court had upheld taking Indian land "by the sword."[35] The Homestead Act of 1862 illustrates this approach. In short, Congress followed its established precedent: it crafted a corporate welfare plan for rich and powerful White persons as well as members of the White general public. More White American affirmative action . . .

Regarding the desperate situation of the former slaves, Congress emulated President Johnson's unfortunate example. Congress refused to help create a firm African American economic foundation. For example, Congress could have confiscated lands of the former slaveholders, compensated the slaveholders, and given confiscated and abandoned farmland to the former captives. After all, while toiling on such land under appalling conditions (for generations!), former slaves had provided free labor. Rather than take a more progressive approach, Congress failed to establish and fund a national program so that the former slaves could purchase and improve land.

In short, neither the federal, state, nor local governments established effective programs to help former slaves achieve another important hallmark of full and equal citizenship—economic self-sufficiency. Instead, many Republicans adopted a laissez-faire economic philosophy, stressing that the ability to work as free laborers would inevitably allow Blacks to save money and develop their own economic strength.

## A Ray of Hope

As the process of Reconstruction continued to evolve, many congressional Republicans perceived a troubling picture. President Johnson had retreated from his decision to oppose allowing prominent former slaveholders and confederates to hold governmental positions of leadership.[36] Furthermore, Johnson had vetoed both the Civil Rights Act of 1866 and congressional legislation creating the Freedmen's Bureau. Johnson's behavior confirmed the fears of Republicans that a clear and present danger existed: *unless effective steps were taken, blood shed during the Civil War would have been shed in vain.* To be sure, many White Republicans did not accept the idea that Blacks were their social, intellectual, or moral equals. Nevertheless, such individuals at least believed that with a fair opportunity to work, Blacks would be able to pull themselves up by their economic bootstraps and prosperity would follow.

The congressional elections in 1866 derailed President Johnson's attempt to increase his political power. Rather than electing Democrats and conservative Republicans, voters chose more progressive Republicans. These congressional leaders gained greater control of the reconstruction process.

To provide a more secure legal structure for recognizing universal freedom and equality, the Congress proposed and the states ratified the Fourteenth Amendment. Section 1 of that Amendment provided that "All persons born or naturalized in the United States and subject to the jurisdiction thereof, are citizens of the United States and of the State wherein they reside."[37] These words constitute the Citizenship Clause of the Fourteenth Amendment. The Citizenship Clause effectively overruled *Dred Scott*, which had held that the Constitution did not recognize African Americans as citizens.

In addition, the Fourteenth Amendment prohibited the states from abridging "privileges or immunities of citizens of the United States."[38] Thus, the Amendment attempted to place the former slaves on the same legal pedestal as White citizens. Furthermore, regardless of citizenship status, the Amendment guaranteed all persons equal protection of the laws and due process of law. In short, the Fourteenth Amendment sought to permanently infuse and entrench President Lincoln's vision expressed in his Gettysburg Address; namely, "A New Birth of Freedom."

In this vein, as noted before, the Civil Rights Act of 1866 explicitly recognized that the Constitution secured to all U.S. citizens

> of every race and color . . . the same right, in every State and Territory in the United States, to make and enforce contracts, to sue, be parties, and give evidence, to inherit, purchase, lease, sell, hold and convey real and personal property, and to full and equal benefit of all laws . . . for the security of person and property, as is enjoyed by white citizens.

The Fourteenth Amendment reinforces and expands the legal protections of the Act.

Unfortunately, in its hands-off approach to Black economic progress, Congress failed to take account of the existing realities within much of the nation and especially in the South. White terrorist organizations like the Ku Klux Klan and the Knights of the White Camelia used tried and tested methods against Blacks and their allies who attempted to exercise leadership (particularly in political and economic matters).[39] The terrorists killed, assaulted, raped, tarred and feathered, and even burned people at the stake. Such terror tactics followed the brutal blueprint used to maintain control of slaves beginning in colonial times and continuing until the end of the Civil War.

In the early Reconstruction period (1869-71), terrorist organizations helped impose white supremacist–oriented governments in Georgia, Alabama, and North Carolina.[40] Many Whites, both North and South, resisted the reality that the Civil War had changed the relationships of the states to the federal government.

Partially in response to the pleas of supporters of the Union (especially former slaves), on April 20, 1871, Congress passed "An Act to enforce provisions of the Fourteenth Amendment" (also commonly referred to as the Ku Klux Klan Act). Among other things, the Act provided civil and criminal remedies for individuals subjected to harassment, intimidation, and violence when such persons attempted to exercise their human rights under the Constitution.[41] President Ulysses S. Grant, in a relatively rare display of political courage on behalf of protecting Blacks, ordered the use of federal troops to suppress Klan violence in some jurisdictions like South Carolina.[42] Attorney General Amos T. Akerman also moved to enforce antiterrorist laws in places like North Carolina and Mississippi.[43]

As previously noted, despite life-threatening challenges, the former slaves demanded the right to participate fully in American society. They were especially eager to exercise the rights to vote, own land, and travel freely. Through the agitation of Blacks and progressive members of the White community, in 1870 the Fifteenth Amendment was ratified, allowing Black males to vote.

In addition, attempts were made to remove state-mandated travel restrictions on former slaves. Immediately after the war, such restrictions had been incorporated into the

Black Codes to ensure a virtually captive Black labor force. Such a workforce could be coerced into working under conditions nearly identical with slavery.[44] Freedom of travel was a crucial human right for Reconstruction-era Blacks. If they found that in a particular place social, political, and economic conditions were too hostile for them to thrive or even to survive, the ability to relocate was essential.

Despite numerous challenges, for a brief shining historical moment more representative Reconstruction governments arose in the South. Under Reconstruction, for the first time, state institutions mandated free state-funded public education, and established asylums for mentally ill persons as well as homes for orphans. Some states provided poor relief. Many Reconstruction governments abolished public whipping posts. Such governments also eliminated property requirements for voting and jury service as well as imprisonment for failure to pay one's bills.[45] In short, some Reconstruction governments made important human rights achievements for their constituents.

Another bright spot in the Reconstruction process involved the work of women. Some women (White and Black) were abolitionists, and, in some cases, suffragists as well. Some women of color who were free before the war helped the newly freed slaves become self-sufficient through education, productive work, and ownership of property. Many middle-class women from the North were particularly supportive of the actions of the newly created Freedmen's Bureau. Women of various hues worked diligently as agents and associates of the Bureau. Such women also served as volunteers in major cities (north and south) as well as in rural areas.[46]

## The Courts: Undependable Refuge in the Storm

When interpreting the Reconstruction laws (especially the constitutional amendments), the federal courts seemed to take one step forward and two steps back. For example, in 1873, in the *Slaughterhouse Cases*, the Supreme Court analyzed the Thirteenth, Fourteenth, and Fifteenth Amendments to the Constitution. The Court said that

> no one can fail to be impressed with the one pervading purpose found in them all, lying at the foundation of each, and without which none of them would have been even suggested; we mean the freedom of the slave race, the security and firm establishment of that freedom, and the protection of the newly-made freeman and citizen from the oppressions of those who had formerly exercised unlimited dominion over him.[47]

By stating that the Constitution safeguarded the rights of Negroes, the Court took a giant step forward compared to *Dred Scott*, which had said that Blacks had no rights that Whites were bound to respect.

However, the *Slaughterhouse* Court proceeded to claim that the Constitution provided two sets of citizenship rights. One set of rights could be exercised by all national citizens. Other rights could only be exercised at the state level. And each state could decide both what those state citizenship rights were and who could or could not enjoy them.

Accordingly, even though the Fourteenth Amendment made the former slaves citizens of the national government, the *Slaughterhouse* Court contended that the rights of citizens at the national level were extremely limited. For example, national citizenship rights encompassed the right to petition the government to change its policies, to have the assistance of the national government if the citizen was in trouble on the high seas or with a foreign government, and to move freely from one state to another. Relatively speaking, these were puny national citizenship rights.

In contrast to pint-sized national rights, the *Slaughterhouse* Court said that the states controlled most meaningful rights of citizenship. Quoting *Corfield v. Coryell*, the

*Slaughterhouse* Court described the rights (or "privileges and immunities") of state citizenship as being

> comprehended under the following general heads: protection by the government, with the right to acquire and possess property of every kind, and to pursue and obtain happiness and safety, subject, nevertheless, to such restraints as the government may prescribe for the general good of the whole.[48]

From the Court's perspective, important matters like making contracts, owning property, and serving on juries were all primarily under state supervision.

The Court recognized that the Fourteenth Amendment was drafted to protect the human rights of former slaves. However, the Court firmly rejected the obvious meaning of the Amendment: specifically, that the Constitution gave Congress broad power to protect the former slaves from the very same state governments that, during Reconstruction, had enacted the Black Codes and similar oppressive state laws. Thus, the *Slaughterhouse* Court spoke with a forked tongue.

The Supreme Court miserably failed to facilitate the primary purpose of the Amendment: securing liberty and justice for all. The Court asked derisively:

> Was it the purpose of the fourteenth amendment, by the simple declaration that no State should make or enforce any law which shall abridge the privileges and immunities of citizens of the United States, to transfer the security and protection of all the civil rights which we have mentioned, from the States to the Federal government? And where it is declared that Congress shall have the power to enforce that article, was it intended to bring within the power of Congress the entire domain of civil rights heretofore belonging exclusively to the States?[49]

A reasonable answer to the Court's questions would have been, "*Yes*! Of course!" State laws created slavery. State laws perpetuated the accumulation of material wealth and political power derived from slave labor. State laws undermined and almost permanently destroyed national unity. And state laws attempted to recreate slavery through Black Codes. In fact, regarding the Thirteenth, Fourteenth, and Fifteenth Amendments, in its own words, the Court had recognized that

> no one can fail to be impressed with the one pervading purpose found in them all, lying at the foundation of each, and without which none of them would have been even suggested; we mean the freedom of the slave race, the security and firm establishment of that freedom, and the protection of the newly-made freeman and citizen from the oppressions of those who had formerly exercised unlimited dominion over him.[50]

In these circumstances, the obvious and only reasonable answer was yes! The Fourteenth Amendment gives the Congress plenary power to protect individual liberty from state oppression. With African Americans and other supporters of Reconstruction being lynched, shot, beaten, and chased out of town often aided and abetted by state officials and former confederates, the answer should have been, emphatically, "Yes, the Fourteenth Amendment expressly gave Congress the authority to protect the human rights of persons living in the United States." The constitutional protection exists especially where the state failed to act or where the state became an instrument of majority tyranny.

The dissenters in *Slaughterhouse* recognized the Court's flawed analysis and said:

> A citizen of a State is now only a citizen of the United States residing in that State. The fundamental

> rights, privileges, and immunities which belong to him as a free man and a free citizen, now belong to him as a citizen of the United States, and are not dependent upon his citizenship of any State ... They do not derive their existence from its [the state's] legislation, and cannot be destroyed by its power.[51]

Moreover, the dissenters pointed out that:

> The amendment does not attempt to confer any new privileges or immunities upon citizens, or to enumerate or define those already existing. It assumes that there are such privileges and immunities which belong of right to citizens as such, and ordains that they shall not be abridged by State legislation. If this inhibition has no reference to privileges and immunities of this character, but only refers, as held by the majority of the court in their opinion, to such privileges and immunities as were before its adoption specially designated in the Constitution or necessarily implied as belonging to citizens of the United States, it was a vain and idle enactment, which accomplished nothing, and most unnecessarily excited Congress and the people on its passage ... But if the amendment refers to the natural and inalienable rights which belong to all citizens, the inhibition has a profound significance and consequence.[52]

The dissent's position would have not only furnished powerful protection for former slaves but also strengthened protection for the rights of all working people (including the butchers in the *Slaughterhouse Cases*). Workers and small business entrepreneurs would have been able to better exercise their rights to freely pursue their vocations.

The Framers designed the Privileges or Immunities Clause of the Fourteenth Amendment to protect former slaves by ensuring that not only were the ex-captives recognized as citizens of the United States but also that they would have the same human rights as other citizens, especially the same rights as Whites. In other words, the privileges or immunities provision of the Fourteenth Amendment limited the ability of the states to oppress the former slaves. The Amendment authorized Congress to protect those rights through enacting appropriate legislation.

The majority's miserly interpretation of human rights under the Fourteenth Amendment conferred the primary protection of the human rights of African Americans upon state governments. Former rebels often dominated these governments or subjected state officials to physical, economic, and social threats. Basically, the Court placed the foxes firmly in control of the chicken coop.

On the same day that the *Slaughterhouse* Court butchered the Privileges or Immunities Clause the Court also decided *Bradwell v. State*. In *Bradwell*, Myra Bradwell, a woman living in Illinois, had passed the Illinois bar exam with high honors, and was qualified to practice law.[53] The Illinois Supreme Court denied Bradwell admission to the state bar. Bradwell sued, alleging that her privileges or immunities of citizenship included the freedom to practice law, and that the state of Illinois had violated her rights under the Fourteenth Amendment.

The Court rejected Bradwell's argument and held that the Privileges or Immunities Clause did not encompass a woman's right to practice law. *Only moments before deciding Bradwell's case*, the *Slaughterhouse* Court narrowly read the meaning of "privileges or immunities of citizenship." Having gutted the Privileges or Immunities Clause, the Court could then more easily rebuff Myra Bradwell's argument that as a U.S. citizen, she had a right to practice law. The *Bradwell* Court seemed convinced that the freedom to choose a vocation was not central to American citizenship. To the extent that citizenship was relevant to practicing law, the Court concluded that individual states could require that a citizen be of a particular gender to be admitted to the state's bar.[54] The practical result: the United States Supreme Court upheld the Illinois court's decision to exclude Bradwell from the legal profession because she was a woman. In essence, after the *Slaughterhouse* Court eviscerated the Privileges or Immunities Clause, the *Bradwell* Court pureed the remaining freedoms.

To make bad matters worse, during its next term, the Supreme Court reaffirmed its unfortunate *Slaughterhouse* rationale. In *Minor v. Happersett*,[55] the Court denied the majority of American citizens—women—the right to vote. On October 15, 1872, in St. Louis, Missouri, Virginia Minor attempted to register to vote in the upcoming November 1872 national elections. When Reese Happersett, the registrar, refused to register her because she was not a "male citizen of the United States,"[56] Minor sued him.

After losing in Missouri state court, Minor appealed to the Supreme Court of the United States. The Supreme Court stated:

> Certainly if the courts can consider any question settled, this is one. For nearly ninety years, the people have acted upon the idea that the Constitution, when it conferred citizenship, did not necessarily confer the right of suffrage. If uniform practice long continued can settle the construction of so important an instrument as the Constitution of the United States confessedly is, most certainly it has been done here. Our province is to decide what the law is, not to declare what it should be.
>
> We have given this case the careful consideration its importance demands. If the law is wrong, it ought to be changed; but the power for that is not with us. The arguments addressed to us bearing upon such a view of the subject may perhaps be sufficient to induce those having the power to make the alteration, but they ought not to be permitted

> to influence our judgment in determining the present rights of the parties now litigating before us. No argument as to woman's need of suffrage can be considered. We can only act upon her rights as they exist. It is not for us to look at the hardship of withholding. Our duty is at an end if we find it is within the power of a state to withhold.
>
> Being unanimously of the opinion that the Constitution of the United States does not confer the right of suffrage upon anyone, and that the constitutions and laws of the several states which commit that important trust to men alone are not necessarily void, we *Affirm the judgment.*[57]

In other words, the *Minor* Court said that voting was recognized and protected by individual states. The bottom line: the *Minor* Court held that the majority of American citizens—women—did not have a federally recognized right to vote.

The *Bradwell* and *Minor* cases buttressed a national legal and social structure that obstructs women's entry into and progress within the legal profession. Indeed, from 1789 to 2008, every American president appointed males to more than 70% of federal judgeships. Moreover, during that time, every president nominated White males to fill a majority of such judgeships. White male affirmative action thoroughly permeated the federal judicial selection process.

President Barack Obama departed from the practice of appointing members of a minority group (White males) to a majority of judgeships. Obama appointed women to over 40% of federal judgeships.[58] Men of color and women of all hues comprised the majority of Obama's judicial appointees. President Donald Trump's federal judicial appointments reflected a return to White affirmative action. White men constitute nearly 65% of Trump's federal judicial appointees.[59]

Halfway through the fourth year of his presidency, President Joe Biden has distinguished himself in a number of ways, including being the first president to appoint more women than men to the federal judiciary. As of July 29, 2024, Biden had appointed 197 federal judges, including 124 women (62.9%). In other words, nearly two-thirds of Biden's appointments are persons from a significant and often underrepresented American majority: women.[60] White women constitute the largest demographic cohort among Biden's 197 judges—46 judges or 23.35%. African American women comprise 16.25% (33 judges). Biden has appointed a record number of American Indian women: three.[61] Biden's appointments in the next several months will determine the extent to which his judicial choices will make a significant difference to the demographic profile of the current federal bench.

In the aftermath of the Civil War, the Court seemed afraid to recognize that individuals from politically weak groups—like women, Blacks, and working persons—had constitutionally protected rights to pursue happiness, for example, through practicing a profession or following a calling. The *Slaughterhouse* and *Bradwell* decisions suggest that the Court feared upsetting the social status quo that had entrenched materially wealthy White men in dominant positions throughout American society.

Whatever the Court's motivation, when the *Slaughterhouse* Court narrowly interpreted citizenship rights, the Court surrendered its important role of protecting human rights under the Constitution. In a government based on separation of powers, the Court is entrusted to interpret the Constitution. The Courts must and should do so to defend the rights of individuals and disadvantaged groups, including minorities who sometimes may be poor, downtrodden, and unpopular. Protecting the rights of the weak against the *legal oppression* of powerful majorities (political bullies) is a primary requirement of equal protection of the law. Concentrated political and economic power in a few hands can lead to laws that oppress vulnerable populations. Unless the courts intercede, centralized political and economic power can—like the old Black Codes—evolve into legal tyranny.

The Panic of 1873 accelerated increasing resistance among White Americans to Reconstruction. In part because of greed and speculative investments related to the railroads and other large economic entities, major financial institutions in the United States collapsed. When major financial institutions like banks failed, many people lost their life savings and were reduced to poverty. In these circumstances, many White politicians viewed requests to alleviate the desperate situation of the newly freed slaves as a nuisance.

Following a brief period of relative calm, throughout the mid and late 1870s, white terrorist forces renewed their efforts to re-enslave or at least to subordinate African Americans to the maximum extent possible. For example, they waged a determined campaign of physical violence to reestablish White domination in Mississippi, Louisiana, and South Carolina. White vigilantes used fraud, lynch ropes, torches, and whips to intimidate and discourage Blacks from voting and to overturn election results that were not to the liking of the local White elite.[62]

Southern political, civic, and religious leaders boldly proclaimed their continued dedication to restoring "white supremacy." Between 1873 and 1877, in Mississippi, Louisiana, Alabama, Georgia, and both Carolinas, "Home Rule" or "Redeemer" governments came to power riding a wave of whips, bullets, and stuffed ballot boxes. These governments opposed the exercise by Negroes of rights like voting, property ownership, and holding jobs other than manual labor. Enjoying the fruits of one's labor as an entrepreneur was viewed by many Whites as a threat. For instance, after he, his wife, and children had been beaten by Klansmen, one Black man in Florida, who was trying to purchase a parcel of land for his family, was told that the Klan did not "allow damned niggers to live on land of their own."[63] Landownership was a hallmark of freedom; the inability to own property was a badge of slavery.

In practical terms, ex-Confederates and their supporters continued their guerrilla war on Reconstruction. Widespread physical violence helped to create state and local governments that deprived Blacks and progressive Whites of their human rights.

Realizing that something needed to be done, the Republican Congress passed the Civil Rights Act of 1875. The Act sought to safeguard human rights, especially those of former slaves by limiting discrimination against Blacks in public accommodations and other spheres of American life. However, court challenges to the Act immediately arose due to substantial resistance among some White members of the public.

In fact, the ratification of the Reconstruction Amendments (Thirteenth, Fourteenth, and Fifteenth Amendments) and passage of the Civil Rights bills of 1866 and 1875 helped to convince many White persons that the basic work of Reconstruction was completed. Such individuals viewed the new laws as having made Blacks equal citizens both in theory and in fact. As Horace Greeley, an outspoken opponent of slavery and fervent supporter of white supremacy, said: it was now time to "Root, hog or die."[64] In other words, the former slaves were on their own: they had to fend for themselves (in an often hostile legal and social environment) without expecting assistance from anyone.

Greeley's abandonment approach to African Americans' human rights struggle garnered significant support in the courts and in electoral politics. For example, in 1872 in Louisiana, following a disputed gubernatorial election, a mob of white militia comprised chiefly of former Confederate soldiers attacked the county seat of Colfax, Louisiana, and slaughtered several hundred African Americans who were defending the town. Congress had recently passed legislation (the Enforcement Act of 1870) which among other things specifically protected voting rights and made it a felony to:

> band or conspire together, or go in disguise upon the public highway, or upon the premises of another, with intent to violate ... this act, or to injure, oppress, threaten, or intimidate any citizen, with intent to prevent or hinder his free exercise and enjoyment of any right or privilege granted or secured to him by the Constitution or laws of the United States, or because of his having exercised the same ...[65]

Indictments were brought against the mobsters. The criminal charges included violating the human rights of African Americans to vote, peacefully assemble, and to bear arms. In *United States v. Cruikshank*,[66] the Supreme Court narrowly interpreted the statutes so that most of the criminal defendants were freed. The Court said that:

> [T]hese counts are too vague and general. They lack the certainty and precision required by the established rules of criminal pleading. It follows that they are not good and sufficient in law. They are so defective that no judgment of conviction should be pronounced upon them.[67]

The Court also stated that:

> The Fourteenth Amendment prohibits a State from denying to any person within its jurisdiction the equal protection of the laws; but this provision does not, any more than the one which precedes it, and which we have just considered, add anything to the rights which one citizen has under the Constitution against another. The equality of the rights of citizens is a principle of republicanism. Every republican government is in duty bound to protect all its citizens in the enjoyment of this principle, if within its power. That duty was originally assumed by the

> States, and it still remains there. The only obligation resting upon the United States is to see that the States do not deny the right. This the amendment guarantees, but no more. The power of the national government is limited to the enforcement of this guaranty.[68]

Regarding equal protection, the Court left primary responsibility to the state governments, which were the principal creators of laws that discriminated based on race. As to racial violence flowing from individuals, the Court's decision disregards section 5 of the Fourteenth Amendment, which grants Congress plenary authority to legislate to ensure equality under the law. Nowhere does the Amendment expressly prohibit federal legislation to prevent individuals from violating the rights of other individuals because of race.

Moreover, the Thirteenth Amendment provides additional constitutional protection from racist behavior of private individuals. That Amendment specifically outlaws enslavement of individuals by other individuals and authorizes Congress to enact appropriate legislation prohibiting individuals from treating others like enslaved persons were treated; for instance, being subjected to assaults, rapes, torture, and murder based on race. Curtailing and punishing such individual actions clearly fall within the scope of the Thirteenth Amendment. The *Cruikshank* Court seemed to have a specific political agenda: to interpret the law to maximize the power of the former enslavers over those formerly enslaved.

A year after the *Cruikshank* decision, the prospect of a society based on liberty and justice for all suffered another significant setback. In 1876, a hotly disputed presidential election between New York's Democrat Governor Samuel Tilden and Ohio Republican Governor Rutherford Hayes culminated in Hayes being elected president by one electoral vote. More specifically, Hayes secured victory because of the electoral votes of three southern states under Republican control: Florida, South Carolina, and Louisiana. Hayes' victory would have been impossible without the votes of African Americans who turned out and voted for him despite threats, violence, and electoral fraud.[69]

Tilden contested the election results. As part of an apparent political deal to smooth the way to Hayes becoming president, through intermediaries, Hayes sent a historic signal to his political opponents: Hayes indicated that he would adopt a hands-off approach to the reestablishment of ex-Confederate-dominated state government under the control of white supremacists.[70] Thus, despite evidence that Republicans had won gubernatorial elections in South Carolina and Louisiana, Hayes recognized Democrats as governors of those states. Moreover, Hayes ordered federal troops to return to their barracks in South Carolina and Louisiana thus ensuring that local supporters of the newly installed state governments would have a free hand in squashing dissent especially from Black Republicans who had supported Hayes' candidacy.

Eminent American historian Eric Foner summed up matters this way:

> [The year] 1877 marked a decisive retreat from the idea, born during the Civil War, of a powerful national state protecting the fundamental rights of American citizens. Yet the federal government was not rendered impotent in all matters—only those concerning blacks.[71]

Thus, like a recurrent nightmare, African Americans had once more furnished the resources—organization, energy, courage, and votes—to advance the careers of persons like Hayes who in turn betrayed the American ideals of liberty and justice for all. As one formerly enslaved person said, state governments dominated by former enslavers promised justice for all: but such promises were "like pie crust: easily broken."[72]

While often discouraging, the news coming from the Supreme Court regarding the human rights of African Americans was not all bad. In 1880, in *Strauder v. West Virginia*, the Court struck down a West Virginia statute limiting jury service to White males who were at least 21 years of age. Under West Virginia's White male jury law, an all-White male jury had convicted the defendant of capital murder. Regarding the purpose of the Fourteenth Amendment, the Supreme Court quoted its prior decision in *Slaughterhouse* as follows:

> The existence of laws in the States where the newly emancipated negroes resided which discriminated with gross injustice and hardship against them as a class was the evil to be remedied, and, by it [the Fourteenth Amendment], such laws were forbidden. If, however, the States did not conform their laws to its requirements, then, by the fifth section of the article of amendment, Congress was authorized to enforce it by suitable legislation.[73]

The Court continued its analysis and stated:

> If this is the spirit and meaning of the amendment ... it is to be construed liberally to carry out the purposes of its framers. It ordains that no State shall make or enforce any laws which shall abridge the privileges or immunities of citizens of the United States ... It ordains that no State shall deprive any person of life, liberty, or property without due process of law, or deny to any person within its jurisdiction the equal protection of the laws. What is this but declaring that the law in the States shall be the same for the black as for the white; that all persons, whether colored or white, shall stand equal before the laws of the States, and, in regard to the colored race, for whose protection the amendment

> was primarily designed, that no discrimination shall be made against them bar [*sic*] law because of their color? The words of the amendment, it is true, are prohibitory, but they contain a necessary implication of a positive immunity, or right, most valuable to the colored race—the right to exemption from unfriendly legislation against them distinctively as colored—exemption from legal discriminations, implying inferiority in civil society, lessening the security of their enjoyment of the rights which others enjoy, and discriminations which are steps towards reducing them to the condition of a subject race.[74]

*Strauder* recognized that the Fourteenth Amendment prohibited legislation that was intended to or had the effect of subordinating Blacks. Accordingly, *Strauder* voided a state law derived from previous ones designed to keep African Americans in bondage.

The Court's support of equality (like pie crust!) soon crumbled. Three years after *Strauder*, in the *Civil Rights Cases*, the Supreme Court ruled that much of the Civil Rights Act of 1875 was unconstitutional. The Civil Rights Act of 1875 had outlawed race discrimination against Blacks in public accommodations, including theaters, inns, and on railroads. Reflecting the mentality of many members of the general White public, the Court stated:

> When a man has emerged from slavery, and by the aid of beneficent legislation has shaken off the inseparable concomitants of that state, there must be some stage in the progress of his elevation when he takes the rank of a mere citizen, and ceases to be the special favorite of the laws, and when his rights as a citizen, or a man, are to be protected in the ordinary modes by which other men's rights are protected.[75]

The Court interpreted the Fourteenth Amendment to apply only to "state action," and then narrowly defined state action to allow race discrimination to flourish. The Court's reading crippled Congress' efforts to establish equal treatment of Negroes. Ensuring that Negroes received the same treatment as White folks (the practical meaning of equal protection of the laws!) was, for the Court in the *Civil Rights Cases*, simply going too far.

In dissent, Justice John Marshall Harlan spoke eloquently against the Court majority's decision to torpedo protection of the rights of the newly freed Blacks:

> My brethren say, that when a man has emerged from slavery, and by the aid of beneficent legislation has shaken off the inseparable concomitants of that state, there must be some stage in the progress of his elevation when he takes the rank of a mere citizen, and ceases to be the special favorite of the laws, and when his rights as a citizen, or a man, are to be protected in the ordinary modes by which other men's rights are protected. It is, I submit, scarcely just to say that the colored race has been the special favorite of the laws. The statute of 1875, now adjudged to be unconstitutional, is for the benefit of citizens of every race and color. What the nation through Congress, has sought to accomplish in reference to that race, is—what had already been done in every State of the Union for the white race—to secure and protect rights belonging to them as freemen and citizens; nothing more. It was not deemed enough "to help the feeble up, but to support him after." The one underlying purpose of congressional legislation has been to enable the black race to take the rank of mere citizens. The difficulty has been to compel a recognition of the legal right of the black race to take the rank of citizens, and to secure the enjoyment of privileges belonging, under the law, to them as a

> component part of the people for whose welfare and happiness government is ordained. At every step, in this direction, the nation has been confronted with class tyranny, which a contemporary English historian says is, of all tyrannies, the most intolerable, "for it is ubiquitous in its operation, and weighs, perhaps, most heavily on those whose obscurity or distance would withdraw them from the notice of single despot." To-day, it is the colored race which is denied, by corporations and individuals wielding public authority, rights fundamental in their freedom and citizenship. At some future time, it may be that some other race will fall under the ban of race discrimination. If the constitutional amendments be enforced, according to the intent with which, as I conceive, they were adopted, there cannot be, in this republic, any class of human beings in practical subjection to another class, with power in the latter to dole out to the former just such privileges as they may choose to grant.[76]

For the most part, Justice Harlan's prescient insights were ignored: some persons continued to equate enacting new laws with practical societal change. Such individuals seemed blind to hypocritical public policies designed to help those who needed it least, like railroads.

Thus, instead of "help[ing] the feeble up, [and supporting] him after,"[77] the Court molded the meaning of the Fourteenth Amendment to benefit the rich and powerful. For example, three years after the Supreme Court took its gigantic backward step in the *Civil Rights Cases*, in 1886 in *Santa Clara County v. Southern Pacific Railway Co.*,[78] the Court fabricated a remarkable interpretation of the Fourteenth Amendment. Chief Justice Morrison "Mott" Waite said:

> The Court does not wish to hear argument on the question whether the provision in the Fourteenth

> Amendment to the Constitution which forbids a state to deny to any person within its jurisdiction the equal protection of the laws applies to these corporations. We are all of opinion that it does.[79]

The *Southern Pacific Railway* Court unanimously proclaimed that the Constitution extended human rights guarantees to railroads. The Court reached this astounding conclusion less than 20 years after the Fourteenth Amendment was ratified to protect the human rights of formerly enslaved Americans.

In deciding the *Southern Pacific Railroad* case, the Court noted that the Congress had given "liberal grants" of land in the state of California to the Southern Pacific Railway Company totaling approximately 11 million acres. Much of that free land was not used for railroad-related business. Instead, the major activities conducted on the land included farming, cattle ranching, and similar endeavors.[80] In this context, the Court also unanimously held that the California State Board of Equalization had improperly taxed property belonging to the railroad. The *Southern Pacific Railway* case was one in an impressive line of Supreme Court decisions stating that railroads and other businesses were persons under the Fourteenth Amendment.

Furthermore, the Court aggressively protected the railroads from state regulation fees. For instance, in the *Minnesota Rate Cases*,[81] the Minnesota state regulatory board required a railroad to impose a charge of 2½ cents per 10-gallon container of milk. The Minnesota Supreme Court held that the decision of the regulatory agency was final and unreviewable.

A divided U.S. Supreme Court reversed the decision of the Minnesota Supreme Court. The U.S. Supreme Court said that the state court ruling conflicted with the Constitution because it meant that the state could impose tariffs on private property so as to take the property without due process of law.[82] Specifically, the Court stated:

> The question of the reasonableness of a rate of charge for transportation by a railroad company, involving as it does the element of reasonableness both as regards the company and as regards the public, is eminently a question for judicial investigation, requiring due process of law for its determination. If the company is deprived of the power of charging reasonable rates for the use of its property, and such deprivation takes place in the absence of an investigation by judicial machinery, it is deprived of the lawful use of its property, and thus, in substance and effect, of the property itself, without due process of law and in violation of the Constitution of the United States; and in so far as it is thus deprived, while other persons are permitted to receive reasonable profits upon their invested capital, the company is deprived of the equal protection of the laws.[83]

The Court's intervention on behalf of the railroads was so aggressive that some academic commentators summarized the Court's role as follows: "For nearly 40 years, the Court was rate-maker and accountant."[84]

When dealing with big businesses and influential members of society like railroad tycoons, the Court's approach was similar to that of the two other branches of government—namely, the Congress and the Executive. As previously mentioned, the Congress and the Executive had granted the railroads over 100 million acres of free property plus millions of dollars in federal grants (free money!) to build a transcontinental railroad.[85] Judicial rulings protective of large businesses signaled that all three branches of government favored the economic elites. Such privileged individuals and organizations were eagerly soliciting and receiving nineteenth-century corporate welfare. All three branches of the government unanimously and enthusiastically agreed to the massive taxpayer subsidized giveaways.

In contrast, Black former enslaved persons were often denied even food rations. One former slave from Texas wrote a searing letter to Massachusetts Senator Charles Sumner, asking why, "whilst Congress appropriated land by the million acres to pet railroad schemes ... did they not aid poor Anthony and his people starving and in rags?"[86] Public officials behaved as though giving starving Blacks free food during a depression would make Blacks lazy and unwilling to work. Public welfare seemed to be reserved for those who needed it least.

Perhaps one should not be surprised by different perceptions of reality flowing from different personal life experiences. Thus, a railroad executive whose company had received millions of acres of public land for free would see life differently than "poor Anthony and his people starving and in rags." Those who had not experienced myriad forms of oppression often believed that once the law changed everyone could immediately and freely exercise their human rights. This belief in instant equality conveniently and tragically overlooked a disturbing reality: *In theory, the law protected formerly enslaved persons; however, in fact, the law often did not.*

Many African Americans perceived the bitter reality that they were being *railroaded* toward a new type of slavery.

In sum, during Reconstruction, Congress and several presidents failed to provide the military and economic support necessary for a new social order in which Blacks would be able to truly become full citizens with Whites and other members of society. In expounding the Constitution to protect the newly freed slaves and those in similar circumstances, the Supreme Court often neglected its responsibility to interpret the Constitution to promote liberty and justice for all. Like any human institution, the Court was, and always will be, imperfect. Recognizing that it was prone to error, if the Court was to err at all in its judicial decision making, it should have erred on the side of the have-nots rather than continuing to error on the side of the haves.

Federal timidity in protecting the human rights of former captives caused the progress of Reconstruction to be slow, uneven, and eventually, in many ways, very modest. Individuals who believed that changes in American human rights law necessarily improved people's lives often overlooked how governmental policies erected obstacles to assisting those most in need. The plight of former enslaved persons is a prime example of wishing that a serious problem would magically disappear.

The lack of both constructive national government leadership and moral courage contributed to creating a toxic national environment. In this context, lynching, exploitation, and unhealthy social myths like white supremacy mushroomed.

A horrific example of what happens when the prevailing society lacks strong moral backbone involves these carefully documented facts courtesy of the Equal Justice Institute:

> EJI has documented 4084 racial terror lynchings in twelve Southern states between the end of Reconstruction in 1877 and 1950, which is at least 800 more lynchings in these states than previously reported. EJI has also documented more than 300 racial terror lynchings in other states during this time period.[87]

Led by courageous and brilliant human rights champion, Bryan Stevenson, EJI continues the struggle for justice in the criminal law system of the United States.[88] Other human rights scholars discovered that in Texas, hundreds more persons, mostly Latinos, were lynched between 1910 and 1920. During this time frame, estimates exist that in the Lone Star State as many as 5,000 Mexican Americans were murdered.[89]

The end of Reconstruction, the rise of all-White Redeemer governments in the South, the widespread disenfranchisement of African Americans, and the lynching of people of color as a tool of American domestic terrorism

Figure 1. Photograph of Sam Hose's body after a mob murdered him (https://jcdean8417.wordpress.com/sam-hose/sam-hose-photo-gallery/#jp-carousel-77).

marked the end of the 1800s. An extraordinary account of the barbaric measures taken to intimidate Blacks and push them back as close to slavery as possible is reflected in the *New-York Tribune* description of the lynching of Sam Hose, which took place in Coweta, Georgia.[90]

> Before the torch was applied to the pyre, the Negro was deprived of his ears, fingers and other portions of his body with surprising fortitude. Before the body was cool, it was cut to pieces, the bones were crushed into small bits and even the tree upon which the wretch met his fate was torn up and disposed of as souvenirs. The Negro's heart was cut in several pieces, as was also his liver. Those unable to obtain the most ghastly relics directly, paid more

> fortunate possessors extravagant sums for them. Small pieces of bone went for 25 cents and a bit of liver, crisply cooked for 10 cents.[91]

In this context, W.E.B. Du Bois was in Atlanta, Georgia, on his way to deliver a letter regarding lynching to Joel Chandler Harris, writer of Uncle Remus story tales. While walking down the street, Du Bois saw some of Sam Hose's amputated fingers and toes being displayed in a local meat market. The sight of parts of Hose's dismembered body emotionally shook Du Bois so much that he decided not to deliver his letter. Instead, he committed himself to a life of activism to address societal problems associated with the color line.[92]

Chapter V

# Hijacking the Right to Vote, and Legalizing Jim Crow

IN THE WAKE OF LYNCHINGS, arson, physical assaults, and other terrorist violence, the Redeemer governments moved to disenfranchise Blacks using literacy tests, poll taxes, and property requirements.[1] In addition, ex-Confederate-friendly state legislation like the infamous grandfather clauses granted voting rights to White grandsons whose granddads were eligible to vote before the Civil War. The grandsons did not have to pass literacy tests or other discriminatory voting requirements.

To ensure that citizens who had been stripped of their rights could not effectively defend themselves, white supremacist leaders used devious methods. In Mississippi (1890), South Carolina (1895), Louisiana (1898), and Virginia (1901-1902), the governing elites convened state constitutional conventions. In each case, only a few hundred delegates (at most) devised methods to rob tens of thousands of Black men (and many poor White men) of their voting rights. The new power brokers dramatically purged the voting rolls in each of these states. For fear that their vote stealing would be reversed, the political establishment refused to allow the public to vote on the new constitutions.[2] In each of these states, after purging the electorate, the rulers proclaimed the new state constitution as being in effect.[3]

In the one convention state in which the new constitution made it to referendum (Alabama 1901), the matter passed because of overwhelming support from majority Black counties! The official tally showed that in heavily Black counties, *36,244 out of 41,695 votes were counted in favor of disenfranchisement*. Obviously, the likelihood of nearly 90% of these voters, voting to deprive themselves of a say in government was as great as a snowball causing a blizzard in hell.[4]

In three Alabama counties, the total number of votes supposedly cast exceeded the number of eligible voters by more than 12,000.[5] The practical result of such outright vote fraud was to ensure that the proposed state constitution would be adopted and that Blacks would be disqualified from voting.

North Carolina used similar methods. After the North Carolina state legislature ratified the work of its vote-stripping convention, the counties with Black voting majorities provided the margin of victory necessary to disenfranchise Black North Carolinians. As one opponent of the North Carolina disenfranchisement campaign said:

> Again, the election law, which seems to be an insurmountable barrier to success, and the thought of having to face Winchester rifles again in the coming campaign, seems to have paralized [*sic*] the energies and efforts of the opposition in this section of the state ... The courage of men, who stood the test in the last election seems to fail them now.[6]

In other words, ballot stuffing and Winchester rifles ruled. The will of the public was sabotaged—literally at gunpoint.

Eliminating Black voters also adversely affected Black participation in the criminal law system. Persons who were not voters were often disqualified from serving as jurors. In this way, disenfranchisement proved to be a double veto of Black human rights.

The case of *Williams v. Mississippi*[7] exemplifies this situation. In *Williams*, the defendant alleged that an all-White male jury had convicted and sentenced him to death by hanging, and that the state had unlawfully excluded Blacks from the jury. State law required that to become a juror one must be registered to vote. Qualifications for voting included (1) having paid all taxes that were due by February 1 before the election; (2) being able to read, understand, or explain the state Constitution; and (3) not having been convicted of certain crimes. By torpedoing Black efforts to vote, the state also disqualified them from serving as jurors.

Despite overwhelming evidence that state governmental officials had eliminated Blacks from the voter and juror rolls, the *Williams* Court said that the state Constitution and statutes "do not on their face discriminate between the races, and it has not been shown that their actual administration was evil, only that evil was possible under them."[8] In fact, the Court put it this way:

> There is an allegation of the purpose of the convention to disfranchise citizens of the colored race, but with this we have no concern, unless the purpose is executed by the constitution or laws or by those who administer them. If it is done in the latter way, how or by what means should be shown. We gather from the statements of the motion that certain officers are invested with discretion in making up lists of electors, and that this discretion can be and has been exercised against the colored race, and from these lists jurors are selected. The Supreme Court of Mississippi, however, decided, in a case presenting the same questions as the one at bar, "that jurors are not selected from or with reference to any lists furnished by such election officers."[9]

In short, the Court signaled that it was likely to uphold state legislation that disenfranchised Blacks unless the state officials were so dim-witted as to promulgate a constitution that baldly stated something like "This provision of the Mississippi Constitution is intended to disenfranchise colored men; state and local officials should implement it accordingly."

In Mississippi, Black voters outnumbered Whites statewide. This contributed to the 1890 Mississippi Constitutional Convention focus on eliminating Black political power.[10] While comprised of 134 delegates,[11] Mississippi's 1890 convention included only one Black. Unlike the 1869 Mississippi Constitution, which was ratified by a statewide vote, state officials did not allow the electorate to vote on the 1892 Mississippi Constitution.

Following adoption of the new constitution, through poll taxes and selectively enforced educational requirements, the Mississippi political elite succeeded in radically reducing the number of Black voters.[12] In doing so, they also disenfranchised many poor White men.

Through the 1890s, and into the twentieth century, this unfortunate scenario, like a bad dream, repeated itself throughout the South. Black men and many poor White ones were rendered voteless. Thus, in 1902 in Virginia, the state Constitution was amended so as to disenfranchise Blacks by imposing literacy tests and poll taxes. At the beginning of the Virginia Constitutional Convention, Virginia State Senator Carter Glass stated:

> "Discrimination!" Why that is what we propose; that exactly, is why this Convention was elected—to discriminate to the very extremity of permissible action . . . with a view to the elimination of every Negro voter who could be gotten rid of, legally, without materially impairing the numerical strength of the white electorate.[13]

In fact, within 100 days of the promulgation of Virginia's new Constitution, over 125,000 Negro voters were purged from the voting rolls.[14] Of the nearly 150,000 Negro voters in the state, by October 15, 1902, only 21,000 remained on the rolls. When the poll tax became effective in 1903, this small remnant of Negro voting strength was reduced even further.[15] Virginia's poll tax statutes provided that to vote in an election, a voter had to pay $1.50 per year for each of the three preceding years. The tax had to be fully paid at least six months before the election was held. The requirement that the poll tax must be paid six months prior to the election was one of many gimmicks designed to trap the unwitting prospective voter.[16]

After making ample provision for disenfranchising Negro voters, and ensuring segregation in public education and transportation, the promulgators of this nefarious document became fearful that if it were submitted to the voters for approval that it would be defeated. Virginia's constitution makers confirmed Lord Acton's perceptive observation: "power tends to corrupt and absolute power corrupts absolutely."[17] As in Mississippi, South Carolina, and Louisiana, Virginia's political elite refused to allow the electorate to vote on the new state Constitution.[18] Following the precedent of other autocrats, Virginia's power brokers boldly proclaimed the Constitution as being in effect.

In *Jones v. Montague*,[19] Negro plaintiffs challenged the newly decreed Virginia state Constitution. The plaintiffs argued that state officials had conspired to deprive them of their rights under the U.S. Constitution, and that the plaintiffs were suffering a legal injury that the Court could prevent.[20]

As in *Williams v. Mississippi*, the U.S. Supreme Court sustained Virginia's travesty.[21] The Court concluded that because the House of Representatives was the judge of its members' qualifications and had seated the persons from Virginia, the Court could not intervene. The Court ignored the heart of the plaintiffs' claim: massive election fraud and blatant race discrimination in the electoral process. If the

Court had decided the case properly, the Court would have ruled that the elections violated both the Fourteenth and Fifteenth Amendments. Then, in light of its ruling to require lawful elections, the Court could have provided the House of Representatives an opportunity to take appropriate remedial measures. In other words, the House should have been afforded an opportunity to address what to do regarding persons who had been seated as a result of electoral fraud and racial discrimination. Instead, the Court essentially swept under the judicial rug Virginia's widespread denial of the right to vote. The Court upheld the state government's strangulation of key individual human rights; namely, the right to vote and have a meaningful say in the political process.

Efforts to suppress the vote of people of color and poor Whites persist today. Since 2008, widespread efforts to limit Americans' right to vote have included legislation in over 30 states requiring prospective voters to overcome obstacles like producing government-issued photo identification even though little evidence of alleged voter fraud exists.[22]

Moreover, the 2012 elections witnessed the spectacle of tens of thousands of Americans standing in lines sometimes as long as eight hours to cast their ballots. Many, though by no means all, of such individuals were persons of color.[23]

In the year following the 2012 elections, the Court decided *Shelby County v. Holder*.[24] The Court eviscerated the Voting Rights Act of 1965. Among other things, the Voting Rights Act required specific states and localities with a history of discrimination against persons of color to present proposed changes in their electoral process to the federal government. Before implementing the changes, the federal government had to evaluate whether the changes had "the purpose [or] . . . the effect of denying or abridging the right to vote on account of race or color."[25] If the federal government found no such race discrimination, the proposed changes could become effective.

The Shelby County, Alabama, local government sued the U.S. government, alleging that Section 4(b) and Section (5) of the Voting Rights Act were unconstitutional.[26] Section 4(b) set out the coverage formula that would cause the Voting Rights Act to apply. Relevant factors included past state and local government racist practices. Examples of such governmental corruption designed to deny African Americans the right to vote included literacy tests, poll taxes, and requiring that voters interpret obscure legal statutes.[27]

In *Shelby*, by a 5-4 vote, the Supreme Court decided that Congress did not have a valid reason to use Section 4(b)'s coverage formula. The *Shelby* Court said that when Congress renewed the Act in 2006: "Congress did not use the record it compiled to shape a coverage formula grounded in current conditions. It instead reenacted a formula based on 40-year-old facts having no logical relation to the present day."[28] Accordingly, the Court ruled that Section 4(b) of the Voting Rights Act was unconstitutional. The Court's decision means that unless Congress revises the coverage formula, states and localities of the United States with an extensive history of race discrimination in voting are now free to experiment with how far they can discriminate.

In a trenchant dissent, Justice Ruth Bader Ginsburg pointed out that in the period leading up to the reauthorization of the Voting Rights Act in 2006, Congress had substantial evidence of state and local official efforts to curb voting of people of color:

> The coverage provision identified a known list of places with an undisputed history of serious problems with racial discrimination in voting. Recent evidence relating to Alabama and its counties was there for all to see. Multiple Supreme Court decisions had upheld the coverage provision, most recently in 1999. There was extensive evidence that, due to the preclearance mechanism, conditions in the covered jurisdictions had notably improved. And there was evidence that preclearance was still having a substantial real-world effect, having

> stopped hundreds of discriminatory voting changes in the covered jurisdictions since the last reauthorization. In addition, there was evidence that racial polarization in voting was higher in covered jurisdictions than elsewhere, increasing the vulnerability of minority citizens in those jurisdictions. And countless witnesses, reports, and case studies documented continuing problems with voting discrimination in those jurisdictions. In light of this record, Congress had more than a reasonable basis to conclude that the existing coverage formula was not out of sync with conditions on the ground in covered areas. And certainly Shelby County was no candidate for release through the mechanism Congress provided.[29]

Justice Ginsburg warned that this type of repressive behavior would happen again.

And she was right. For example, in 2016, a number of states hamstrung voter participation by reducing polling places and opportunities to vote early as well as requiring strict voter identification requirements. While several federal courts struck down such restrictions,[30] a number of government procedural vote shackles were found constitutional. Systematic voter suppression efforts (and possible foreign governmental interference?)[31] helped to propel Donald Trump to narrow victories in highly contested states like Wisconsin, Florida, and North Carolina.[32] Similar vote suppression activities continue in other states like Georgia, Texas, and Ohio.[33]

While the *Shelby* case effectively put much of the Voting Rights Act of 1965 on life support, the Court has not yet pulled the judicial plug. In *Allen v. Milligan*,[34] the Court upheld a plaintiffs' claim under Section 2 of the Voting Rights Act of 1965. The *Allen* plaintiffs alleged that the state of Alabama had unlawfully diluted the voting strength of Black Alabamians. The *Allen* Court noted that Alabama has a history of polarized racial voting: frequently White voters and Black voters vote in blocs but for different candidates. In the *Allen* case, the Alabama legislature had apportioned Alabama's seven congressional districts such that six would be majority White and one majority Black. Given the historical legacy of voting along skin color lines, in practical terms, the Alabama legislature ensured that in six of the seven congressional districts, White voters would be able to elect their preferred candidate.

In fact, statewide, roughly five of every seven Alabama voters are White; two of seven are Black. The plaintiffs presented evidence that the Alabama legislature could have created two districts with sufficient African American voting populations to give Black voters in those districts the same opportunity that White voters had: that is a good chance to elect a representative of their choice.

During the trial of the case, a three-judge trial court took extensive evidence. In an opinion of over 200 pages, the court found that the Alabama legislature could have drawn seven districts using accepted redistricting methods that would have five districts in which White voters would likely have been able to choose a candidate of their choice, and two districts in which Black voters would have been able to do likewise. The lower court ordered the state to not implement the redistricting plan because the plan violated Section 2 of the Voting Rights Act.

On appeal to the Supreme Court, by a 5-4 majority the Supreme Court upheld the lower court ruling. As amended in 1982, Section 2(b) of the Voting Rights Act states:

> (b) A violation of subsection (a) is established if, based on the totality of circumstances, it is shown that the political processes leading to nomination or election in the State or political subdivision are not equally open to participation by members of a class of citizens ... in that its members have less opportunity than other members of the electorate

> to participate in the political process and to elect representatives of their choice. The extent to which members of a protected class have been elected to office in the State or political subdivision is one circumstance which may be considered: Provided, That nothing in this section establishes a right to have members of a protected class elected in numbers equal to their proportion in the population.[35]

Protected classes are comprised of groups of individuals who historically have suffered state-sponsored discrimination in the electoral process.

The *Allen* Court explained the practical situation in which Section 2 applies as follows:

> Individuals . . . lack an equal opportunity to participate in the political process when a State's electoral structure operates in a manner that "minimize[s] or cancel[s] out [their] voting strength." . . . That occurs where an individual is disabled from "enter[ing] into the political process in a reliable and meaningful manner" "in the light of past and present reality, political and otherwise." . . . A district is not equally open, in other words, when minority voters face—unlike their majority peers—bloc voting along racial lines, arising against the backdrop of substantial racial discrimination within the State, that renders a minority vote unequal to a vote by a nonminority voter.[36]

Historically, governmental officials who engage in race-based redistricting frequently seek to ensure that White voters have the greatest opportunity to elect persons of their choice and voters of color have the least. Among other things, Section 2 seeks to mitigate such vote dilution. In *Allen*, the Court took pains to point out that Section 2 does not require proportional representation along the color line:

> Forcing proportional representation is unlawful and inconsistent with this Court's approach to implementing § 2. The numbers bear the point out well. At the congressional level, the fraction of districts in which black-preferred candidates are likely to win "is currently below the Black share of the eligible voter population in every state but three." . . . Only one State in the country, meanwhile, "has attained a proportional share" of districts in which Hispanic-preferred candidates are likely to prevail. . . . That is because as residential segregation decreases—as it has "sharply" done since the 1970s—satisfying traditional districting criteria such as the compactness requirement "becomes more difficult."[37]

As a matter of fact, Section 2 has very limited impact. More specifically, the Court noted that in the past dozen years, there have only been about 10 successful cases, and those cases involved local statehouse races near Milwaukee and Houston. The Court observed: "Since 2010, plaintiffs nationwide have apparently succeeded in fewer than ten § 2 suits. . . . And 'the only state legislative or congressional districts that were redrawn because of successful Section 2 challenges were a handful of state house districts near Milwaukee and Houston.'"[38]

In short, currently Section 2 constitutes a relatively small legal shield to combat the wide-ranging voter suppression tactics used to prevent persons of color from wielding political power non-violently through the ballot box.

In the twenty-first century, cases like *Shelby* exemplify how the Roberts Court is following historical precedent by issuing decisions that frustrate efforts to promote liberty and justice for all. The Court's ruling has an especially negative impact on voting access for marginalized groups (like people of color).

In like manner, in the late 1800s, the Court supported the movement to reverse national progress toward equality under the law. Instead, the Court substituted the Founders' White affirmative action agenda. The most infamous post–Civil War White affirmative action decision involved a civil rights test case intended to persuade the U.S. Supreme Court to rule that segregation in public transportation was unconstitutional. The lawsuit backfired in spectacular fashion. In *Plessy v. Ferguson*, Homer Plessy, an African American who, according to court records, was seven-eighths White and looked like a White person, was arrested for riding in the Whites-only section in a Louisiana railway car. At least one account of Plessy's arrest states that Plessy identified himself by saying to the streetcar conductor: "I have to tell you that, according to Louisiana law, I am a colored man."[39]

Plessy filed suit challenging the local segregation statutes. In an eight-to-one decision the U.S. Supreme Court ruled that the Constitution permitted racial apartheid. The Court held that the Louisiana race segregation statutes were *not unreasonable*. The Court said that if the segregation laws discriminated in a demeaning manner, the root of the problem was primarily in the minds of Blacks. Specifically, the Court said that Blacks had chosen to look at and interpret the statutes as degrading to Blacks. The majority stated:

> We consider the underlying fallacy of the plaintiff's argument to consist in the assumption that the enforced separation of the two races stamps the colored race with a badge of inferiority. If this be so, it is not by reason of anything found in the act, but solely because the colored race chooses to put that construction upon it.[40]

This tortured logic failed to consider the practical negative effects of state-established apartheid. The Court ruled that the segregation statutes did not violate the Fourteenth Amendment's Equal Protection Clause.

In dissent, Justice John Marshall Harlan argued that the real impact of the segregation statutes was that Blacks were perceived as being so debased and inferior that Blacks must be prevented from associating with White citizens:

> Sixty millions of whites are in no danger from the presence here of eight millions of blacks. The destinies of the two races, in this country, are indissolubly linked together, and the interests of both require that the common government of all shall not permit the seeds of race hate to be planted under the sanction of law. What can more certainly arouse race hate, what more certainly create and perpetuate a feeling of distrust between these races, than state enactments, which, in fact, proceed on the ground that colored citizens are so inferior and degraded that they cannot be allowed to sit in public coaches occupied by white citizens? That, as all will admit, is the real meaning of such legislation as was enacted in Louisiana.[41]

Three years later in *Cumming v. Richmond County Board of Education*,[42] the U.S. Supreme Court had an opportunity to address what was meant by "separate but equal." In *Cumming*, a local Georgia school board funded segregated elementary and high school education for both Blacks and Whites. Later, the school board closed the Black high school. Having deprived Blacks of a government-funded high school education, the school authorities funded a larger number of Blacks receiving an elementary school education. The board claimed that it lacked funding for a public high school for Blacks. In contrast, at taxpayer expense, the *board continued providing funds for both elementary and high school education for Whites*.

Black parents sued the school board. The Black parents argued that as long as authorities failed to furnish a high school for Blacks, the local school authorities must stop subsidizing two high schools for White students. In other words, the Black parents petitioned the Court to order the school board to treat White students and Black students the same way. The parents contended that having two taxpayer-supported high schools for Whites but none for Blacks violated the Constitution's equal protection requirement.[43]

The Supreme Court ruled that the plaintiffs failed to prove that the local public school authorities had exercised their discretion based on racial prejudice against Blacks. Practically speaking, the Court's decision meant that the board could use taxpayers' monies to fund White high school education while simultaneously eliminating all funding for Black high schools. Stated another way, according to the *Cumming* Court, the school authorities did not violate equal protection by closing the Black high school and using taxpayer money to pay for White children's high school education. Bluntly stated, a school board could take money "saved" from closing a Black high school and use the funds to maintain and improve free public high school education for Whites.

The Court said that it would have been a different case if the Black parents had sued and requested that the Court order school authorities to allocate revenues for a Black high school.[44] Apparently, to some members of the Court, such an approach seemed more acceptable than asking the Court to close the White school.

In addition to discrimination against African Americans in jury selection, public accommodations, voting, and education, White individuals attempted to physically intimidate Blacks who were exercising their rights to contract and work. For example, in *Hodges v. United States*,[45] a mob of White men in Arkansas marched on a sawmill and drove six Black men off their jobs, thereby preventing the Blacks from exercising their right to contract with other individuals for gainful employment. The assailants were convicted under federal statutes protecting Blacks from terrorist activities by groups like the Ku Klux Klan and the Knights of the White Camellias.

On appeal to the United States Supreme Court, the majority of the Court reversed the lower court's convictions. The Court stated that the Fourteenth Amendment only applies to discriminatory state action. According to the majority, the mob behavior was not state action: the mob was a group of individuals who violated the rights of Blacks.

As to the Black workers' Thirteenth Amendment argument, the Court stated that the Thirteenth Amendment simply abolished slavery.[46] According to the Court, the Amendment was not intended to prohibit the type of racially based crimes that defendants committed in the *Hodges* case. Relying on this reasoning, the *Hodges* Court held that the trial court did not have the authority to convict the White assailants under the civil rights statutes.

In a strong dissent, Justice Harlan argued that the Thirteenth and Fourteenth Amendments applied to the situation. The Fourteenth Amendment applied because it protected Blacks from being assaulted because of their color. Congress could pass legislation to remedy such hate crimes. In addition, Justice Harlan argued that under the Thirteenth Amendment, one of the incidents of slavery was that Blacks were unable to contract. Accordingly, Congress could legislate to prevent private individuals from interfering with Blacks' contract rights. Harlan contended that merely because the Blacks were Black, the vigilantes had forced the Blacks to quit work and thereby violate their employment contracts.[47]

The Court's decisions in cases like *Williams*, *Plessy*, *Cumming*, *Jones*, and *Hodges* all undercut Blacks' attempts to exercise their civil rights. These and similar Supreme Court decisions demonstrated at least one thing: regarding the rights of Blacks, instead of its motto of "Equal justice under law," the Court had effectively posted a large sign: "Justice for Whites Only!"

Chapter VI

# Late Nineteenth-Century Land Grabs

As the nineteenth century closed, the Supreme Court of the United States adopted a hands-off approach to disenfranchisement, segregation, juror discrimination, and other forms of legal oppression of Blacks. Meanwhile, other branches of government like Congress continued to pursue what amounted to a national skin color–based wealth transfer program. Principal features of the program involved removing lands from the hands of Mexican Americans and Native Americans and conferring the property upon White Americans.

A specific example of Congress's late nineteenth-century wealth transfer program from Native Americans to European Americans involved the General Allotment Act of 1887. The Act authorized the president of the United States to allot on an individual basis, parcels of land on Native American reservations "whenever in his opinion any reservation or any part thereof ... is advantageous for agricultural and grazing purposes."[1] Thus, the Act allowed the executive branch of the federal government to divide reservation land into relatively small parcels. After slicing up Indian lands, the government deemed most of the land as "surplus" and sold it to non-Indians.

In practice, the Act served as a convenient legal fig leaf to effect a massive wealth transfer of reservation land to White persons who wanted to become farmers, ranchers, or both. In some cases, such land wound up in the hands of speculators trying to make a quick buck.[2] The non-Indians received cheap, valuable land, the U.S. Treasury received some revenue from the land sales, and the native peoples, as usual, received a raw deal.

According to the United States Department of Interior: "In 1887, tribes held 138 million acres. Forty-seven years later, in 1934, they owned 48 million acres."[3] Some scholars estimate that over two-thirds of Native American land was lost through public policies like the General Allotment Act.[4] The government policy devastated Native American groups as the government took their lands and provided Native American little material benefits. The bottom line: by shrinking the size of the land upon which Native American could live, the U.S. government sabotaged Native Americans' traditional ways of life.

As we mentioned before, following the Mexican-American War (1846-1848) concerns arose about Mexican American property rights in areas like California. However, as a result of the war, the United States not only obtained California but also Nevada, Arizona, New Mexico, as well as parts of Colorado and Utah. In this context, numerous Mexican American–related land controversies continued. In 1891, to resolve land disputes in the New Mexico Territory, Congress established the Court of Private Land Claims (the Land Claims Court). The Land Claims Court used a process similar to the one adopted 40 years earlier regarding Mexican lands in California.

Justice F. Wilbur Stone, one of the judges of the Land Claims Court, stated that the court confirmed only 87 of 301 Mexican American land claims. The 301 claims involved 36 million acres. The 87 confirmed claims entitled the former Mexican owners to a total of 3 million acres, less than 10% of the disputed land. By denying most Mexican American claims, the Land Claims Court allowed the national government to effectively confiscate 33 million acres from the Mexican American population and transfer the land to Anglo-Americans.[5] Yet another example of White American affirmative action. Indeed, Judge Stone candidly described the New Mexico Territory as "a region illimitable in the undeveloped wealth of its coal, metals, agriculture and health giving climate."[6]

Furthermore, according to Stone, the Land Claims Court's activities resulted in the court receiving "the highest commendation as well from the Department of Justice at Washington as from the Bar, the press and the people within its jurisdiction, whose interest are directly effected by its adjudication."[7] Undoubtedly, Mexican Americans who witnessed the court conferring their property upon Anglos saw matters quite differently. The legal title that Mexican American citizens held under prior Mexican and Spanish governments proved ineffective to protect Mexican American land ownership. In New Mexico, as was the case in California—despite its treaty responsibilities—the U.S. government failed to vigorously defend the property rights of its Mexican American citizens.

Under the United States Constitution, the courts are supposed to be a refuge for justice. America's new citizens of Mexican origin sought protection there. Regrettably, the United States Supreme Court furnished little help to ensure that Mexican Americans would exercise significant legal authority over land that they had historically possessed.

For instance, in 1897, in *United States v. Sandoval*,[8] the Supreme Court refused to uphold the Mexican government's land grant to the town of San Miguel del Badoe. The Mexican grant had created a commons outside of the town for farming, recreation, and other municipal purposes. While Mexican authorities intended that the commons would directly benefit the local government and residents, the Court said that the land reverted to the U.S. government.[9] The land could be disposed of in whatever manner the national government saw fit, including cheap sale or grant to private speculators.

The effect of the *Sandoval* case was a significant wealth transfer from Mexican American communities to the Anglo-dominated national government. As a consolation prize, the *Sandoval* Court upheld a Mexican government land grant to approximately 51 individuals.

The Mexican American land grant controversies (now over 170 years old) persist. Not long ago, a U.S. Government Accountability Office report concluded that the United States has met its treaty obligations involving Mexican American land grants. The report has been vigorously challenged by well respected scholars as "a whitewash and a slap in the face."[10]

Professor A.S. Dillingham provides a sobering perspective regarding both Mexican and American claims to lands of indigenous peoples:

> Today, as we reflect on the legacy of the 1848 [Guadalupe Hidalgo] treaty and the national borders it created, we would do well to consider from what vantage point we narrate this history and its meaning. If we move beyond national stories and center the histories of Indigenous people, these events look very different. How we remember this history is just as important as what we remember. Nationalist perspectives make it impossible to imagine a world without borders and the racism and inequality that they perpetuate.[11]

In the meantime, transfer of public lands to privileged groups continues. According to an October 2020 report of the Wilderness Society Action Fund, the Trump administration sold leases for approximately 5.4 million acres of public lands to extractive industries like gas and oil companies. The administration also sold another 5.3 million acres of public waters to similar businesses. It is estimated that 8.3 billion metric tons of carbon dioxide might be produced from the fossil fuels collected through these leases.[12]

In addition, the Trump administration increased the size of groups able to engage in recreational activities on what had been relatively unspoiled wilderness areas.[13] Up to 50 persons per group could participate in four-wheel drive vehicle sports in such places. Some observers saw the administration's actions as an attempt to confer large swaths of public lands upon a relatively small group of wealthy developers, speculators, and well-connected political associates.[14] Could this be yet another example of White American affirmative action? Research seems warranted regarding the identity of those obtaining such governmental largesse. Furthermore, in the public interest, it is appropriate to evaluate the terms of the leases. For instance, inquiry is merited as to the amount that leaseholders have agreed to pay versus the market value of the leases.

Despite many commendable achievements, past American sins have haunted us into the present. We now turn to some more recent sins that are rooted in American history and need acknowledgment.

Chapter VII

# Harvesting Bitter Fruits

IN THE 1920S, in response to the pervasive patterns of segregation permeating American society, a group of social activists (including Oliver W. Hill) decided to challenge the unjust segregation laws.[1] The following narrative draws heavily and sometimes quotes verbatim (without punctuation) from Oliver W. Hill's autobiography, *The Big Bang:* Brown v. Board of Education *and Beyond: The Autobiography of Oliver W. Hill, Sr.*[2]

The decision to challenge segregation laws stemmed in part from a conversation in the late 1920s between Mordecai Johnson, president of Howard University, and Justice Louis Brandeis of the United States Supreme Court. Brandeis reportedly told Johnson that very frequently when Negro lawyers had meritorious cases, the record was so inadequate that the Court could not take the case.[3]

As a result of their discussion, Johnson decided to make Howard University School of Law a first-class law school. A primary focus of Howard's mission, as envisioned by Johnson, would be to train Black lawyers to properly prepare cases and develop adequate records for achieving success in the Supreme Court.

Johnson selected Charles Hamilton Houston to lead this law school project. Houston had graduated from the well-regarded "M Street" High School in Washington, D.C. (M Street High was the predecessor to Dunbar from which Mr. Hill graduated.) Houston went on to Amherst College where he graduated Phi Beta Kappa, and then taught English in the Commercial Department at Howard University. Houston helped pressure the War Department to create a military facility to train Black officers to lead Black troops in World War I. Houston became an army officer, suffered a number of indignities while fighting for this country (including being nearly lynched in France by some White enlisted men), and returned to the United States in 1919.[4]

After the war, Houston attended Harvard Law School. At Harvard, he became the first Negro admitted to the *Harvard Law Review*, and graduated with honors. He also continued at Harvard for his post-graduate education and earned a doctorate in juridical science.[5] Houston wrote his dissertation under Felix Frankfurter, who would later become a Justice of the United States Supreme Court.

Houston had helped litigate *Corrigan v. Buckley*,[6] a suit challenging private discrimination against Negroes in real estate transactions. The case went to the United States Supreme Court, and the Court dismissed the appeal, claiming that it lacked jurisdiction. By narrowly interpreting the Fifth, Thirteenth, and Fourteenth Amendments, the Court in effect upheld the racially exclusive language. Houston was active with the National Association for the Advancement of Colored People (NAACP) and was a good leader of the fight for positive change. That probably attracted him to Mordecai Johnson.

Houston decided to convert Howard Law School from a part-time evening law school to a full-time day program. He established a strong core of lawyers whose ideas and ideals coincided with his. They were dedicated to teaching and training the incoming Howard Law School students. For example, William H. Hastie Jr., a graduate of Harvard Law School, served as a member of the faculty.[7] Hastie subsequently had many other accomplishments, including helping to draft legislation for increased self-government in the Virgin Islands, serving as governor of the Virgin Islands, becoming the first appointed Negro federal judge in the United States,[8] and being appointed to the United States Court of Appeals for the Third Circuit.

The faculty also included Leon A. "Andy" Ransom, who had graduated from Ohio State University Law School where he received academic honors and was a member of the Order of the Coif. He later received a doctorate in juridical science from Harvard.[9] Ransom also litigated and won a number of important cases in the United States Supreme Court like *Hale v. Kentucky*[10] and *Chambers v. Florida*.[11]

In addition, in the early 1920s, a young philanthropist, Charles Garland, inherited a very sizable estate and decided to establish a trust fund to benefit the NAACP. The trust helped to further the NAACP's work in seeking to end segregation—whether by law or custom.

As a result of the grant from the Garland Fund, and at the suggestion of Charles Hamilton Houston, Nathan Margold of Harvard Law School was selected to conduct a study to determine the best course for the NAACP to achieve its civil rights goals. Margold suggested that suits be filed simultaneously throughout the South[12] to challenge the segregated public school systems.

Houston accepted Margold's recommendation on challenging unequal educational opportunities; however, Houston determined that filing multiple suits was infeasible. Houston modified the plan and decided to initially attack segregation within the bounds of the existing law. By making the local officials live up to the holding that *Plessy* dictated—not only separateness but also equality—Houston argued that the White governmental officials would recognize that the public could not afford to maintain equal dual school systems. Once school officials recognized that dual equal public schools were financially infeasible they would (eventually) move to desegregate the schools. In the 1930s, this was a tactical decision because the ultimate goal was eliminating racial segregation—root and branch.

In 1933, an early case in North Carolina presented possibilities to challenge segregation in education. Thomas Hocutt, a Negro student at the North Carolina College for Negroes (now North Carolina Central University in Durham), applied and was denied admission to the School of Pharmacy at the all-White University of North Carolina.

Two Negro lawyers, Conrad Pearson and Cecil McCoy, filed a suit on behalf of Hocutt. William Hastie helped to try the case.[13] Hastie was the second Black to serve as an editor of the *Harvard Law Review* and at that time was serving as a part-time faculty member at Howard Law School. In part because James E. Shepard, the president of North Carolina College for Negroes, refused to release Hocutt's transcripts, Hocutt was unable to prevail in court.[14] Despite this minor setback, the NAACP continued its campaign in challenging segregation.

The North Carolina litigation began during the Great Depression as Mr. Hill was completing law school (1933). By that time, a firmly entrenched racial spoils system had been established favoring the political and economic development of White Americans while undermining that development for people of darker colors.[15]

For example, in 1934, Congress passed and President Roosevelt signed legislation creating the Federal Housing Administration (FHA). From the day it was created and for nearly 30 years afterward, the FHA refused to make housing loans to Blacks who wanted to move to new developments in the suburbs. The FHA's official policy was reflected in its *Underwriting Manual*, which stated, "*if a neighborhood is to retain stability, it is necessary that properties shall continue to be occupied by the same social and racial classes.*" This FHA language mandated race segregation (at all costs!) using federal taxpayer funds. In fact, the FHA expressly recommended "subdivision regulations and suitable restrictive covenants."[16] If a single Black family lived on a block, or if the neighborhood had experienced "infiltration of Jews," the federal government urged and often required that private lenders deny mortgage financing.[17] At the same time, the FHA loaned taxpayer money exclusively to many Whites who wanted to escape the central cities to enjoy a suburban life of better schools, jobs, and other opportunities.[18] In essence, the FHA used federal tax revenues to enforce segregation policies against Blacks and other social pariah groups.

Thus, the FHA racial preference facilitated wealth accumulation by Whites who could purchase homes that appreciated in value. This typical White American affirmative action program strangled economic progress by Blacks and other social outcasts. Official federal government policies ensured economic catastrophes for people of color.

Past government segregation schemes (like the FHA housing requirements) continue to affect our society today. In their pathbreaking work on wealth inequality along America's color line, Dean Melvin Oliver and Professor Thomas Shapiro point out:

> One infamous housing development of the period—Levittown—provides a classic illustration of the way blacks missed out on this asset accumulating opportunity. Levittown was built on a mass scale, and housing there was eminently affordable, thanks to FHA's and VHA's accessible financing, yet as late as 1960 "not a single one of the Long Island Levittown's 82,000 residents was black."[19]

During the Great Depression, another federal housing segregation program, the Home Owners' Loan Corporation, loaned taxpayer money to White home owners. Like the FHA, the Home Owners' Loan Corporation refused such loans to Blacks and created a system of "redlining." Even now the redlining process makes it virtually impossible for many Blacks to obtain loans. Indeed, many lenders have taken matters further by targeting neighborhoods comprised of residents of darker colors for subprime (predatory) loans.[20] During the Great Recession, African Americans and other persons of color lost hundreds of billions of dollars when unscrupulous lenders foreclosed subprime loans against these home owners. For such individuals, their homes represented their principal source of material wealth—the nest egg for themselves and their children. Frequently, that nest egg was scrambled.

By maintaining segregated neighborhoods, the federal government continued its long-standing policy of devising wealth accumulation programs to allow millions of Whites to realize the American dream. Specifically, the dream included owning real estate, accumulating material wealth, and sending their children to better schools. Simultaneously, federal housing policies confined many Blacks and other people of darker color to ghettos in which their choices were restricted to renting or attempting to repair aging homes.[21] Typically such homes generated less tax revenues. In much of the United States, real estate taxes are the primary source of school funding. Accordingly, inner city children had and have fewer educational resources to compete with their more materially advantaged suburban peers. Stated differently, as had been the case since colonial times, the national government legally confined persons of darker color to the back of America's segregated social bus.[22]

We now focus on additional background information on early twentieth-century civil rights struggles. In the 1935 case of *Pearson v. Murray*,[23] on behalf of Donald Murray (an African American), Charles Hamilton Houston and Thurgood Marshall filed suit to desegregate the Maryland state law school located in Baltimore. Marshall was Houston's assistant as well as Mr. Hill's law school classmate and lifelong friend. Both Marshall and Hill were proteges of Houston.

In the *Murray* case, the primary practical question that the court had to decide was whether Murray could attend Maryland's state-supported public law school. Alternatively, would the court rule so that Murray would have only two practical choices: (1) accept state funds from Maryland, leave the state and study law elsewhere, or (2) give up his plans to pursue a legal career? Maryland did not pay transportation or living expenses for Negroes required to study out of state. Houston and Marshall achieved a successful outcome as the state court ordered Murray's admission to the University of Maryland School of Law.

In planning its antisegregation strategy, NAACP leaders and legal staff continuously attempted to educate the public and the courts, including the Supreme Court. The civil rights lawyers sought good cases and endeavored to make strong records to avoid another *Plessy v. Ferguson* Supreme Court decision.

*Missouri ex rel. Gaines v. Canada*[24] reflected the difficult battle in the late 1930s. *Gaines* involved civil rights advocates' attempts to enforce the separate but equal doctrine. In *Gaines*, a Negro student, Lloyd Gaines, was denied admission to the all-White University of Missouri School of Law. Speaking for a divided Court, Chief Justice Hughes stated, "it was as an individual that he was entitled to the equal protection of the laws, and the State was bound to furnish him within its borders facilities for legal education substantially equal to those ... afforded for persons of the white race."[25]

In the school cases, *Gaines* was the first major NAACP litigation victory at the Supreme Court level. After the case was decided, plaintiff Lloyd Gaines mysteriously disappeared. He was never seen again. While foul play was never confirmed or denied, it was strongly suspected.

In the struggle to obtain equal rights in the area of employment discrimination, Houston conceived the idea of having congressional hearings to obtain relevant data. Congressman Adam Clayton Powell Jr. helped the civil rights struggle by holding hearings involving discriminatory practices in the railroad industry.

Powell's congressional hearings established evidence of a pattern of collusive decisions going back to the beginning of the twentieth century. All-White unions and all-White railroad management collaborated to eliminate the Black railroad workers involved in operating the trains. Such Black workers included engineers, firemen, brakemen, and trainmen. When the firemen's jobs were considered especially difficult, dangerous, and degrading, the White railroad workers shied away from them. However, with advances in technology and the advent of the diesel engine, such jobs became more attractive. Instead of frantically shoveling coal with a raging fire and smoke all around, diesel engines allowed firemen to sit serenely in the cabs of the locomotives with nothing more difficult to handle than a small oil can.

After World War II, President Harry S. Truman ran into substantial congressional resistance from segregationists—some referred to themselves as Dixiecrats. In his effort to promote civil rights for Negroes, Truman had appointed a committee to study the U.S. racial situation. In 1948, in its well-known report "To Secure These Rights,"[26] the committee made numerous specific recommendations, including the creation of a civil rights division in the Justice Department to protect the rights of all citizens, the establishment of similar agencies at the state level, passage of a federal anti-lynching law, a review of the nation's wartime detention policy, and voting rights for Native Americans in New Mexico and Arizona. Furthermore, the committee recommended abolition of the poll tax, protection of the right to vote in primaries, the end of segregation in the Panama Canal Zone, and the creation of a permanent Civil Rights Commission to propose measures for continuing change.[27]

Truman endorsed the committee recommendations and aroused the ire of segregationists led by J. Strom Thurmond of South Carolina. Thurmond threatened to organize a Dixiecrat Party in opposition to Truman's election unless Truman desisted from these democratic activities. When Truman stood firm and refused to withdraw the 12 points for adoption by the National Democratic Convention, the Dixiecrats walked out of the convention, organized the Dixiecrat Party, and nominated Strom Thurmond as their candidate for president. By splitting the Democratic Party's base in the South, it was anticipated that Thurmond's maneuver would make it easier for New York Governor Thomas Dewey to defeat Truman. Undaunted, and over the objection of General Dwight D. Eisenhower and others, Truman later issued an Executive Order integrating the armed forces.

These actions took place against the backdrop of dynamic changes in human history. For example, in 1948, the United Nations adopted the Universal Declaration of Human Rights. The Declaration is an international document outlining the standards by which civilized nations aim to live. The Declaration affirms universal freedom and equality: in other words, liberty and justice for all. At the same time, all around the globe, colonialism was being dismantled. The United States looked ridiculous because of its many segregationist governmental policies. In essence, even after two world wars, including one that was supposed to "make the world safe for democracy," democracy seemed to be progressing faster nearly everywhere except in the United States.

Moreover, in analyzing America's post–World War II situation it was evident that the separate but equal litigation was resulting in newer inferior school facilities for Negroes. To ensure inferior new Negro schools, the White school boards constructed schools with wide-ranging ridiculous combinations of rooms. For example, some schools had one room used for cafeteria and gymnasium, or one room used for cafeteria, gymnasium, and the auditorium.

For instance, in Prince Edward County, Virginia, where one of the cases consolidated in the *Brown* decision arose, at the African American high school (Robert Russa Moton High School) there was one room used as a gymnasium and auditorium (see Figure 1).

Frequently, on paper there existed what was in fact a non-existent science department. Thus, even when authorities purported to have a science department, the equipment was meager and facilities totally inadequate to study zoology and botany.

Figure 1. Robert Russa Moton High School gymnasium and auditorium (note the basketball goals on the back wall of this picture). Courtesy Robert Russa Moton Museum, https://motonmuseum.org/about/the-moton-story/.

In the White communities, the schools had separate children's libraries, cafeterias, and science facilities.

Thus, for example, in Prince Edward County, the Farmville High School for White students had a commodious space used as an auditorium (see Figure 2).

While progress at the secondary school level was discouraging, in the graduate school cases the NAACP won victories.[28] *Sipuel v. Board of Regents of the University of Oklahoma* and *McLaurin v. Board of Regents of the University of Oklahoma* established the right of Negroes at the graduate level to participate fully in the educational process.

At the same time, following World War II, many veterans took advantage of the GI Bill to seek further academic

Figure 2. Farmville High School auditorium.
Courtesy Encyclopedia of Virginia,
https://encyclopediavirginia.org/farmville-hs-auditorium/.

and vocational training. For Black GIs who had risked their lives to "make the world safe for democracy" the bitter reality was that the doors of taxpayer-funded segregated public colleges and universities throughout many states remained shut to all Blacks, including veterans. Those same doors swung open widely to welcome returning White GIs.[29] In a perceptive, stimulating law review piece, Anthony Platt stated matters this way:

> A similar double-standard of racist and sexist practices for veterans was imposed after World War II when the 1944 GI Bill enabled some 7.8 million, mostly white, male veterans to afford higher education with the help of free tuition and supplies, a

> living subsidy (including additional payments for children), and low-interest loans for housing. The GI bill, as former University of California President Clark Kerr noted, was a "new entitlement" that heralded the "great age of federal initiatives." By 1947, veterans accounted for almost 50% of all U.S. college enrollments, thus setting the stage for the upward mobility of Irish and other ethnic Americans into stable working class and public sector jobs, and Jews into academia and other professions. According to social historian Karen Brodkin Sacks, "educational and occupational GI benefits really constituted affirmative action programs for white males because they were decidedly not extended to African Americans or to women of any race."' The few thousand African Americans who used the GI Bill to go to college were mostly tracked into segregated, inferior colleges.[30]

Thus, in actual practice, the GI Bill constituted race- and gender-based preference, which allowed World War II veterans like President George H.W. Bush and Chief Justice William Rehnquist to attend any college in the United States.[31] Simultaneously, the law prevented their Black comrades in arms (for instance, Oliver W. Hill) from taking advantage of the same opportunity.

After the war, rather than seeking to dismantle segregated public education, the national government of the United States continued to subsidize a national White American affirmative action program characterized, among other things, by a racial quota system. Under the quota, the federal government gave institutions of higher learning taxpayer money to reserve 100% of entering and graduating classes for White GIs (and other White applicants). For example, many states, especially in the South, mandated segregation in public schools and universities.

By law, Blacks could not compete for places in such institutions. Even in elite schools that were nominally opened to Black GIs, unofficial quotas kept the population of Black students (as well as those of other outcasts, like Jews) at token levels.[32]

Many activists thought that in higher education, segregationists would furnish less resistance because students would probably be more mature and the school officials would likely be more liberal minded. It did not work out that way in part because segregationists politicized the situation and adopted all kinds of bizarre and foolish tactics. Their antics included forcing George McLaurin, a lone Negro graduate student at the University of Oklahoma, to sit outside the regular classroom to obtain instruction.[33] McLaurin was also compelled to eat by himself in the cafeteria when no one else was scheduled to dine and to study at a desk in the mezzanine section of the library. McLaurin was prohibited from using the desks in the library reading room.[34]

Nevertheless, the mid twentieth century began to witness significant change. After *Sweatt v. Painter*,[35] the Texas law school case, it seemed like the Court was prepared to overrule *Plessy*. In *Sweatt*, the Court had accepted the plaintiff's argument regarding the makeshift law school and the criteria for a good law school. Chief Justice Frederick Vinson said:

> Whether the University of Texas Law School is compared with the original or the new law school for Negroes, we cannot find substantial equality in the educational opportunities offered white and Negro law students by the state. In terms of number of the faculty, variety of courses and opportunity for specialization, size of the student body, scope of the library, availability of law review and similar activities, the University of Texas Law School is superior. What is more important, the University of Texas Law School possesses to a far greater degree, those

Figure 3. George W. McLaurin. This photograph shows how he was segregated to the anteroom of a classroom in 1948 after his admission to the formerly all-White University of Oklahoma. From the Library of Congress.

> qualities which are incapable of objective measurement but which make for greatness in a law school. Such qualities, to name but a few, include reputation of the faculty, experience of the administration, position and influence of the alumni, standing in the community, tradition and prestige. It is difficult to believe that one who had a free choice between these law schools would consider the question close.[36]

In *Sweatt*, Chief Justice Vinson discussed the intangible qualities necessary for equal educational opportunity. The *Sweatt* Court seemed open to rule regarding elementary and secondary schools like the Court had done with professional schools. The Court appeared poised to overturn segregation *per se*. Accordingly, at the NAACP convention held in Boston in the summer of 1950, it was decided to challenge segregation *per se*.

Charles Hamilton Houston had developed such an excellent, adaptable strategy that even after his death in April of 1950, the momentum for constructive change continued. In carrying out the objectives of the 1950 NAACP National Convention, Thurgood Marshall filed the *Clarendon County* case in South Carolina to desegregate the segregated county public schools.

A special three-judge federal court was impaneled to hear the case. Over Judge J. Waites Waring's dissent, the lower court upheld segregation. The case was appealed to the United States Supreme Court, which remanded the case to the three-judge court on a technicality.

The *Brown* civil rights litigation resulted in an evolution of Houston's earlier plans. For example, Robert Carter, Thurgood Marshall's assistant, thought that sociological evidence would help the litigation strategy. Carter and Johnny Davis (a prominent Negro social scientist who taught political science at Lincoln University in Oxford, Pennsylvania) collaborated in developing this idea using sociological and psychological research.

In the South Carolina case, Dr. Kenneth Clark testified, and in the Virginia case both Kenneth Clark and his wife, Dr. Mamie Clark, testified. They convincingly demonstrated the damaging effect of segregation on Negro school children.

For example, Kenneth Clark had several dolls—some were Black and others were White. Clark asked Negro schoolchildren a number of questions. For instance, the children were requested to choose the dolls they liked best, or the ones that were the prettiest, or the good dolls. Overwhelmingly, the children chose the White dolls. However, when the same children were asked to identify the bad dolls, the ugly dolls, the worst dolls, they chose the ones that most resembled themselves. These tests were further developed by Drs.

Marian Radke and Helen Trager, and helped to illuminate the devastating effect on Negro children of an educational system and society that was thoroughly segregated and racist.

In April 1951, 16-year-old Barbara Johns led a student walkout in Prince Edward County, Virginia, to protest substandard educational facilities at the all-Black Robert Russa Moton High School. Johns' courageous actions are further chronicled in *The Big Bang,* Brown v. Board of Education, *and Beyond*.[37] The students' bravery, that of their parents, and others in the Prince Edward community culminated in a lawsuit, *Davis v. County School Board of Prince Edward*,[38] which was consolidated as one of five cases that the Court heard as a unit in *Brown*.

Following the Supreme Court's remand of the South Carolina case, the Topeka, Wilmington, and Prince Edward cases came up for Supreme Court review. The Clarendon County case came back to the Supreme Court as well as the District of Columbia case. With all five cases before it, the Supreme Court consolidated the litigation with *Brown* as the lead case.

The Topeka, Prince Edward, Clarendon County, and Wilmington cases were filed under the Fourteenth Amendment, challenging the separate but equal precedents. The issue in all four cases was fundamentally the same: whether segregation in the public schools was constitutional.

The fifth case originated in the District of Columbia.[39] Under the existing judicial interpretations, the Fourteenth Amendment did not apply to the District of Columbia because the District of Columbia is not a state. Those were legal distinctions.

All of the cases challenged segregation in the public schools. Thurgood Marshall argued strenuously for the abolition of segregation *per se* in all of these cases. His was the general argument attacking segregation at its constitutional roots. In addition, the other members of the civil rights team argued the specific facts and circumstances of the individual cases.

After the first argument of the consolidated cases, the Supreme Court could not agree on what to do about segregation *per se* in the public schools. Chief Justice Vinson agreed to Frankfurter's suggestion that the Court delay a decision.

One of the crucial points was how the Court chose to interpret the Constitution. Many civil rights activists believed that the appropriate method for interpreting the Constitution was to view and treat it as a living document. In short, the Court needed to interpret the Constitution to meet existing needs. This could be done by determining what general principles underlie constitutional provisions and then applying those principles to specific facts. Thus, for example, a fundamental objective of the Fourteenth Amendment was to establish equality of civil rights among citizens of the United States. When applied to the specific situation of public schools, the equality principle would lead to a desegregated school system, especially where history and practice had taught us that segregated schools were inherently unequal. In addition, the Supreme Court in *Plessy* was just plain *wrong*.

Houston's basic plan continued to be followed. That was, you use whatever techniques, knowledge, strategies, and insights that circumstances required.

During the year of the re-argument, Chief Justice Vinson died. President Eisenhower appointed Earl Warren as Chief Justice of the United States Supreme Court. Warren succeeded in his primary objective, of overruling *Plessy v. Ferguson* through a unanimous Supreme Court opinion. Warren's approach was both objective and positive. Without his perseverance in achieving a unanimous opinion, the decision would likely have been that of a divided court, perhaps six to three or five to four. Nevertheless, segregationists were, and still are, critical of Chief Justice Warren.

Moreover, in those days, many White persons supported segregation for political, social, or economic reasons. In fact, most racial segregationists not only maintained their malicious personal attitudes toward Negroes but also insisted that other White persons publicly demonstrate a similar attitude.

On Monday, May 17, 1954, a bulletin came over the radio saying that the Supreme Court was announcing its decision in the school segregation cases. Chief Justice Warren started talking and listeners heard the Court rule that racially segregated schools deprived minority children of equal educational opportunity. There soon was much rejoicing in many parts of the country. Racially segregated schools were inherently unequal.

In numerous cities in response to the Supreme Court and lower federal courts desegregation decisions, many White residents fled to the surrounding counties to avoid desegregation. This mid-twentieth-century example of White flight occurred not only in Virginia and other parts of the South but also nationwide.

At the same time, some cities like Richmond, Virginia, attempted to annex surrounding predominantly White counties to maintain a White electoral majority. Thus, for instance, in the early 1960s the Richmond City Council tried to annex portions of Henrico and Chesterfield Counties. The Virginia state courts ruled in favor of the city, allowing it to annex part of Henrico County provided the city paid the county $40 million in compensation.

The city decided this price was too expensive. City officials concluded that they should focus their energies on pursuing an annexation lawsuit against Chesterfield County. During subsequent litigation, evidence obtained in discovery revealed that Mayor Phillip J. Bagley conspired with Chesterfield officials to dilute Negro voting strength. Bagley agreed to annex Chesterfield County property containing a number of White voters rather than annex a more sparsely populated area of county property. The more lightly settled part of the county included property owned by the DuPont Company and had a better tax base. Bagley's actions demonstrated that maintaining the political power of White folks outweighed the community's interest in economic development and in a fair resolution of issues presented by evolving social conditions.

A suit was also filed during the early 1970s to allow the school boards to ignore county district lines in carrying out the Supreme Court's mandate to desegregate schools. Judge Robert Merhige ruled in favor of the plaintiffs but the Fourth Circuit reversed. During this period Justice Lewis Powell along with Justice William Rehnquist had been nominated and confirmed to the Supreme Court. When the case got there Powell decided not to participate in the case but Rehnquist did. The Court was equally divided, which meant that the decision of the Fourth Circuit to reverse Merhige stood.[40]

To make matters worse, in 1974, the Supreme Court decided *Milliken v. Bradley*, a case in which the trial court found that local government officials created segregated schools in Detroit. To remedy the violation of students' rights, the court ordered comprehensive relief, including desegregation of surrounding predominantly White school districts.

The Supreme Court struck down the trial court decision. The Court said that the remedy for the Detroit school district's violation of the students' constitutional rights must be limited to the boundaries of the Detroit school district. In other words, the students' constitutional rights and remedies stopped at the county line.

Interdistrict busing like the trial court ordered in Detroit was not a novelty. During the days of segregation, Virginia had numerous precedents compelling the busing of Negro students to maintain segregation. Black children were bused within local jurisdictions as well as across city and county lines to ensure they attended segregated schools. Indeed, Virginia had long-standing legislation providing for regional school boards to facilitate and maintain racially segregated public schools.

Moreover, state and local officials across the former Confederacy defied the Supreme Court's decision in *Brown* and continued forced busing to maintain segregation. As a personal example, beginning in September 1958, I road school buses past the all-White Botetourt Elementary School in Gloucester, Virginia, which was less than two miles from my home. Each day I road to Thomas C. Walker High School, which was approximately five times farther away than Botetourt. Thomas C. Walker served Black elementary and high school students. Meanwhile, White students in Gloucester attended one of three segregated elementary schools nearest their homes. Rather than being crammed into one facility like their Black peers, the White students had both separate elementary schools and a separate high school.

While many factors contributed to the desegregation of school systems in more rural areas in the South, at least three developments merit attention. First, some legal victories occurred because of the courage and determination of African American parents, children, attorneys, and a small group of equally courageous and determined White persons. In this regard, S.W. Tucker and Henry L. Marsh III, Oliver W. Hill Sr.'s law partners, won the *Green v. New Kent County* Supreme Court case, which ruled that school boards had to devise desegregation plans designed to work now.[41]

Second, under the leadership of President Lyndon B. Johnson, the Department of Health, Education and Welfare threatened to terminate federal funding to school systems that maintained apartheid systems of education.

Finally, the tragic murders of Martin Luther King Jr. and Senator Robert F. Kennedy seared the national conscience. Many Americans decided that enough was enough—and that blatant segregation practices must end.

Looking back a half century, if the Supreme Court had had the courage to rule in favor of remedies including busing across city and county lines to desegregate the schools, it is reasonable to believe that most of the White flight would have stopped. There would not have been any place for the White parents to run to avoid having their children go to school with Negro children. Some political compromise could have been worked out. Instead, the Court limited the constitutional rights of students who had suffered state-sponsored racial discrimination which helped keep the students bottled up in ghettos. The Supreme Court rulings promoted virtually segregated suburbs. The Court gave its stamp of approval to White flight and continuing racial segregation.

The rise in real estate values in the 1970s only worsened government-sponsored inequality between White suburbanites and urban dwellers who were predominantly persons of color. In America, ownership of residential real estate constitutes a major source of family wealth.[42] In that vein, a 2002 Pew Hispanic Center Report illuminates contemporary examples of the effects of persistent race discrimination. The Pew report stated that the median net worth of Hispanic or Latino households was only 9% of that of White households; and the median net worth of Blacks was approximately 6% of that of Whites.[43] In other words, Whites, on average, have 11 times more wealth than Hispanics and 16 times more wealth than African Americans.

An even more recent Pew Hispanic Center Report pointed out that in the aftermath of the Great Recession (2005-2009), the median net worth of Hispanic or Latino households as well as African American households sharply declined. In 2011, the median net worth of White households was 18 times greater than that of Latinos (up from 11 times greater in 2002). Versus African Americans, the wealth of White households was 20 times greater in 2011 (up from 16 times greater in 2002).[44]

In fact, a longitudinal study of approximately 1,700 families over a 25-year period (1984-2009) revealed some interesting facts. Conducted by the Institute on Assets and Social Policy at Brandeis University, the study showed that the wealth gap between Whites and Blacks nearly tripled from $84,000 on average in 1984 to $256,000 in 2009. The principal factors contributing to the accelerating disparity included significant differences in levels of home ownership, education, and material inheritance.[45] Primary causes of disparities in these areas include lending policies that contribute to persistent and pervasive housing segregation, the low minimum wage and lack of enforcement of equal pay laws, insufficient child care resources for working parents, and inequitable tax policies that provide great benefits for the materially wealthy.[46]

Melvin Oliver and Thomas Shapiro have summarized the effects of pervasive governmental and private discrimination against Blacks as follows:

> What is often not acknowledged is that the accumulation of wealth for some whites is intimately tied to the poverty of wealth of most blacks. Just as blacks have had "cumulative disadvantages," whites have had "cumulative advantages." Practically, every circumstance of bias and *discrimination* against blacks has produced a circumstance and opportunity of positive gain for whites. When black workers were paid less than white workers, white workers gained a benefit; when black businesses were confined to the segregated black market, white business received the benefit of diminished competition; when FHA policies denied loans to blacks, whites were the beneficiaries of the spectacular growth of good housing and housing equity in the suburbs. The cumulative effect on such a process has been to sediment blacks at the bottom of the social hierarchy and to artificially raise the relative position of some whites in society.[47]

In other words, Oliver and Shapiro elegantly describe White American affirmative action.

Other examples of *de facto* governmental race discrimination policies include the Social Security Act of 1935. For decades the Act excluded many people of color from coverage. Such dark folks disproportionately comprised farm laborers and domestic workers. The law hobbled the efforts of these hard-working, long-suffering individuals to care for themselves and accumulate material wealth to transfer to their posterity.[48]

In addition, to qualify for benefits, the welfare system requires impoverished people to divest themselves of nearly all material assets. This discourages wealth accumulation and enlightenment through education. For example, in the early days of the welfare system, beneficiaries were handicapped in their educational development because they were denied common resources like radios. The welfare system has encouraged and perpetuated dependency and ignorance.[49] To make bad matters worse, the failure of this society to insist on a living wage for workers ensures that a secondary economy literally indebted to criminal elements will flourish. In these circumstances, the law has taken a cruel but not unsurprising twist. Thousands of Black and Brown persons have been incarcerated for selling marijuana and as a result are saddled with the crippling, life-limiting weight of a felony conviction. Now many state governments have legalized the sale of recreational marijuana: and persons with access to capital can earn millions of dollars through selling marijuana without fear of conviction of a felony.

The effects of America's past system of legal apartheid have been devastating. Primarily because of conscious or subconscious racism and sexism the talents and skills of the majority of Americans have been underdeveloped. Individuals of color have often been thought of as lazy, shiftless, and stupid; and women were supposedly weak, silly, and timid. Class stereotypes further complicated matters. Such gross misperceptions cut across color and gender lines. For example, class bias is reflected in well-known infamous, denigrating terms like "poor White trash."

Today, as we are nearly midway through the third decade of a new century and a new millennium, the legacy of a racial and gender spoils system lingers. For instance, White males are a minority group comprising approximately 30% of the nation's population,[50] nevertheless, they account for 95%-97% of senior managers of Fortune 1000 industrial and Fortune 500 companies,[51] 75% of the U.S. senators,[52] and the majority of tenured professors.[53] In addition, at the end of the twentieth century, White males were receiving over 90% of the federal government's funding for prime public contracts.[54]

Another striking example of modern White male affirmative action is reflected in two reports commissioned by the Virginia Department of Minority Business Enterprises. During the five fiscal years beginning with 1998 and extending through 2003, in procuring goods and services from private business, the Commonwealth of Virginia spent only 0.44% of its budget with minority-owned businesses. In other words, less than half a penny on each taxpayer's dollar was spent with minority businesses to obtain goods and services needed by the state. Similarly, the Commonwealth spent only 1.27% of its procurement budget with women-owned businesses. That means that the state spent more than 98% of its procurement budget with firms that were owned by White males. Stated differently, $0.98 of each taxpayer's dollar was spent with White male–owned businesses. In short, women of all complexions and men of color got two cents on each taxpayer dollar.

A more recent disparity study for the Commonwealth of Virginia published in 2011 showed that from 2006 to 2009, White males received 98% of the Commonwealth's dollars paid to persons in the following businesses: (1) prime construction contractors, (2) architecture and engineering prime consultants, (3) professional services prime consultants, and (4) goods and supplies prime contractors.[55] Even regarding subcontractor contracts, during the July 1, 2006–June 30, 2009, time period, White men received the lion's share of such funding—85%.[56]

## A Note on Congress and the Courts

Toward the end of the twentieth century, Congress recognized that serious social and economic inequities exist and that America's bountiful talents are interspersed from sea to shining sea. Talented Americans are found in every color, gender, and social class. Accordingly, Congress created programs to specifically include the majority of Americans who had been effectively locked out of the government contracting process. For instance, Congress mandated in the Surface Transportation and Uniform Relocation Assistance Act of 1987 (the Surface Transportation Act) that the Department of Transportation should expend "not less than ten percent" of the federal appropriation "with small business concerns owned and controlled by socially and economically disadvantaged individuals."[57] The Surface Transportation Act included in its definition of "socially and economically disadvantaged individuals" women, Blacks, Hispanics, Asia Pacific persons, subcontinent Asians, and Native Americans.[58] The Act presumed that individuals within these categories were disadvantaged. All totaled, individuals in such categories comprise approximately two-thirds of America's population. The Act did not limit itself to such individuals. In fact, the Act sought to help all disadvantaged individuals, including White males, to obtain government contracts.

Collectively, women, people of color, and economically disadvantaged White males comprise well over 70% of America's population.[59] The Surface Transportation Act set aside 10% of funding for the overwhelming majority of Americans who are not materially wealthy White males. The legislation allowed up to 90% of the Surface Transportation Act's monies to be spent on businesses owned by non-disadvantaged White males. Stated differently, rich White men could receive 90% of the funding. In the competition for federal contracting dollars, Congress attempted to modestly balance the economic scales and to energize underdeveloped sectors within America's economy.

In *Adarand Constructors v. Pena*,[60] the Supreme Court stepped in and held that courts must apply extremely onerous standards to justify federal programs to redress pervasive inequities flowing from government-facilitated (and sometimes mandated) racial discrimination. Justice Sandra Day O'Connor wrote:

> All governmental action based on race—a group classification long recognized as "in most circumstances irrelevant and therefore prohibited," ... should be subjected to detailed judicial inquiry to ensure that the *personal* right to equal protection of the laws has not been infringed. These ideas have long been central to this Court's understanding of equal protection, and holding "benign" state and federal racial classifications to different standards does not square with them.[61]

The *Adarand* Court seemed indifferent to the real-world problems confronting Congress. Consequently, the Court narrowly interpreted Congress' authority to encourage fair competition between individuals from groups that have historically been "haves" versus those from groups that have been "have-nots."

In dissent, Justice John Paul Stevens said:

> The consistency that the Court espouses would disregard the difference between a "No Trespassing" sign and a welcome mat. It would treat a Dixiecrat Senator's decision to vote against Thurgood Marshall's confirmation in order to keep African Americans off the Supreme Court as on a par with President Johnson's evaluation of his nominee's race as a positive factor. It would equate a law that made black citizens ineligible for military service with a program aimed at recruiting black soldiers. An attempt by the majority to exclude members of a minority race from a regulated market is fundamentally different from a subsidy that enables a relatively small group of newcomers to enter that market. An interest in "consistency" does not justify treating differences as though they were similarities.[62]

A more enlightened Court took a different view of the historical realities of American life and history in *Grutter v. Bollinger*.[63] In *Grutter*, the United States Supreme Court scrutinized whether in the higher-education context, admissions officers may consider an applicant's race in attempting to create a diverse student body. By a five-to-four majority, the Supreme Court ruled that admissions officers may incorporate race as one of many factors in a flexible, individualized evaluation of an applicant's request for admission. Giving prospective students that type of individualized attention is constitutional.[64] The Court specifically noted that:

> Context matters when reviewing race-based governmental action under the Equal Protection Clause.... Not every decision influenced by race is equally objectionable and strict scrutiny is designed to provide a framework for carefully examining the importance and sincerity of the reasons advanced by the governmental decision maker for the use of race in that particular context.[65]

Addressing the concern of the dissenters that in effect the university's admissions program constituted racial balancing or a quota system, Justice O'Connor pointed out that:

> When using race as a "plus factor" in university admissions, a university's admissions program must remain flexible enough to ensure that each applicant is evaluated as an individual and not in a way that makes an applicant's race or ethnicity the defining feature of his or her application. The importance of this individualized consideration in the context of a race-conscious admissions program is paramount....
>
> Here, the law school engages in a highly-individualized, holistic review of each applicant's file, giving serious consideration to all the ways an

> applicant might contribute to a diverse educational environment. The Law School affords this individualized consideration to applicants of all races. There is no policy, either *de jure* or *de facto*, of automatic acceptance or rejection based on any single "soft" variable.[66]

The Court also pointed out that the law school takes seriously diversity factors aside from race:

> The Law School frequently accepts non-minority applicants with grades and test scores lower than underrepresented minority applicants (and other non-minority applicants) who are rejected ... This shows that the law school seriously weighs many other diversity factors besides race that can make a real and dispositive difference for non-minority applicants, as well. By this flexible approach the law school sufficiently takes into account, in practice as well as in theory, a wide variety of characteristics besides race and ethnicity that contribute to a diverse student body.[67]

The Court noted that the First Amendment protects freedom of thought, and that by admitting a diverse student body, institutions of higher learning could carry out one of their fundamental objectives: promoting a wide-ranging and vigorous intellectual discourse.[68] To help promote academic excellence especially through vigorous intellectual cross-fertilization of differing ideas, perceptions, and experiences, universities and other institutions of higher education could, in their admissions processes, take diversity into account.[69] The Court would defer to the judgment of university admissions officials in the absence of a showing that such officials were not acting in good faith.[70]

The *Grutter* majority pointed out that race-conscious admissions programs must have "reasonable durational limits."[71] Noting that 25 years have passed since Justice Lewis Powell stated that race could be considered in achieving student body diversity in higher education, the Court said, "we expect that 25 years from now, the use of racial preferences will no longer be necessary to further the interest approved to date."[72]

Responding to the majority's optimistic (and perhaps unrealistic) wishes about the duration of affirmative action programs, in a concurring opinion joined by Justice Stephen Breyer, Justice Ruth Bader Ginsburg stated:

> [I]t remains the current reality that many minority students encounter markedly inadequate and unequal educational opportunities. Despite these inequalities, some minority students are able to meet the high threshold requirements set for admission to the country's finest undergraduate and graduate educational institutions. As lower school education in minority communities improves, an increase in the number of such students may be anticipated. From today's vantage point, one may hope, but not firmly forecast, that over the next generation's span, progress towards nondiscrimination and genuinely equal opportunity will make it safe to sunset affirmative action.[73]

Following *Grutter*, the Court retreated from its decision to support desegregation of institutions of higher education and promote equal educational opportunity for persons at the bottom of the societal ladder in the United States. For instance, in *Fisher v. Texas*,[74] Abigail Fisher, a White high school graduate, applied to the University of Texas at Austin and was denied admission. Fisher claimed that the university unconstitutionally discriminated against her and other White applicants because the university considered applicants' race in the admissions process. The lower courts ruled against Fisher.

By a 4-3 vote, the Supreme Court upheld the university's admissions process. Writing for the majority, Justice Anthony Kennedy pointed out that the University of Texas at Austin was seeking to diversify its student body, that nearly 80% of undergraduate classes with five or more students contained no African American students or had only one Black student in them, and that the university had tried a number of other nonracial admissions programs to no avail. The Court said that when Fisher applied for admission, 75% of the freshman class consisted of students who finished in the top 10% of their Texas high school graduating class.

Fisher fell below the 10% threshold. Approximately 25% of the University of Texas at Austin freshman class fell into Fisher's (non–top 10%) category. Accordingly, like many other Texas high school students who graduated below the top 10%, Fisher had to compete for one of the relatively few remaining seats in the entering freshman class.

In deciding who would be admitted to the remaining 25% of the class, University of Texas at Austin admissions officers considered a number of factors, including the applicant's test scores; grades; letters of recommendations; written essays; resume; leadership; community service; special circumstances, including socioeconomic status; which language members of applicant's household spoke; and race. According to Justice Kennedy, in this context, race was "a factor of a factor of a factor." Stated another way, race mattered but only in a limited set of circumstances.

On this basis, the Court concluded that the university had met the stringent standard for use of race to achieve diversity—that is, race was considered in narrowly tailored situations. Only in such confined limits did race affect the outcome of admissions decisions. In other words, everyone had an opportunity to have a holistic, individualized evaluation of her application. In fact, the Court endorsed the trial court's conclusion that "[a]s the Defendants point out, the consideration of race, within the full context of the entire application, may be beneficial to any UT Austin applicant—including Whites and Asian Americans."[75]

Many aspects of *Fisher* are troubling. Before returning to a discussion of the *SFFA* cases, I will point out only one significant problem that *Fisher* presents. The University of Texas at Austin has a well-documented, extensive legacy of racial discrimination. That unfortunate heritage extends back at least to the *Sweatt* case. In *Sweatt*, decided in 1950, the Supreme Court held that Texas failed to meet the Constitution's equal protection standard. As noted previously, the *Sweatt* Court said that:

> What is more important, the University of Texas Law School possesses to a far greater degree those qualities which are incapable of objective measurement but which make for greatness in a law school. Such qualities, to name but a few, include reputation of the faculty, experience of the administration, position and influence of the alumni, standing in the community, traditions and prestige. *It is difficult to believe that one who had a free choice between these law schools would consider the question close.*[76]

A casual glance at historic pictures of the exterior of the University of Texas Law School Building (Figure 4) versus the storefront provided for prospective African American lawyers (Figure 5) reinforces the Court's conclusion: It is difficult to believe that one who had a free choice between these law schools would consider the question close.

Accordingly, the *Fisher* Court's decision is deeply ironic: the Court demands that this particular university meet a nearly impossible standard to remediate the continuing impact of race-based discrimination that it practiced. This is especially troubling since as the Court noted:

Figure 4. University of Texas Law Building

> [A]lthough admissions officers can consider race as a positive feature of a minority student's application, there is no dispute that race is but a "factor of a factor of a factor" in the holistic-review calculus.[77]

Stated another way, the fierce resistance to such minimal programs as that at the University of Texas at Austin reflects a relentless drive to eliminate programs that help to ensure that student bodies in public institutions reflect the diversity of the general public whose tax dollars fund such institutions. The net effect of such resegregation campaigns is to ensure wider opportunities for persons from materially wealthy backgrounds and individuals with good personal connections. Protecting such perks of privilege comes at the expense of competent individuals without those kinds of advantages. Evidence of the lengths to which privileged persons will go to consume every piece of the societal pie is reflected in recent scandals in which such persons have

Figure 5. School of Law of the Texas State University for Negroes (circa 1947)

engaged in bribery, fraud, and other dishonorable activities to obtain entrance into selective institutions of higher education.[78]

As promised, we return to the two *SFFA* cases that the Court decided in 2023. The Harvard and UNC cases bore the intended fruit: protecting the privileges of materially well-to-do White persons. By a six-vote majority in each case, the Supreme Court effectively overruled *Grutter* and *Fisher*. The Court held that the Harvard and UNC affirmative action plans were unconstitutional. Pointing to *Grutter*, the *SSFA* Court said that the use of race in higher education admissions must further a compelling interest and be narrowly tailored.

> Any exception to the Constitution's demand for equal protection must survive a daunting two-step examination known in our cases as "strict scrutiny." ... Under that standard we ask, first, whether the racial classification is used to "further compelling governmental interests." ... Second, if so, we ask whether the government's use of race is "narrowly tailored"—meaning "necessary"—to achieve that interest.[79]

The Court opined that:

> [T]he interests [the universities] view as compelling cannot be subjected to meaningful judicial review. Harvard identifies the following educational benefits that it is pursuing: (1) "training future leaders in the public and private sectors"; (2) preparing graduates to "adapt to an increasingly pluralistic society"; (3) "better educating its students through diversity"; and (4) "producing new knowledge stemming from diverse outlooks." ... UNC points to similar benefits, namely, "(1) promoting the robust exchange of ideas; (2) broadening and refining understanding; (3) fostering innovation and problem-solving; (4) preparing engaged and productive citizens and leaders; [and] (5) enhancing appreciation, respect, and empathy, cross-racial understanding, and breaking down stereotypes." ...
>
> Although these are commendable goals, they are not sufficiently coherent for purposes of strict scrutiny.[80]

According to the Court, when a university considers an applicant's race in the admissions process, the university must do so in a way that is sufficiently "measurable to permit judicial [review]."[81] The Court did not define or describe what such "measurable and concrete" admissions processes would look like.

Further, the Court argued that Harvard and UNC used race in a stereotypical fashion. For instance, the Court contended that the universities' "racial" group classification system was too imprecise and treated persons from diverse demographic backgrounds as though they were exactly the same. So, for instance, the Court objected to the use of the term "Asian" as being too imprecise because: "[B]y grouping together all Asian students ... respondents are apparently uninterested in whether *South* Asian or *East* Asian students are adequately represented, so long as there is enough of one to compensate for a lack of the other."[82]

Moreover, the Court recoiled at what the Court perceived as a "negative" use of race. From the vantage point of the Court, considering race would result in a class with more African Americans and Latinos. Such an outcome constituted a "negative" for White and Asian students for as the Court stated pointedly, "College admissions are zero sum."[83]

Finally, the Court contended that neither Harvard nor UNC had identified a concrete date upon which their programs would end. In these circumstances, the Court summed up the reasons for its decision as follows:

> [T]he Harvard and UNC admissions programs cannot be reconciled with the guarantees of the Equal Protection Clause. Both programs lack sufficiently focused and measurable objectives warranting the use of race, unavoidably employ race in a negative manner, involve racial stereotyping, and lack meaningful end points.[84]

In an impassioned, trenchant dissent, Justice Sonia Sotomayor wrote that in prior cases:

> The Court has explained that a university can consider a student's race in its admissions process so long as that use is "contextual and does not operate

as a mechanical plus factor." ... The Court has also repeatedly held that race, when considered as one factor of many in the context of holistic review, "can make a difference to whether an application is accepted or rejected." [citation omitted] After all, race-conscious admissions seek to improve racial diversity. Race cannot, however, be "'decisive' for virtually every minimally qualified underrepresented minority applicant.... That is precisely how Harvard's program operates."[85]

Moreover, Sotomayor pointed out that:

Consistent with the Court's precedents, Harvard properly "considers race as part of a holistic review process," "values all types of diversity," "does not consider race exclusively," and "does not award a fixed amount of points to applicants because of their race." ... Indeed, Harvard's admissions process is so competitive and the use of race is so limited and flexible that, as "SFFA's own expert's analysis" showed, "Harvard rejects more than two thirds of Hispanic applicants and slightly less than half of all African-American applicants who are among the top 10% most academically promising applicants."[86]

As to North Carolina's program, Sotomayor said:

The limited use of race at UNC thus has a smaller effect than at Harvard and is also consistent with the Court's precedents. In addition, contrary to the majority's suggestion, such effect does not prove that "race alone ... explains the admissions decisions for hundreds if not thousands of applicants to UNC each year." ... As the District Court found, UNC (like Harvard) "engages a highly individualized, holistic review of each applicant's file, which considers race flexibly as a 'plus factor' as one

> among many factors in its individualized consideration of each and every applicant."[87]

Stated simply, race is not "a defining feature of any individual application."[88]

Justice Sotomayor argued that the lower courts had conscientiously determined the material facts and applied the law to those facts. Justice Sotomayor also pointed out that the anti–affirmative action arguments the Court rejected in *Grutter* prevailed in the *SFFA* cases. Justice Sotomayor summarized the legal landscape as follows:

> At bottom, the six unelected members of today's majority upend the status quo based on their policy preferences about what race in America should be like, but is not, and their preferences for a veneer of colorblindness in a society where race has always mattered and continues to matter in fact and in law.[89]

In the Harvard case, Justice Ketanji Brown Jackson recused herself. In the UNC decision, Justice Jackson participated, and in a brilliant thumbnail historical and jurisprudential summation dissented. Among other things, Justice Jackson analyzed the societal impact of the infamous *Dred Scott* decision, the historical reasons for and scope of the Fourteenth Amendment, as well as race-conscious congressional human rights legislation enacted following the Civil War to help formerly enslaved persons.[90] Justice Jackson perceptively illuminated the malign role of the Supreme Court in choking the promise of equality in decisions like the *Civil Rights Cases* and *Plessy*.[91] Extending her historical overview to modern times, Justice Jackson also evaluated the role of the Congress and other national policy makers in conferring benefits along the color line. For example, Justice Jackson said:

> [N]ationwide, it was FHA's established policy to provide "no guarantees for mortgages to African Americans, or to whites who might lease to African

> Americans," irrespective of creditworthiness. No surprise, then, that "[b]etween 1934 and 1968, 98 percent of FHA loans went to white Americans," with whole cities (ones that had a disproportionately large number of Black people due to housing segregation) sometimes being deemed ineligible for FHA intervention on racial grounds. The Veterans Administration operated similarly.[92]

Justice Jackson elucidated how these modern examples of government sponsored race discrimination against persons of color continue to impact America today:

> [I]t is significant that, in so excluding Black people, government policies affirmatively operated—one could say, affirmatively acted—to dole out preferences to those who, if nothing else, were not Black. Those past preferences carried forward and are reinforced today by (among other things) the benefits that flow to homeowners and to the holders of other forms of capital that are hard to obtain unless one already has assets.[93]

Justice Jackson furnished the following poignant example of present practical and measurable effects of governmental race-based housing policies:

> Just four years ago, in 2019, Black families' median wealth was approximately $24,000. For White families, that number was approximately eight times as much (about $188,000). These wealth disparities "exis[t] at every income and education level," so, "[o]n average, white families with college degrees have over $300,000 more wealth than black families with college degrees." This disparity has also accelerated over time—from a roughly $40,000 gap between White and Black household median net

> worth in 1993 to a roughly $135,000 gap in 2019. Median income numbers from 2019 tell the same story: $76,057 for White households, $98,174 for Asian households, $56,113 for Latino households, and $45,438 for Black households.
>
> These financial gaps are unsurprising in light of the link between home ownership and wealth. Today, as was true 50 years ago, Black home ownership trails White home ownership by approximately 25 percentage points. Moreover, Black Americans' homes (relative to White Americans') constitute a greater percentage of household wealth, yet tend to be worth less, are subject to higher effective property taxes, and generally lost more value in the Great Recession.
>
> From those markers of social and financial unwellness flow others. In most state flagship higher educational institutions, the percentage of Black undergraduates is lower than the percentage of Black high school graduates in that state.[94]

In a haunting (indeed prophetic!) voice regarding the majority's decision, Justice Jackson declared:

> UNC has thus built a review process that more accurately assesses merit than most of the admissions programs that have existed since this country's founding. Moreover, in so doing, universities like UNC create pathways to upward mobility for long excluded and historically disempowered racial groups. Our Nation's history more than justifies this course of action. And our present reality indisputably establishes that such programs are still needed—for the general public good—because after centuries of state-sanctioned (and enacted) race discrimination, the aforementioned intergenerational

> race-based gaps in health, wealth, and well-being stubbornly persist.
>
> Rather than leaving well enough alone, today, the majority is having none of it. Turning back the clock (to a time before the legal arguments and evidence establishing the soundness of UNC's holistic admissions approach existed), the Court indulges those who either do not know our nation's history or long to repeat it. Simply put, the race-blind admissions stance the Court mandates from this day forward is unmoored from critical real-life circumstances. Thus, the Court's meddling not only arrests the noble generational project that America's universities are attempting, it also launches, in effect, a dismally misinformed sociological experiment.
>
> Time will reveal the results. Yet the Court's own missteps are now both eternally memorialized and excruciatingly plain.[95]

Stated in different words, Justice Jackson's opinion highlights examples of what this book has referred to as White American affirmative action.

Condemning modest programs to help the most vulnerable persons in society diverts attention from White American affirmative action. Richard Delgado describes such tactics cogently:

> For more than 200 years, white males benefited from their own program of affirmative action, through unjustified preferences in jobs and education resulting from old-boy networks and official laws that lessened the competition. Today's affirmative action critics never characterize that scheme as affirmative action, which of course it was. By labeling problematic, troublesome, and ethically agonizing a paltry system that helps a few of us get ahead, critics neatly take our eyes off the system of arrangements

that brought and maintained them in power, and enabled them to develop the rules and standards of quality and merit that now exclude us, make us appear unworthy, dependent (naturally) on affirmative action.[96]

## A Sobering Assessment

In retrospect, had the courts and legislatures been more willing to use effective measures to remedy past discrimination, by now this society would have adjusted to equal opportunity as the law of the land. Obviously, affirmative action would have been a temporary measure and after the inequalities had been remedied, it would no longer have been necessary.

The issue basically boils down to fairness. We live in a society in which material and other resources are *not* allocated on an equitable basis. So we must evaluate the material as well as non-material resources that each person has. Then we need to ask: How can we fairly evaluate how well each person has done with the resources available to her? After doing so, we are required to make a prediction (prophesy) regarding how well she is likely to do if given additional opportunities.

In helping to redress America's shameful legacy of race, gender, and class discrimination, the Congress, the Executive Branch, and courts each have important roles. Thus, the Constitution empowers Congress to legislate so that as a society we can address today's inequitable conditions that are rooted in past (and present) unjust discrimination. For instance, University of Virginia School of Law Professor Kimberly J. Robinson has cogently argued that the Congress should recognize a federal right to education. In doing so, Congress would also ensure that ultimately each public school student in the United States had access to an excellent education and that resources would be equitably allocated to achieve this goal. Moreover, such a program could be implemented incrementally. State-level initiatives could test which approaches work best in varying contexts.[97] Of course, as Professor Danielle

Wingfield has cogently argued, initiatives to ensure good quality public education for all students is likely to encounter modern day vestiges of Massive Resistance.[98]

Likewise, almost completely segregated pools of contractors still exist. Such nearly all-White groups function like economic cartels and dominate the contract procurement process at both the state and national levels. To use a homespun example, if you found a turtle on the top of a tall fence post, how do you think it got there? When have you seen a turtle climbing fences? Would it be more sensible to assume the turtle received some assistance? Like the turtle, the White males who (in the 1980s) received roughly 90% of national government transportation contracts had benefited from intergenerational privileges propelling them to the top. Where, as in Virginia,[99] the percentage of prime contract dollars garnered by White males exceeds 95%, it is even clearer that favoritism along color and gender lines exists. To redress such gross disparities, state officials should establish programs that target business entities that can fulfill reasonable contract requirements but have not (or only rarely) received government contracts.

Turning to the role of the Executive Branch, the President and the President's subordinates must vigilantly enforce laws to ensure that each person can reach her maximum potential. Accordingly, the Executive should promote policies targeted to help the majority of this nation who come from disadvantaged backgrounds—namely, women, men of color, and less materially wealthy White males.

Under the Constitution, despite the legislature and the Executive's failure to protect individual rights, those rights still exist. Even when the political branches of government, dominated by a majority political faction, seek to squash such rights, the rights remain.[100] Unfortunately, in practice vulnerable persons may find it impossible to fully exercise their human freedoms.

Finally, in these circumstances, the courts confront several important constitutional challenges. First, courts need to recognize that the Constitution protects individual liberty from the tyranny of the majority. In the United States, a relatively small group of materially well off White males claim to speak for the (White) majority. Second, the Constitution requires courts to protect the interests of the victims of discrimination (for example, social scapegoats like members of the LBGTQ+ community). Third, the Constitution mandates respect for the separation of powers between the legislature, the Executive, and the courts. Fourth, while respecting separation of powers, the courts must also defend civil liberties.

Executing these judicial obligations is especially important where persons of color compete with persons whose families were not confronted with race discrimination, and who have a 250-year head start. The late visionary economist Lester Thurow put matters as follows:

> Imagine a race with two groups of runners of equal ability. Individuals differ in their running ability, but the average speed of the two groups is identical. Imagine that a handicapper gives each individual in one of the groups a heavy weight to carry. Some of those with weights would still run faster than some of those without weights, but on average, the handicapped group would fall farther and farther behind the group without the handicap.
>
> Now suppose that someone waves a magic wand and all of the weights vanish. Equal opportunity has been created. If the two groups are equal in their running ability, the gap between those who never carried weights and those who used to carry weights will cease to expand, but those who suffered the earlier discrimination will never catch up. If the economic baton can be handed on from generation to generation, the current effects of past discrimination can linger forever.[101]

On a similar note, Oliver W. Hill said this:

> I make no apologies about advocating affirmative action where necessary because I see how the United States government is willing to send white youngsters as well as black ones to foreign countries to risk injuries and their very lives to fight for democracy. If this country can risk the lives of its young people for democracy on "foreign shores," why can't some white people in America temporarily suffer a little inconvenience or sacrifice a little more economically so that on these shores we can develop a society in which a person's color or ethnic classification becomes immaterial. Why is it that many affirmative action critics are unwilling to give back the considerable material benefits that they have inherited through centuries of discrimination? They want to keep the benefits and privileges of racism, and are unwilling to make some temporary sacrifices or experience some transitory inconvenience for the common good. Where is their patriotism? There ought to be fair opportunities for all, and a sharing of power and resources at all levels of our society.
>
> Moreover, time has shown that affirmative action was and is still needed. Over fifty years after *Brown* and over forty years after enactment of the Civil Rights Acts, we still do not have a level playing field regarding employment, education, business, social or political opportunities.[102]

Denial needs to stop. Blame needs to stop. It's time to face facts. This book has tried to outline a few salient facts. Why not make at least two decisions? First, why not face facts with humility and courage? Second, let's resolve to create a civilized society.

As part of a civilized society, for the foreseeable future, compensatory (affirmative action) steps will remain necessary. Such programs can allow persons from disadvantaged groups to compete on a level playing field.

Such a society is a threat to some persons who feel entitled to rule this nation—in fact, even to rule the world. They feel that they as individuals, as well as persons who resemble them physically, economically, and in other ways, are inherently better than others.

In contrast to such elitist (and in some cases white supremacist) thinking, we affirm that a civilized society:

- resolves its conflicts without resorting to war,
- recognizes that we are all part of one human family, and
- allocates resources so that each person can achieve her maximum potential as well as live a happy life.

To accomplish these objectives, as human earthlings in the twenty-first century, we can and must create a renaissance in human relations.

As a step toward achieving such a renaissance, we turn to a repeating problem: What events in our shared history should we celebrate and how?

Chapter VIII

# Toward Truth and Reconciliation in the United States: Preliminary Thoughts on Confederate Heritage, Heresy, and History

IN THE UNITED STATES, hot disputes about race, enslavement, heritage, and history have become commonplace. Such disputes have carried over from the twentieth century into the first decades of the twenty-first. We wish to help lessen individual and societal distress revolving around these recurring flash points. Accordingly, this chapter evaluates the behavior of three former Confederate military officers following the Civil War. From our standpoint it makes more sense to deal with an ex-Confederate's legacy by focusing on what the person did to reunite the United States rather than what he did to destroy it. In that context, we consider the post–Civil War activities of former Confederate General Robert E. Lee, former Confederate General William Mahone, and former Confederate Chaplain Lewis Downing.

This chapter's discussion on Mahone and Downing benefited from the outstanding contributions of two recent University of Richmond School of Law graduates, Chris Evangel, Esq., and Flannery O'Rourke, Esq.

Figure 1. Confederate General Robert E. Lee
in Confederate Uniform.
(Photo Credit: Library of Congress)

## Confederate General Robert E. Lee

At the close of the twentieth century, in June 1999, a controversy erupted in Richmond, Virginia, regarding a large banner that was hung on the wall of the Richmond Canal. The banner portrayed Confederate General Robert E. Lee wearing a Confederate military dress uniform complete with a star on the lapel of his officer's coat. This banner referred to Lee as "General Lee." The Lee banner was one of about a dozen others displayed on the Richmond Canal Walk.[1]

After vigorous protest from some members of the Richmond community, the Lee banner was removed. Two local civic organizations (the Richmond Historic Riverfront Foundation and the Richmond Renaissance) convened a panel to solicit public input as well as make recommendations to City

Figure 2. Photograph of Firebombed Lee Mural
(Courtesy *Richmond Magazine*, August 18, 2022, Cover)

Council for resolving the controversy.[2] A commission was formed. Several months later, after extensive discussion and debate, the Richmond City Council approved a new banner. The principal difference between the original banner and the second one was that the original banner was produced based on a picture of Lee made during the Civil War. The second banner used a different picture of Lee in front of his civilian residence following the War. The second presentation of Lee was remarkably similar to the original one and likewise referred to Lee as "Robert E. Lee, General."[3]

On the night of January 17, 2000, Martin Luther King Jr.'s national holiday, someone firebombed the second Lee banner (see Figure 2).

The arson was widely condemned. The arsonist was never apprehended.

Lee's banner was hung a third time. Richmond's mayor at the time, Tim Kaine, established a commission to make recommendations to the City Council whenever future matters might arise involving "public historical interpretation."[4] The Lee banner no longer hangs on the Canal Walk.

Throughout the Lee banner controversy, some persons argued that Lee's image should have been displayed on the Canal Walk in Confederate military dress, and that he should be referred to as "General Robert E. Lee." They argued that such a portrayal of Lee is part of our American heritage or of southern American heritage or at least of Confederate heritage. More recently some supporters of retaining Confederate statues, pictures, and similar symbols in public places have claimed that such items reflect "culture." To remove such items is condemned as attempts to "cancel culture."

Others contended that a mural of Robert E. Lee in the heart of Richmond only served to remind persons, especially African Americans, of armed, violent attempts to enslave them. Historically, Richmond functioned as a major commercial hub for America's domestic slave trade in which family members were literally ripped from their loved ones' arms sometimes never to be seen again during this earthly life cycle. Thus, to some individuals, removing Confederate symbols was (and is) not an attempt to cancel culture. It was (and is) an attempt to cancel racism (or at least some of racism's concrete manifestations).

Yet other persons asserted that it was time to stop arguing about the meaning of the symbols and move forward. In other words: "Let sleeping dogs lie. Put the past behind us and move on." Such individuals argued that to progress we should not erect more public murals of controversial figures like Lee. They said we should seek greater community—human unity—not division.

Since the Robert E. Lee mural controversy, numerous other fiery public debates have exploded regarding what to do about public monuments and statues erected to honor Confederate leaders as well as the numerous schools, forts, and other public places named after them. Likewise, the display of the Confederate battle flag in public spaces (as was the case for years on the grounds of the South Carolina state capital) has been a trigger for vigorous and sometimes disruptive disagreements.

Sadly, not long ago, a group of white supremacists organized a "Unite the Right" rally in Charlottesville, Virginia. Among other objectives, the supremacists sought to prevent the Charlottesville City Council from removing or covering statues of Confederate leaders in a public park. Among the statues in the park, was one of Confederate General Lee. Violence erupted involving the white supremacists and persons opposing them.

One of the white supremacists deliberately rammed his car into a group of fleeing counterdemonstrators. Among those the neo-Nazi struck with his car was 32-year-old Heather Heyer. Ms. Heyer, a young paralegal, had been nonviolently expressing her disapproval of the actions of the white supremacists. Tragically, Heyer died of injuries inflicted upon her when the killer crushed her with his car.[5]

The recent litany of similar events reflects what feels like America's new civil war.[6] The catalogue of human tragedies grows distressingly longer and more outrageous. A few of the more well-known examples of twenty-first-century American domestic terrorism include:

1. The massacre during a Bible Study of 11 African American worshippers at Mother Emanuel AME Church in Charleston, South Carolina.
2. The slaughter during Sabbath Services of 10 Jewish congregants at the Tree of Life Synagogue in Pittsburgh.
3. The ambush and murder of 23 mostly Latino shoppers at a Walmart store in El Paso, Texas.

4. The premeditated killing of 10 African American shoppers in a grocery store in Buffalo, New York.
5. The deadly rampage in the Atlanta, Georgia, metropolitan area ending in the slaying of 7 Asian Americans.
6. The atrocious murder of 19 young school children and 2 of their teachers in Uvalde, Texas;
7. And by the time you read these words, in the United States alone, there will have been numerous additional, predictable, heartbreaking mass killings.

The list of racist and anti-Jewish hate crimes is accelerating. In response, President Joe Biden forcefully condemned this "senseless carnage." Widespread outrage has not prevented the atrocities from mushrooming into a Wild West kind of national shootout with defenseless children and peaceful community members as the frequent victims. The disrespect for the lives of Jews and persons of color has metastasized into mainstream White societal circles. The killing of 52 persons at a country music festival in Las Vegas is a sad reminder of the pervasive nature of America's societal *dis-ease*.

In these circumstances, we continue to grapple with the complex, sometimes horrible history of our nation's complicated racial past. At times the struggle—a possible national reckoning—can be gut-wrenching and painful. Nevertheless, that same history also furnishes us with opportunities. We can learn together. In learning together, we also can start the process of healing as local, state, and national communities. In that spirit, this book now suggests that as a national community, we commit to make peace with one another. One modest constructive step in the peacemaking direction involves recognizing the contributions of Robert E. Lee and other Confederate leaders *following the Civil War*. Let's focus on positive steps such individuals took to rebuild and reunite the United States.

## Haunting Questions

We begin by asking ourselves why are some of us continuing to glorify the military misdeeds of ex-Confederate leaders? Why do some extol taking up arms and "levying war against the United States"? Even today, some elected officials who have sworn to uphold the Constitution have called for "civil war," including armed insurrection against the U.S. government.[7] The Constitution has a name for levying war against the United States: treason! What is the point of emphasizing and attempting to defend treason? Why encourage plots, schemes, and rallies to snuff out the American experiment? Why prevent the creation of a society of liberty and justice for all?

While it is true that Confederate soldiers valiantly fought, bled, and died, we need to remember why. They died attempting to split the United States and establish a new nation whose constitution explicitly protected "Negro slavery." Article I, Section 9, Clause 4 of the Constitution of the Confederate States of America said: "(4) No ... law denying or impairing the right of property in negro slaves shall be passed." Similarly, Article IV stated: "The Confederate States may acquire new territory ... In all such territory the institution of negro slavery, as it now exists in the Confederate States, shall be recognized and protected [by] Congress and by the Territorial government; and the inhabitants of the several Confederate States and Territories shall have the right to take to such Territory any slaves lawfully held by them in any of the States or Territories of the Confederate States." The drafters of the Constitution of the United States did not expressly state that the Constitution was designed to promote and protect slavery, in contrast, the Confederate Constitution forthrightly acknowledged that its foundation was based on preserving as well as propagating slavery.

In these circumstances, why is laying down one's life for such a lost cause—holding members of the human family captive and ruthlessly exploiting them—a reason to celebrate? Why shouldn't we mourn such massive and tragic losses?

We have no illusions: the ideas in this book are only a partial start toward a constructive, therapeutic approach to truth and reconciliation. Our suggestions are imperfect—very far from the last word.

## Fact Versus Fiction

By the eve of the American Civil War, for over 200 years, slavery—sometimes referred to as "The Peculiar Institution"—had evolved into a primary feature of "the Southern way of life." In contrast to sometimes benevolent renditions of the nature of slavery in the United States, the autobiographies of formerly enslaved individuals like Virginia lawyers, Thomas Calhoun Walker and George Washington Fields testify to the contrary.[8]

Moreover, in light of the stout legal fortifications defending slavery, one can only speculate why the Confederates sought to destroy the Union. This book does not attempt to discuss the many possibilities in detail. For instance, we do not analyze whether Confederates were principally attempting to:

- ensure the expansion of slavery,
- create broad power for individual states like Virginia to determine their own destiny, or
- guarantee the existence of institutions to perpetually enslave humans.

Alternatively, could the reasons have been a combination of all the preceding possibilities, or something else?

In many respects, what is really at issue involves differing views about race. Such discussions often touch on personal family matters. For example, how did one's ancestors conduct themselves during the era of American chattel slavery? What did those ancestors (grandparents, grand uncles and aunts, cousins, and others) do to end or preserve enslavement of African Americans? Answers to such questions differ in part because individuals often perceive events differently. When family stories appear in these discussions, the conversation can become explosive.

For instance, during the first year of comprehensive desegregation in my high school, one of my White classmates casually mentioned that his great-grandfather had been a slaveholder. The classmate continued by saying that his relative had been "a good master." I wondered how good could a person be who held someone else by force and worked the captive until death without allowing the captive to do what the slaveholder took for granted: go and come as you please, receive compensation for work, have a say in how and what laws are made. We remained on good terms. However, we had very different perceptions revolving around enslavement and race. Such differing perspectives can lead to "blowups" between individuals—emotionally draining experiences yielding more heat than light. The interpersonal disagreements can negatively affect relations between people of good will. Emotional walls sometimes appear—then harden. We retreat behind color lines. And then, all too often, we dig in.

In this country today, we see the consequences of such hardening of the arteries of communication. Many persons seem to believe that removing Confederate statues dishonors the lives of Confederate warriors. In contrast, others perceive governmental decisions to remove the statues as an attempt to dishonor war as an instrument to enslave humans.

Why not speak frankly? There is no doubt that Confederate soldiers had many good human traits, such as kindness, courage, and honesty. However, such soldiers also had a common human flaw: like many of us, they failed to treat other humans with the same respect that they demanded for themselves. Taking up arms to perpetuate slavery manifests profound disrespect—contempt—for an enslaved person's humanity. In the case of Confederate fighters, the persons they treated with contempt sometimes included

Confederates' own enslaved children who were referred to as "children of the plantation." Others who Confederates' disrespected by defending slavery were Confederates' enslaved mistresses and relatives.[9]

It is especially tragic that Confederate soldiers died. Nevertheless, one can try to respectfully ask a hard question: Is it possible for a person to dishonor himself by fighting for the freedom to destroy the lives of others? In short, why should we not learn from the mistakes of our ancestors? Not only can we, but we must.

In that spirit, we humbly suggest that individuals concerned with healing the United States illuminate instances following the War in which former Confederate military and civilian leaders behaved honorably. Examples might include: assisting formerly enslaved people to obtain land, protecting the right to vote, and resisting or at least not promoting the fairy tale of white supremacy. When we are able to identify evidence of such constructive community building, those positive actions should be acknowledged. Those types of examples can furnish historical precedent upon which to build.

Admittedly, in seeking truth and reconciliation, we take risks. Nevertheless, we must try our best. Whether we choose to acknowledge it or not, situations like the Lee controversy continue and are likely to recur. So we ask: How should this type of situation be handled? In answering this question, we bear in mind that words matter. The facts that the words describe matter, too.

## Defining Terms

First, let's define important terms. We begin with heritage. Some individuals argue that "heritage" is a justification for placing Robert E. Lee's portrait and other symbols honoring former Confederates in public places. To support hanging Lee's banner on the Canal Walk, this heritage argument was advanced by a number of persons, including former Ku Klux Klan leader David Duke.[10]

Arguing that "it's my heritage" presents problems. Many people often use the same word to mean different things. That leads to confusion. To reduce unnecessary misunderstandings, we use the *Oxford English Dictionary* definition of heritage: "That which comes from the circumstances of birth; an inherited lot or portion; the condition or state transmitted from ancestors."

But what is our "inherited lot or portion; the condition or state [of affairs]" that our ancestors have transmitted to us? If we view ourselves as all members of the human race—human earthlings—we have a partial answer to the question of what is heritage. We have inherited the same old human challenge: how to live together on planet earth without destroying each other. We have sufficient weapons (nuclear, chemical, and biological) to destroy all humankind. In the twenty-first century our survival as a human race is at stake.

Human survival—the necessity of solving our conflicts non-violently—is complicated enough. To make matters even worse, we have competing views of what is heritage and what is hateful. Moreover, code words like heritage are sometimes replaced with different words with similar meanings. For instance, some persons have recently been employing "culture" as a substitute term for heritage. When referring to Confederate symbols, some modern Confederate sympathizers thunder "don't cancel our culture!"

Whether "culture" or "heritage" is employed to defend Confederate iconography in public spaces, other individuals see such symbols as an example of racist oppression. Indeed, such items are perceived as links along an unbroken chain in places like Virginia stretching back at least to the 1660s. Unfortunately, in 1865 when the Civil War officially ended two centuries of American enslavement, the societal and legal chain of misery evolved into the societal handcuffs known as segregation or American apartheid.

Of course, people's perspectives and interpretations of historical events can differ dramatically. When we cannot agree on what we perceive as happening (what's going on) our differing perceptions almost inevitably lead to conflict.

To deal with the dilemma of heritage, humans must do several things conscientiously and simultaneously. First, we must seek and salvage the constructive contributions of our ancestors. Second, we must acknowledge their misdeeds. Third, where we disagree with one another, we must resolve to live together without resorting to violence. Using this type of careful thinking, we can make wiser choices.

As a test case for this way of decision making, let's return to the question: What should be done about displays of images of former Confederate leaders like Robert E. Lee?

## Another Lee Portrait

Until recently a life-size portrait of Confederate General Robert E. Lee hung on the wall of the Louisa Circuit Court located in Louisa County, Virginia. The portrait directly faced the judge and was in clear sight of the jury. The picture portrayed Lee in a Confederate military uniform with a large sword on his hip and wearing thigh-length nineteenth-century military boots.

The Louisa Circuit Court portrait was hung a few years after the 1901-1902 Virginia State Constitutional Convention during which Virginia State officials disfranchised over 120,000 African American males. The so-called Virginia Constitutional Convention excluded African Americans from participating in its deliberations. The purpose of the convention's brazen power grab was clearly articulated by Virginia state senator (later United States Senator) Carter Glass. Glass stated:

> Discrimination! Why that is exactly what we propose; that exactly is why this Convention was elected—to discriminate to the very extremity of permissible action ... with a view to the elimination

Figure 3. Portrait of Confederate General Robert E. Lee on rear wall of Circuit Court of Louisa County, Virginia. (photo credit: The Central Virginian)

> of every Negro voter who could be gotten rid of, legally, without materially impairing the numerical strength of the white electorate.[11]

Glass said:

> This plan will eliminate the darkey as a political factor in this state in less than 5 years ... [T]he article of suffrage which the conventional will adopt today does not necessarily deprive a single white man of the ballot but will inevitably cut from the existing electorate four-fifths of the Negro voters.[12]

The prophecy of Carter Glass proved to be an understatement. Rather than nearly 80% Negro voters being defrauded of the right to vote as Glass predicted, the actual number was closer to 90%.

In cases like Confederate General Lee's Louisa County courthouse portrait, we must ask: What justification exists for displaying such a portrait today? Stated differently, why have a likeness of a former Confederate military leader in full military dress displayed in any court? In all courts—state and federal—each person is entitled to equal protection of the law.

In *Commonwealth v. Darcel Murphy*, a Louisa Circuit Court capital murder case, defense counsel, Doug Ramseur, Esq., filed a motion asking the court to remove the portrait of Robert E. Lee from the courtroom. Among other things, the defense argued that Lee is a cultural icon of the Confederacy and as such symbolizes the Confederacy's central objective of maintaining the enslavement of African Americans.[13] The defense contended that the Lee portrait was a "badge or incident of slavery," and therefore violated the Thirteenth Amendment.

Moreover, defense counsel asserted that the Lee portrait also transgressed the Fourteenth Amendment, which guarantees equal protection of the laws to all persons in the United States. Counsel stated:

> There is no greater offense to the Equal Protection Clause than government favoritism of one race over another. The display of the [portrait of] Robert E. Lee in his Confederate uniform in addition to the other displays in the courtroom presents a clear message that his service on behalf of the Confederacy in order to preserve slavery is respected and honored by the justice system of Louisa County. Clearly, the display of this portrait is a state action that affects a suspect class in a discriminatory manner and was placed with a discriminatory purpose.[14]

Finally, the defense said that in this courtroom context, conducting a capital trial would be unfair. Such proceedings violate the United States Constitution's due process requirement (as well as Virginia's Constitution). This would especially be the case where the court is trying an African American who was facing a possible death sentence in a court dominated by an imposing military portrait of Robert E. Lee. After all, Lee led Confederate forces that shed blood to maintain slavery and white supremacy.[15]

After careful consideration, the Louisa Circuit Court initially rejected defense counsel's motion. In the court's first letter opinion, the court stated: "the function upon which the Court has primarily focused ... is its service as a forum for the trial of civil and criminal matters ... [T]he courtroom has served that primary function reasonably well."[16]

The Louisa Circuit Court asserted further that "[t]he second function of the courtroom ... is its service as a place of honor for those whom the citizens of Louisa County have decided to commemorate over the decades."[17] The Louisa Circuit Court also acknowledged that "the institution of slavery was, and is, indefensible. Those who played an active role in defending the indefensible face substantial difficulty in escaping the harsh judgment of history."[18] Nevertheless, the court contended that "[t]he concern of the Defendant in this case is really not what this portrait depicts, but who it depicts."[19]

The court further observed:

> [T]here are many who admire the real or perceived qualities of General Lee. The most significant representation of that admiration is the fact that he is one of the few individuals, Virginian or otherwise, who have received the honor of having a Virginia state holiday observed in their honor. It is difficult for the Court to accept that nothing other than the implied original and continuing racism of the Virginia General Assembly supports that distinction. Being so honored makes a compelling case for the inclusion of the portrait.[20]

The court concluded that what should be done about Lee's portrait was a political decision for the Board of Supervisors of Louisa County.[21]

The Lee portrait saga did not end with the Honorable Court's first decision. The court later reconsidered and reversed its ruling. The court especially noted a number of significant developments. One new and important fact was the Virginia General Assembly repealed a statute that had created a state holiday honoring Confederate generals Robert E. Lee and Thomas "Stonewall" Jackson. The court said:

> The Court is aware of the General Assembly's action abolishing the Lee–Jackson Holiday. The Court is aware of the General Assembly's amendment of Virginia Code § 15.2-1812 to give localities their control over the disposition of war memorials. In the Court's view, these are precisely the types of action which the Court alluded to in its November 15, 2019, opinion holding that these matters were properly political matters to be addressed by the people's elected representatives.
>
> The Court continues to believe that matters of this nature would be best addressed by the people's elected representatives . . . rather than the unelected judge.[22]

The Court also stated:

> While Robert E. Lee's place in history has been controversial, undoubtedly, for some time, the tenor of that debate has changed remarkably in the ten months which have passed since the Court last addressed the issue. The image of Robert E. Lee has gone from one being deemed unworthy by some of being honored because of his significant role in a war which had a goal of preserving the institution of slavery to one of abiding racial prejudice and hatred which bears some level of responsibility for the real ills suffered by African American citizens some 150 years after his death. Despite the existence of

> legislative remedies to effect the removal of statues of Lee and other Confederate icons, criminal mayhem directed at those symbols is implicitly, and in some instances explicitly, condoned by some Commonwealth and municipal officials.
>
> Given this, the Court is compelled to conclude that the level of controversy surrounding the image of Robert E. Lee is sufficiently intense that it is foreseeable that it may impair the fair administration of justice. More importantly, given the significantly prevalent image of Robert E. Lee as a figure of racial hatred and prejudice, the Court is compelled to conclude that such image is unwelcoming to many of the African Americans, and others, who are compelled to appear in our courtroom as litigants, witnesses, jurors, attorneys, and judges.[23]

On this basis, the court ordered the Lee portrait to be removed. While overdue, the court's decision is a welcomed breath of fresh air for those who believe that justice must not only be done, but manifestly seen to be done.

Moreover, as defense counsel brilliantly argued during the Lee portrait court hearing, the Louisa Circuit Court is part of a third, equal, separate, and independent branch of government. In a court, the majority of the general public does not have the legal authority to determine what happens to the rights of unpopular individuals. Criminal defendants charged with capital murder (just like everyone else) have individual human rights secured by the Constitution of the United States. These individual rights are protected from the biases and passions of the majority. All judicial officers—state and federal—must faithfully interpret the Constitution.

To put it bluntly, the Constitution secures equal protection and due process of law as individual rights. Those rights cannot be abrogated by the vote of the people or Board of Supervisors of any jurisdiction. The court should have granted defense counsel's motion to remove the portrait of

Lee in a Confederate military uniform because it violated the defendant's right to a fair trial in a judicial environment that does not spotlight historic images of persons hostile to the defendant's life and liberty.

In these circumstances, the defendant's objection was both to whom and to what the Lee portrait depicts. Lee's life-size courtroom portrait exalted a Confederate military officer in battle regalia who led hundreds of thousands of troops in a war to destroy the United States of America. If successful, Lee's actions would have sliced the United States into two nations: one slave and the other free. Lee fought to create a new nation that would ensure continuing enslavement of African Americans like defendant Darcel Murphy.

## What to Do with Lee and Other Ex-Confederate Leaders

Situations like the Robert E. Lee military portrait occur frequently. So, what should be done? Is there no possibility of Lee being appropriately depicted in a public place—particularly a court? Stated differently, we must ask: What justification exists today for displaying a portrait of a Confederate leader like Lee in a public governmental space? Such public spaces encompass courts, legislative halls, and executive branch sites like the White House. These governmental places should be welcoming to all people of each jurisdiction.

At its root we are asking a fundamental question: How do we treat one another as we wish to be treated? How can we act in a way that is respectful of someone else's humanity?

To resolve these and similar dilemmas, we must first carefully weigh Lee's accomplishments in the scales of history. After doing so, this book outlines suggestions of how to deal with dilemmas like that confronting the Louisa Circuit Court. Hopefully, these suggestions contribute to a more constructive approach to promote community reconciliation and healing.

## Lee at the Crossroads

Here we focus mainly on two sets of Robert E. Lee's major decisions. First, we analyze Lee's actions immediately before the Civil War. Some of those acts contributed to widening the breach in national unity. Second, we evaluate Lee's behavior to restore the Union following the war. Lee's performance as a Confederate military leader is of limited historical interest. True, leading armed insurgents against the government of the United States had momentous legal implications. *Under the Constitution "levying war against [the United States]" constitutes treason.*[24] But spending lots of time talking about whether Lee was a traitor or his prowess as a military leader is unnecessary. Accordingly, our analysis begins with background information leading to Lee's decision to levy war against the United States. After that analysis, this book will consider Lee's behavior following the War.

### *The Unrepentant Lee*

In weighing Lee's behavior, we first consider the negative side of the historical scales. Our assessment includes the following.

By March 30, 1861, a number of deep southern states had declared that they intended to leave the Union. Those states had established a rebel "government" with a military wing. Lee was aware of these facts and that the threat of civil war was increasing daily. While Lee knew that secessionists were attempting to split the Union and that war might erupt at any time, on March 30, 1861, United States Army Lt. Col. Robert E. Lee accepted a commission from President Abraham Lincoln promoting Lee from lieutenant colonel to colonel.

During the two weeks after Lincoln promoted Lee to colonel, several more southern states joined the seceding crowd. Secessionists' escalated their war against the United States by attacking Fort Sumter, South Carolina. In response to this military assault, on April 15, 1861, President Lincoln issued an order mobilizing a militia of 75,000 individuals. Lincoln intended to use the militia units to save the Union from dissolution.

Two days later, April 17, 1861, Virginia cast its lot with the secessionists. The following day (April 18, 1861), through an intermediary, President Lincoln offered the newly promoted Colonel Lee the opportunity to command the 75,000-man army to restore law and order. Colonel Lee declined.[25]

On April 20, 1861, two days after refusing the offer to lead a force to preserve the Union, Lee wrote a letter resigning his commission from the United States Army. On the same day, Lee accepted an invitation to meet with representatives from Virginia's breakaway government. Two days later, on April 22, 1861, Lee was technically still a United States Army Colonel. On that day, Lee accepted a commission as a major general in Virginia's rebel army.[26] At this point, Lee was an officer in two opposing armies. On April 25, 1861, three days after he accepted the major generalship in Virginia's army, United States Army Colonel Lee's discharge from the United States Army became effective.

This sequence of events raises troubling concerns. For example, when Lincoln offered Lee the command of the Union army, did Lee have or expect a similar offer from Virginia's secessionist leaders? In fact, on May 14, 1861, less than a month after submitting his resignation from the United States Army, Lee accepted the position of Brigadier General in the Army of the Confederacy.[27]

Lee's military expertise and family prestige (his father had been a noted Revolutionary War figure and former governor of Virginia) make it reasonable to believe that Lee could have exerted some influence on Virginia secessionists to not betray the Union. It is hard to evaluate what effect Lee's intervention might have had on efforts to persuade secessionists to remain in the Union. Nevertheless, it is clear that the vote for succession (88-55) was not overwhelming. A change of 17 votes would have reaffirmed Virginia's allegiance to the United States.

From the beginning, many perceptive persons saw that Virginia would become (1) splintered, (2) the battleground for much of the bloody conflict, and (3) a participant in an effort destined to fail. From the first day, secession from the Union was truly a lost cause.

If he had chosen to do so, Lee could possibly have dissuaded secessionists from military action by pointing out that the southern states lacked both the resources and infrastructure to maintain a drawn out military campaign. Moreover, Lee could have counseled Virginia's leaders regarding the substantial risk that if Virginia seceded from the Union, the western third of the state would secede from Virginia.

One could hypothesize endlessly. Would Lee's intervention have kept Virginia in the Union? We do not know however, little evidence exists that Lee did much to keep the United States *united.* Lee used his substantial military talents to mastermind an armed rebellion. "Levying war" against the United States *equals treason under the Constitution.*

Furthermore, as has been discussed previously, what is not disputed is this: slaveholders already had significant legal protections ingrained in the Constitution. Such protections included constitutional protection of the international slave trade for 20 years, which allowed slaveholders to build a massive inventory of cheap human labor. In addition, the Constitution of the United States increased slaveholder representation in the House of Representatives and the Electoral College, as well as ensured federal help in capturing slaves and suppressing insurrections. Finally, the Framers designed a process for amending the Constitution that in practice would ensure that slavery could last indefinitely.

## *Weighing Lee's Behavior in the Scales of History: The Negative Side of the Scales*

Evaluating the negative side of the scale of history, Lee accepted a military commission from the governor of Virginia and willingly joined the rebels' attempt to forcibly and unlawfully overthrow the government of the United States. Lee's misuse of his combat talents extended the war, as well as contributed to untold additional killings, maimings, and tremendous human misery.

For many people today, as primary leader of the Confederate military forces, Lee's name conjures up the image of a defender of slavery. To many supporters of the "southern way of life," Lee remains a hero. Prominent features of such a way of living included embracing racial segregation, lynching, the Ku Klux Klan, White Citizens' Councils, and other acts promoting white supremacy. This idea of heritage is reflected in former Klan leader David Duke's visit to Richmond, Virginia, urging the reestablishment of the "General Lee" mural. Similarly, among other things, the August 11-12, 2017, "Unite the Right" rally in Charlottesville, Virginia, and its deadly aftermath represented white supremacists' attempts to affirm and glorify Lee's military efforts as well as those of other Confederate leaders. In short, for many who supported Jim Crow laws, disenfranchisement, massive resistance, and lynching, Lee is a cultural idol.

## Repentant Lee?

Having evaluated some of the negative aspects of the Lee heritage, we turn to some of his positive activities. At the end of the Civil War, Robert E. Lee surrendered. In addition, he pointedly rejected suggestions to continue a bloody guerrilla-style conflict against the U.S. government.[28] The perceptive, liberal, and conciliatory attitude of President Lincoln as implemented by General Ulysses S. Grant influenced Lee to act in many ways like a "born again" bridge builder between North and South, and to a modest extent, between Blacks and Whites.

To help smooth the transition from armed violence to peace, with President Lincoln's support and encouragement, Grant paroled Lee and the members of the Confederacy's Army of Northern Virginia. The parole recognized that Lee and other Confederate fighters were prisoners of war.[29] The parole allowed the former rebels to return home immediately provided they obeyed the law. To assist them in beginning their new lives, if they owned a horse or mule, each ex-Confederate soldier could take such an animal home with him. Former Confederate officers were even allowed to retain their sidearms.

Not long after these peaceful measures had been implemented, Lee received and initially declined the offer of the Board of Trustees to become the president of Washington College in Lexington, Virginia. Lee recognized his significant shortcomings and feared that if he accepted the Trustees' offer, his previous unpatriotic activities would inhibit and embarrass that institution's rebuilding program. Lee particularly felt uneasy about how northerners generally and philanthropists more particularly would accept him becoming president of the college. In the aftermath of a devastating conflict, Lee knew that for the college to survive, it would need significant financial support from such sources. Lee deserves commendation and respect for his self-knowledge and humility as well as his willingness to put Washington College's well-being above his own personal interests.

While Lee hesitated initially, the Trustees persisted in urging Lee to reconsider. Lee recognized the opportunity to repent and redeem himself, and seized the opportunity to remove the blemish on his name. Lee rejected an offer of an annual salary of $10,000 to head an insurance company and instead accepted an annual salary over six times smaller ($1,500) as Washington College president. The college also promised Lee a residence. Lee wound up personally having to supervise much of the renovation of the dilapidated lodgings allotted to the college president.

Furthermore, Lee turned aside invitations from various quarters to run for governor of Virginia and to oppose General Grant in the presidential election of 1868. Lee never openly criticized the Confederacy. Nevertheless, to his credit, following the War, Lee also refused to publicly participate in most partisan political activities. Moreover, and repeating for emphasis, after the Civil War, Lee could have led an armed insurgency against the United States. He did not. After conceding defeat at Appomattox, Virginia, Lee was not like some modern-day insurrectionists—namely, a sore loser. Similarly, when his military adversary, former General Ulysses Grant won the presidency, Lee accepted the will of the voters. He did not try to overthrow a validly elected national government.

In fact, rather than pursue potentially more lucrative and prestigious offices, Lee worked with great diligence and energy as Washington College president to improve the academic standards and the stature of the college. To expand the endowment and course offerings of the college, Lee tenaciously worked to rehabilitate the widely held image that he was a traitor. Lee persuaded northern philanthropists to assist in revitalizing the college.

Under Lee's administration, courses in commerce and journalism were added to the curriculum, and plans were made to develop an astronomy department as well as to enhance practical scientific course offerings. The commerce and journalism courses were among the first offered in American colleges. Lee's initiatives formed the basis for Washington and Lee's well regarded School of Commerce, Economics and Business, as well as its Department of Journalism and Mass Communications.

In addition, Lee quadrupled the student body, which had numbered only 83 on the eve of the Civil War, and he more than tripled the 5-person faculty. Lee was also instrumental in recognizing the versatility and value of legal education. In that regard, Lee succeeded in forging an agreement with Judge John W. Brockenbrough to merge Brockenbrough's Lexington Law School with Washington College. The Lexington Law School became a division of Washington College in 1870.[30]

While serving as president of Washington College, Lee confronted an especially delicate situation. One night several students from Washington College came to a business owned by a local Union Civil War veteran. The students beat on the shuttered doors and windows. They also threatened to kill the former soldier. Lee participated in an investigation of the incident and gave those involved an opportunity to withdraw from the college or be expelled.[31] Lee refused to tolerate actions that bordered on mob violence. Lee also appreciated the practical need to control rowdy students who were under the watchful eye of Union troops.

Lee's dedicated service to the college convinced the trustees to expand the institution from a college to a university. His death only five years after assuming the presidency of Washington College probably occurred for several reasons, including Lee's devoted, unrelenting college-related work. In recognition of his efforts, after his passing, the trustees added his name to that of the university.

Moreover, several anecdotes outside of the educational arena reflect favorably on Lee's character following the Civil War. These accounts merit consideration. For instance, it has been widely reported that shortly after the end of the War, when other White Christians in Richmond, Virginia, refused to accept communion with a Black brother in Christ, Lee strode forward and did so. This episode accented the genuineness of his faith.[32]

Similarly, when an embittered Confederate sympathizer asked Lee what to do about a tree that she had on her property that especially reminded her of the War, Lee is reputed to have replied, "My dear madam, cut it down, and forget it!"[33] This directive indicated Lee's desire to move beyond the ill will flowing from what has been the bloodiest conflict ever to occur in the United States.

## Conclusion

After evaluating some of the praiseworthy and blameworthy qualities of Robert E. Lee's contributions to American society, it comes down to this: as we progress through the third decade of a new millennium, we need to be honest: die-hard segregationists have continued to resist true equality of opportunity. Some of them attack the relatively modest affirmative action programs that seek to ensure that individuals from America's shutout groups can participate on an equal basis in their pursuit of happiness.

Despite such continuing obstacles, great progress has been made in the United States. For instance, in some parts of this nation, we have witnessed the first generation of persons of darker color in nearly 400 years become adults without being the targets of government-imposed segregation. They have attended public schools and universities, worked in jobs, as well as lived in neighborhoods, formerly reserved exclusively for Whites. Fifty years ago, in many parts of the country, this was impossible. Moreover, increasingly, persons who do not closely resemble the Founding Fathers have earned significant positions of authority. Nevertheless, racist laws and practices (as well as their effects) die slowly.

So, we return to the issue of how, if at all, a Confederate leader like Robert E. Lee can be appropriately recognized in a public space like the Louisa Circuit Court or other venues where governmental functions take place. A portrait of Robert E. Lee in a Confederate military uniform with a large sword sends a message that Robert E. Lee was a military warrior fighting to (1) establish the Confederate States of America as an independent nation, and (2) destroy the United States of America by force, and (3) establish a new nation founded on liberty and justice for White persons only.

To place such a symbol in a honored public place creates major unnecessary problems. The Constitution of the United States says, "Treason against the United States, shall consist only in levying War against them, or in adhering to their Enemies, giving them Aid and Comfort." Lee clad in a Confederate military uniform symbolizes an individual determined to wage war against the United States so as to dismember and destroy the Union. Based on the words of the Constitution itself, as previously mentioned, Lee's behavior during the Civil War has a legal name that rhymes with reason . . .

Moreover, Lee's behavior as a military leader bent on establishing a new government grounded on race hatred and oppression is at war with the bedrock of America's democracy—freedom and justice for all. Lee's portrayal in military dress in a courthouse is anything but benign: it is malign. Such a portrait communicates a clear and present danger to justice for every person entering such a public space.

Every moment that the image of former Confederates in Confederate military uniforms or similar attire remain staring at members of the general public in governmental buildings and on governmental grounds is a moment in which the government of all the people abdicates its duty to uphold the Constitution against those who tried and others who are attempting to dismember the United States.

In these circumstances, if the portrait of Robert E. Lee were to be displayed on the walls of any courtroom or any similar governmental venue in the United States, Lee should be portrayed in civilian dress, which he wore following the Civil War. That's the time in which Lee and the whole nation had, to a limited degree, embraced Lincoln's vision "that this nation, under God, shall have a new birth of freedom—and that government of the people, by the people, for the people, shall not perish from the earth."[34]

Before moving on to consider two other former Confederate military officers, we note that another historic sketch adorns the walls of the Louisa Circuit Court. That sketch portrays Louisa County born, African American educator, attorney, and political leader John Mercer Langston. The relatively small, modest, and inconspicuous drawing of Langston is located on the Louisa courthouse wall not too far from where once hung the domineering portrait of Lee. Langston was born free in the mid-1820s and moved to Ohio after the death of both his White father and his mother, who was a woman of color. Educated at Oberlin College, Langston became a lawyer and advocated vigorously for the Union cause during the Civil War.

Not long after the close of the War, Langston became the founding dean of the fledging Howard University School of Law in Washington, D.C.[35] In that capacity, Langston helped to furnish legal educational opportunities for individuals, particularly African Americans. Later, Howard University School of Law graduated many African American lawyers who helped to propel American society forward toward a more sane and civilized future and away from regrettable past misdeeds. The list of distinguished Howard University lawyers is too long to be reproduced here but certainly Thurgood Marshall, Spottswood Robinson, Pauli Murray are historic Howard University School of Law alumni: and, of course, the person who inspired this book—Oliver White Hill, Esq. They and many others rewrote America's human rights script for the better.

John Mercer Langston also served briefly as vice president and acting president of Howard University. Later he was instrumental in the founding of the Miner Normal School, which helped prepare African American women for teaching positions.[36]

Subsequently, Langston returned to Virginia where in December 1885 he accepted a commission to become the president of the Virginia Normal and Collegiate Institute for Negroes.[37] Virginia Normal and Collegiate Institute later evolved into the well respected educational institution Virginia State University. He resigned from the Virginia Normal and Collegiate Institute position two years later. In 1888, Langston won election to the United States House of Representatives. However, because of widespread voting fraud, voter intimidation, and election tampering, Langston's opponent was initially declared the winner. To help rig the election against him, Langston's opponents had created segregated voting lines so that White persons who were heavily outnumbered could quickly vote using one line. In contrast, African Americans had to wait in another much longer line for several hours. As Langston's opponents intended, many African Americans were denied the right to vote because they were still in the lines as the polls closed.[38]

Langston contested the result and prevailed after drawn out litigation and hearings in the House of Representatives.[39] The entrenched opposition from ex-Confederate leaders and sympathizers made it impossible for Langston to assume his seat in the House of Representatives until only a few months remained in his term.

While Langston's tenure in Congress was short, he introduced landmark legislation to create a national university for African Americans. The mission of this institution of higher learning was to

> educate and to train young men and women in all the branches of the highest scholarship and in all the callings of general industry, art, and trade, fitting all students graduating therefrom for the best possible industrial effort and scholarly professional labor in life.[40]

Langston also offered a constitutional amendment to require a literacy test for prospective voters. Langston crafted his amendment for at least two reasons. First, the most obvious justification was to help ensure a more informed electorate. The proposed amendment's second and less obvious rationale was to force southern states to support public education. Langston knew that many White men were illiterate and would not be able to vote unless the states adequately funded public schools. Langston recognized that state legislatures would have been more supportive of funding public education to lift White men into the voting ranks. Langston also believed that his amendment would have disproportionately benefited Black men because due to slavery and continuing racist educational practices, Black illiteracy rates were higher.[41] While Langston's proposed amendment would have expanded voting opportunities for men, the amendment would not have broadened the franchise to include women.

After introducing his federal legislation, Langston soon faced reelection. Due to continuing electoral chicanery, including vote fraud and voter intimidation, Langston was defeated in his attempt to retain office. Such political corruption typified many elections in the post–Reconstruction South. Regrettably, using similar vote dilution shenanigans, and targeting persons of color, members of state legislations in 45 states have recently introduced *legislation to tilt (rig?)* elections in favor of a small (predominantly White) oligarchic group.[42]

In sum, Langston's drawing deserves to be on the Louisa County Circuit courthouse walls. Lee's portrayal as a Confederate army officer does not.

As part of a limited truth and reconciliation process, we should forthrightly confess that Lee and his Confederate colleagues committed criminal acts that should be condemned. The perpetrators, Lee included, should be extended what we all need—*forgiveness.*

Having carefully weighed the matter, we are convinced that Robert E. Lee merits positive recognition for his behavior *following the Civil War*. Lee distinguished himself as a progressive educator. Unfortunately, Lee's supporters and detractors fail to give Lee adequate praise for his role as an educator and conscientious peacemaker. Indeed, not long before his own death, John Elrod, a past president of Washington and Lee University pointed out that "[t]hose who have studied his life know that Lee took much greater pride in his role as educator, mediator and conciliator."[43]

By insisting on honoring Confederate General Lee in military dress, Lee's supporters disrespect Lee. Washington College President Lee desired to put the division and bitterness of the Civil War behind us, and move forward toward a united future. As we look for a way out of the quicksand of intolerance and narrow-minded thinking, we recognize that forgiveness of confessed misdeeds is crucial to the establishment of a civilized community. As Desmond Tutu pointed out in his book *No Future Without Forgiveness*:

> To forgive is not just to be altruistic. It is the best form of self interest. What dehumanizes you, inexorably dehumanizes me. Forgiveness gives people resilience, enabling them to survive and emerge still human despite all efforts to dehumanize them.[44]

Accordingly, we recognize positive accomplishments of college president Robert E. Lee, and say to the worshipers of Confederate military leader Lee, in our judgment, you would do best to take General Douglas MacArthur's advice given to old soldiers and let your worship of Lee as a Confederate leader "just fade away." Confederate attempts to preserve slavery and overthrow the government of the United States is not American heritage—it is American horror.

Perhaps a fitting way to remember Robert E. Lee is the portrait of him as president of Washington College shown in Figure 4.

Come on! Can we talk? Why have we not learned that Hitler's Nazi movement showed there is nothing noble about fighting for white supremacy and similar "big lies"? Nevertheless, how can we dispute that "big lies" matter? They often have deadly, enduring, and even global consequences.

In sum, through carefully weighing the positive and negative contributions of historical figures like Robert E. Lee, concerned individuals can properly recognize the legacy of such controversial persons. We can and must salvage the healing aspects of our sometimes hurtful collective heritage.

## Alternatives to Lee

The behavior after the Civil War of at least two other former Confederate military officers merit close scrutiny. We should commend some of the postwar activities of

Figure 4. College President Robert E. Lee in his study at Washington College (Courtesy PBS, American Experience, available at https://www.pbs.org/wgbh/americanexperience/features/lee-gallery/)

Confederate General William "Billy" Mahone and of Confederate Chaplain Lewis Downing. We begin with Mahone.

## William "Billy" Mahone

In 1826, William "Billy" Mahone was born in Southampton County, Virginia. Mahone's father, Fielding Mahone, was a businessman who owned a farm, general store, and a local tavern. William Mahone's mother, Martha Drew, worked primarily in the home.

At first, Fielding Mahone homeschooled his son, Billy. As a teenager, Billy supplemented the homeschool education of his father by attending a nearby private school.

Later, Billy Mahone matriculated at Virginia Military Institute (VMI). At VMI, Mahone excelled in physical science and engineering. His record regarding courses in the humanities was undistinguished. After graduating from VMI, Mahone had a short stint teaching high school in Caroline County, Virginia.

Subsequently, Mahone applied for and received a job as chief engineer for the Norfolk and Petersburg Railroad. In part because Mahone devised an innovative way of transporting goods through the Great Dismal Swamp, he quickly advanced through the Norfolk and Petersburg Railroad ranks. At the age of 33 Mahone ascended to the position of president and chief engineer of the railroad.

When the Civil War erupted, Mahone swiftly joined the Confederate forces and rose to the rank of Brigadier General. In the fall of 1863, while still serving in the Confederate armed forces, Mahone was also selected to become a member of the Virginia State Senate from Norfolk. He attended his first Virginia State Senate session in the spring of 1864.

A few months later, during the Battle of the Crater in Petersburg, Virginia, troops under Mahone's command captured and summarily executed African American Union soldiers taken as prisoners of war.[45] One eyewitness account written by a Confederate soldier stated that more Blacks would have been murdered but for Mahone's personal appeal to some of his troops:

> Bayoneted, knocked on the head by the butts of muskets. all would have been killed had it not ben for Gen. Mahone, who would beg our men to spare them. one fellow in our Brigade killed several. The Gen. told him for gods sake stop. Well, Gen. let me kill one more, he deliberately took out his pocket knife and cut ones throat. Great many of the yankees officers, even Negroes, were killed on the spot.[46]

Following the Civil War, Robert E. Lee reportedly said that slavery was over forever and that the former Confederate soldiers should go home and go to work.[47] This account of Lee's perspective is consistent with the story of Lee telling a woman who had bad memories of the War whenever she looked at a particular tree to "cut it down, and forget about it." Lee recognized that the preservation of slavery, the primary reason for fighting to split the Union, could not be achieved. Taking a pragmatic approach Lee decided that the best thing for former Confederates was to adjust to changed circumstances. Practically speaking that meant many White persons would need to acclimate themselves to a new society that did not rely on enslavement of others as its principal foundation.

Mahone's post–Civil War behavior is consistent with Lee's advice. After using his sword in a futile attempt to dismember the United States, Mahone laid the sword down. Less than four months after surrendering at Appomattox, Mahone was able to negotiate the return of the Norfolk and Petersburg Railroad from the control of the U.S. military. Mahone, a recently defeated former Confederate general, resumed his position as president of the Norfolk and Petersburg Railroad.[48] In late 1865 Mahone was also elected president of the South Side Railroad, which ran through southern Virginia. The South Side Railroad had played an important role in the Confederate military effort to destroy the Union.[49]

How was it that Mahone, a leading Confederate army officer and a Confederate state senator, could so easily resume his pre–Civil War activities?

Glad you asked.

As previously mentioned, at the close of the Civil War President Lincoln advocated that members of the Union reunite with and forgive former Confederates on generous terms.[50] For example, Lincoln proposed that if at least 10% of the persons eligible to vote in 1860 in a rebel state swore an oath of allegiance to the United States Constitution and swore their support for the abolition of slavery, that the national government would protect the new 10% government from invasion or domestic violence. In addition, persons swearing Lincoln's proposed oath would be fully pardoned unless they were high-ranking Confederate military or civilian officers. Under Lincoln's plan, ex-Confederates could regain all of their property with one important exception: ex-Confederates could not re-enslave their workers.

In short, Mahone benefited from President Lincoln's and General Grant's conciliatory approach, which was later implemented by President Andrew Johnson. Along with other persons who waged war to disunite the United States, Mahone received grace extended from political decision makers who decided not to prosecute his treasonous acts. Instead of imprisonment or death, Mahone was instead quickly restored to a leading position in the business community of the post–Civil War South.

As a leading business leader, Mahone was no stranger to political intrigue. Evidence exists that in the 1869 Virginia elections, Mahone participated in a deceitful plan to have J.D. Harris, a prominent African American, nominated for lieutenant governor on the Republican Party ticket.[51] Mahone knew that Harris' presence on the Republican ticket would spark a broad White male backlash in favor of the Conservative Party candidates. Because White male voters outnumbered Black male voters, Mahone hoped to orchestrate both the nomination and election of a Conservative gubernatorial ticket.

Mahone's plan worked and a slate of candidates were elected who were successful in ensuring that most former Confederate supporters could vote. Due in part to Mahone's efforts, the post–Civil War electorate in Virginia included many former Confederate military personnel like himself who had attempted to destroy the United States.[52]

According to Nelson Blake, one of Mahone's principal biographers, during the Virginia gubernatorial campaign of 1873, Mahone again engaged in several underhanded practices:

[Mahone] was credited with various types of strategy in order to control the negro vote and aid the Conservative cause. One of these was the use of tissue ballots by Conservative voters. These ballots were so thin that a number of them could be used in place of a single ballot of the usual thickness. When tissue ballots were used, it often happened that the number of votes cast in an election outnumbered those who were registered to vote. This made it necessary to reduce the votes to the number of registered voters. A man was selected for this purpose and carefully blindfolded. Being in sympathy with the Conservatives he made it a point to withdraw none of the tissue ballots. As a result of this chicanery a large number of the negro ballots were extracted and their vote was correspondingly decreased. [Conversations with Senator Carter Glass, Lynchburg, Virginia.] Another scheme of Mahone's to lessen the negro vote was made possible by his employment of hundreds of negroes on his railroad. On election day he would send out a train crew of negroes to make repairs on some portion of the track. Their return home would be delayed until late at night, making it impossible for them to take part in the election. Other schemes, as well, were resorted to in order to reduce, or to control, the negro vote. [Conversations with Dr. C.S. Dodd, Petersburg, Virginia. Mahone Collection. R.F. Walker, Richmond, to William Mahone, July 1, 1873.] These steps were taken by Mahone in a sincere belief that the end justified the means, and that the triumph of the Conservative candidate was essential to the best interests of the State. These methods, open to criticism as they are, were certainly no more objectionable than the use of intimidation and fraud in many other southern states during the same period.[53]

These vote fraud tactics suppressed the African American vote and facilitated the election of conservative White candidates.

In Virginia's 1873 statewide elections, Mahone supported the Conservative Party candidate, former Confederate General James Lawson Kemper. The Conservative Party swept to power statewide, and predictably made it more difficult for many Virginians to vote.[54] For example, the Conservatives resurrected the poll tax, which muffled the right to vote of economically distressed males in Virginia.

Compounding the societal situation confronting many Virginians, Virginia and much of the United States suffered an economic depression. The economic downturn exacerbated the Commonwealth's already compromised financial condition.

In these circumstances, Mahone felt strongly that it was a mistake to pay Virginia's pre–Civil War debt in full. The majority of the Commonwealth's tax revenues went to pay the past debt rather than invest in the future through funding public education as well as repairing and rebuilding transportation infrastructure.

During the antebellum period, Virginia's state-funded free schools were commonly looked down on as "pauper schools." No self-respecting White family would send its children to such schools. After the war many White persons retained this traditional hostility to the public schools.

Moreover, several other objections to public schools were cited. For instance, anti–public education advocates argued that the public school system was of foreign origin imposed on former Confederates by their Union conquerors. Some opponents of public schools argued that the purpose of the schools was to break down social ranks and establish the equality of the races. In any event, public school detractors contended that the experiment was much too costly to be tried while the Commonwealth was in such an impoverished condition.[55]

The Commonwealth's debts were owed principally to large bondholders, many of whom lived in the United Kingdom as well as in some northern states. The Commonwealth's debt strangled the ability of the state to quickly recover from the ravages of war.

In addition, the economic depression of 1873 led to Mahone's railroads being forced into bankruptcy. Mahone suffered substantial personal financial loss. In this context, Mahone turned from supporting the Conservative Party and helped to create a new political coalition commonly referred to as the Readjusters. The Readjusters forged a coalition of middle- and working-class Whites as well as Blacks. Led by Mahone, in the 1879 elections the Readjusters took control of both houses of the Virginia State Legislature.[56]

The Readjusters delivered on their campaign promises. They wasted no time in passing legislation to substantially cut the state debt, increasing funding for public schools, abolishing the whipping post, and establishing elections based on voting by secret ballots rather than by voice. The Readjusters also amended Virginia's Constitution to eliminate the poll tax.

A lasting contribution of the Readjuster legislature occurred when Delegate A.W. Harris, an African American member of the Virginia General Assembly from Petersburg, introduced legislation that when enacted, resulted in the creation of the Virginia Normal and Collegiate Institute.[57] This institution later became Virginia State University.[58] Harris was also a lawyer and respected community leader who graduated from Howard University School of Law.

According to renowned historian and former University of Richmond President Edward Ayers, the Readjuster Party in Virginia stood out for one reason in particular: during the Reconstruction period, the Readjuster Party was the only progressive political organization in the former Confederacy to win statewide office and effect significant reforms. Ayers states:

> Yet only Virginia under Mahone was able to put together a broad coalition that effectively wielded statewide power for even a short time. The fault lines in the other coalitions, lines of race, subregion, and doubt, widened under Democratic charges of disloyalty to race and region. Established Republicans were reluctant to share offices with erstwhile Democrats, and the Republican administrations in Washington reconsidered the wisdom of handing out patronage to independents who were no more able to claim a victory than the regular Republicans had been. No other anti-Democratic leader in the South possessed the connections and the acumen of William Mahone. The task of forging a new coalition overwhelmed everyone else who tried, and no other insurgent party came up with an issue that bridged the class and racial divides of the New South. The Democrats did not hesitate to return to the methods they had used to gain power in the seventies. Wielding fraud, bribery, and intimidation, they gave their opposition little time or space in which to develop a coherent and long lived party.[59]

In 1881, the Readjusters in the Virginia General Assembly elected William Mahone to the United States Senate. At the national level, Mahone was the pivotal vote in an equally divided Senate. Choosing to caucus with the Republican Party, Mahone's vote facilitated national Republicans' agenda and allowed Mahone to direct federal resources to help revitalize the physical infrastructure in Virginia. For example, in a thoughtful biography, Professor John Chappo points out that Mahone supported capital improvements to public buildings in Virginia municipalities as well as enhancements for wharfs, harbors, and rivers.[60]

Mahone also rewarded his supporters at the local level with patronage jobs. According to Professor James Tice Moore, under Mahone's Readjusters:

> The debt revolt also created hundreds of jobs for the racial minority. Black teachers took charge of the education of their race, frequently displacing whites; Negro doctors and professors held important posts at the new state institutions; blacks served as government clerks, prison guards, and postal workers. After a decade of political impotence, the freedmen shared the benefits of a civil rights revolution.[61]

Compared to the prior negligible patronage appointments made under Conservative Party administrations, the number of African Americans receiving such positions under Mahone's Readjusters was remarkable.[62]

However, Mahone's coalition split apart largely because of effective Conservative Party attacks based on race. The Conservatives marketed themselves as the party of white supremacy, gave themselves a new name—Democrats—and argued that the Readjusters supported Africanization as well as Black political domination of Whites. In 1883, these appeals along with a race riot in Danville, Virginia, near the time of the election, galvanized the White vote in favor of the former Conservatives who regained control of both houses of the Virginia State legislature.[63] In 1885, the Conservatives, again masquerading under the label of the Democratic Party, won the governorship. In doing so the more conservative party—the Democrats—gained control of all branches of the state government.

Evidence also exists that Mahone contributed to dividing his own coalition along the color line. He actively engaged in efforts to sabotage the congressional candidacy of African American lawyer, educator, and former diplomat, John Mercer Langston.

According to Langston's autobiography, Mahone objected to having an African American represent the congressional district in which Mahone lived. Langston asserted that Mahone methodically implemented a plan that denied

Langston the Republican Party nomination for Congress. When Langston managed to get on the ballot as an Independent, Mahone conspired with White Democratic Party members to defeat Langston at the polls.[64] Ultimately, as noted before, Langston was seated. Langston was imminently qualified. However, Mahone and other White Readjuster opposition to Langston's candidacy helped to undermine Republican/Readjuster Party unity.

In this vein, also contributing to the Readjusters' demise was Mahone's authoritarian leadership style. Mahone demanded strict allegiance of Readjuster Party members to the Readjuster platform that he had created. In response, some former Readjuster Party leaders and members deserted Mahone as well as the Readjuster Party. The Readjuster coalition gradually disintegrated. In 1887, the Conservative-controlled Virginia legislature refused to reelect Mahone to the United States Senate.[65]

## Comparing and Contrasting Lee and Mahone

When briefly comparing and contrasting Robert E. Lee and William Mahone, a few things stand out. First, to the credit of Lee and Mahone, when the Civil War ended, they both laid down their weapons. In doing so, they spared an already bloodied nation the trauma of intense, pervasive, organized, violent insurrections. Lee and Mahone set positive examples of former soldiers who chose to put away their swords and pursue more peaceful endeavors. Such examples might well have encouraged their former Confederate military comrades to do likewise.

In addition, both Lee and Mahone helped to contribute to broader post–secondary educational opportunities although for different constituencies. At Washington College, Lee helped to establish three new academic divisions: a Law School, a Department of Commerce, and a Department of Journalism, as well as a variety of undergraduate course offerings in diverse areas, including business, journalism, modern languages, applied mathematics, and natural sciences. He also substantially increased both Washington College's student body and faculty. In so doing, Lee helped to propel the college forward into becoming a more modern educational institution. Of course, like many other private colleges and universities of the time, Washington College served a privileged minority: the college was an all-White male institution.

Washington and Lee University subsequently has made an indelible imprint locally and well beyond.

Mahone contributed to broadening educational opportunities on wider and deeper levels. He played a significant role in establishing public primary and secondary schools in Virginia. Mahone helped to ensure that these public schools were much better funded than antebellum pauper schools. His efforts made it possible for economically disadvantaged persons of all complexions to obtain the benefit of a public school education.

Mahone facilitated more educational possibilities for a particular subset of Virginians who had historically been excluded from taxpayer-funded public education—namely, African Americans. The Readjusters helped to increase by severalfold the number of public schools and teachers for African Americans. By supporting legislation that established the Virginia Normal and Collegiate Institute for Negroes (later Virginia State University), the Mahone-led Readjusters extended public education opportunities to African Americans at the post–high school level. Mahone ensured that taxpayer dollars would no longer support public education for Whites only. However, the public schools were segregated on the basis of race. Race segregation made it easier for governmental officials to discriminate in favor of White students and against students of color.

Mahone's practical constructive influence on the lives of people in Virginia was more extensive than Lee's. For instance, Mahone supported the enactment of laws that reformed the social order by ridding Virginia of the slave-era relic of terror and oppression—the public whipping post. The whipping post was a sadistic public place where persons who sought to escape the brutality of enslavement could be tortured by being brutally beaten or (even killed) while other enslaved persons were forced to witness the terrifying spectacle.

Furthermore, Mahone headed a political party that succeeded in widening access to political participation through the abolition of the poll tax. Abolishing the poll tax helped to facilitate access to voting for impoverished persons of all skin tones. In addition, by eliminating the requirement that votes be cast publicly by voice, more vulnerable persons could vote their conscience secretly. The secret ballot insulated such persons from intimidation by employers, vigilantes, and others who sought to influence their electoral choices.

Moreover, Mahone set an important public example in political affairs by treating African Americans with a modest measure of respect. African Americans who worked for the Readjuster Party, like their White counterparts, were rewarded with federal patronage jobs. For Mahone, treating African Americans with respect had limits: Mahone steadfastly rebelled against supporting John Mercer Langston, an African American, as Mahone's congressman. Like many politicians, then and now, race sometimes trumped party.

Political opponents used allegiance to white supremacy as a litmus test to help destroy the Readjuster Party. Nevertheless, Mahone refrained from publicly espousing a doctrine of White domination.

Mahone was a man of his times.

All things considered, Mahone's contributions were more worthy of emulation than Lee's. An important consideration in preferring Mahone's post–Civil War record to Lee's is Mahone's important work to create and propel a progressive multichromatic ("rainbow") political coalition. Relative to other political alliances of its era, the Readjuster Party embraced some constructive ideas that improved the lives of most Virginians to this day. The Readjusters did so following the bloodiest war in American history.

## Lewis Downing[66]

Lewis Downing began his life's journey in 1823 in Tennessee. His ancestors were Cherokees, English, and Irish. Located geographically in the southern states, the Cherokee Nation was heavily influenced by its White American neighbors. The Cherokees adopted the regrettable American practice of enslaving human beings.

Cherokee enslavement had some notable differences. For example, some Cherokee laws were harsher against enslavers than the enslaved. Noted historian Theda Perdue says:

> The paucity of laws governing the behavior of masters and slaves in the preremoval Cherokee slave code stands in stark contrast to the multitude of provisions of the white antebellum South. Noticeably lacking in the Cherokee code are laws dealing with insubordination and rebellion, and the majority of punishments are reserved for the masters and not the slaves. The law penalized the person who bought goods from slaves, the masters who allowed their slaves to buy or sell liquor, and the whites or Indians who married slaves. Even the hysteria which usually accompanied any suggestion of sexual relationships between white women and blacks is missing, and white or Indian women who indulged in interracial sex suffered fourteen fewer stripes than men. The discrepancies between the slave code of the Cherokee Nation and the codes of the white society which many Cherokees were trying to emulate can only be explained in terms of the enduring power of Cherokee cultural traditions.[67]

Nevertheless, even though only a minority of Cherokees were slaveholders, those who did hold slaves were very influential. Eleven of the twelve signers of the Cherokee Constitution were slaveholders.[68]

As a teenager, Lewis Downing became a refugee: he and his family were forcibly removed from their home and trod the Trail of Tears to Indian Territory, which later became the state of Oklahoma. Downing came under the influence of Baptist missionaries and converted to Christianity. At the age of 21 he became a Baptist minister and pastor of the Flint Baptist Church in Adair County, Oklahoma. Downing also had substantial interaction with the Keetoowah Society, which advocated maintenance of Cherokee cultural practices and values.[69]

In the early 1840s, Downing became active in Cherokee political affairs and served as a Senator in the Cherokee legislature. He aligned himself with the Cherokee's Principal Chief, John Ross, who advocated that the Cherokees remain neutral in the impending American Civil War.

In the aftermath of the Union soldiers' retreat from Cherokee territories and the advance of Confederate armed forces toward the Cherokees' land, Principal Chief Ross decided to ally the Cherokee Nation with the Confederacy. A number of Cherokees, especially Cherokee slaveholders, endorsed Ross' position. Some Cherokees who identified with the Confederacy formed their own regiment.

On the other hand, Downing sympathized with the Union cause. He nevertheless joined a Cherokee regiment in the Confederate armed forces. However, Downing's regiment was principally comprised of persons who were inclined, if the opportunity arose, to support the Union. Such an opportunity arose early in the Civil War. In March 1862, the Confederates suffered a significant defeat at Pea Ridge, Arkansas. Several months following the Confederate loss, Downing, who was a Chaplain, led 200 Cherokee Confederate soldiers to cross battle lines and join the Union Army.[70] Downing became a lieutenant colonel fighting for the Union.[71]

Downing also was a leader in helping the Cherokee Nation to adopt an emancipation proclamation that freed enslaved persons held by citizens of the Cherokee Nation. Because a significant number of materially wealthy Cherokees were slaveholders, many Cherokee slaveholders rejected the Cherokee Emancipation. Accordingly, in practice the Cherokee Emancipation had little effect.

Shortly after the Civil War, in 1866 the U.S. Congress ratified a treaty that fractured Cherokee landownership. Rather than one large reserve, Cherokee land was splintered into thousands of parcels, most of which were 160 acres.[72] In the 1866 Treaty, Congress also provided for a section of Cherokee lands to be divided among Blacks formerly enslaved by the Cherokees. Much of Cherokee land that was not parceled out in these relatively modest allotments wound up in the hands of railroads and non-Cherokee individuals.

In the wake of the Civil War and substantial societal upheaval, Lewis Downing sought to unite the Cherokee Nation. Downing was elected Principal Chief in 1867. Downing sought to reconcile Cherokees who supported the Union with those who fought for the Confederacy. He also tried to ensure that African Americans formerly enslaved by Cherokees received the land that Congress mandated by statute. And he advocated that members of the Cherokee Nation embrace formerly enslaved African Americans as citizens.

For many reasons, Downing's efforts met with limited success. He introduced, but was unable to garner sufficient support to pass, legislation that would have alleviated conditions faced by formerly enslaved African Americans. For instance, Downing's initiatives would have helped to upgrade substandard segregated schools and address the lack of support for orphaned children. In his first State of the Union Address to the Cherokee Nation, Downing said: "Our laws should be uniform, the jurisdiction of our Courts should be the same over every part of our Nation and over every individual citizen."[73]

In 1871, shortly after being reelected, Principal Chief Lewis Downing died.[74]

## Final Notes on Three Former Confederate Soldiers

A few final comments are in order. After surrendering at Appomattox, Confederate General Robert E. Lee stopped participating in armed fighting to destroy the United States. In doing so, Lee set an important example for soldiers formerly under his command. In addition, we need to highlight Lee's post-war activities as a forward-thinking educator.

Like Lee, former Confederate General William Mahone modeled constructive steps toward peacemaking when he too laid down his arms. Furthermore, Mahone made noteworthy contributions to boost Virginia's public education and physical infrastructure.

Finally, former Confederate Chaplain Lewis Downing stands out for his courage and wisdom in leading 200 Confederate soldiers across battle lines to join the Union forces. In so doing, Downing helped his "flock" to serve their country in a way that better honored their sacrifice and promoted a society dedicated to universal justice. He made determined efforts to promote healing within the Cherokee Nation and to integrate African American freed persons into the Cherokee community. Downing's efforts bore limited fruit.

## Facing the Future

Regarding our human heritage, what should we keep and what should we forsake?

The struggle about what to do with images of former Confederate leaders like Robert E. Lee symbolizes challenges not only in the United States but worldwide. In the United States, we need to tell a more complete story of U.S. history. Where possible, we should highlight facts that point toward unity and reconciliation rather than discord and societal disunion.

In the global context, competing stories involving different perceptions and interpretations of heritage plague our small cosmic spaceship that we call planet earth. For instance, the government of Israel and Hamas are engaging in a brutal, escalating armed conflict that already has resulted in psychological trauma to hundreds of thousands of Israelis and Palestinians with no clear end in sight. Unknown numbers of innocent civilians have died. Competing versions of history and current events undermine peacemaking. Likewise, different perceptions of the past as well as the present fuel the massacre of vulnerable human beings in Sudan. Similar competing and conflicting stories exist in Bosnia, Sri Lanka, South Africa, and Iraq. Existing conflicts between Russia and Ukraine as well as impending ones involving China and Taiwan threaten to explode, metastasize, and imperil human survival.

The examples could be multiplied almost endlessly. Even the "facts" of history are in dispute—some people still are trying to prove that American slavery was not all that bad and others contend that the Holocaust never even happened.

# Epilogue

## Reflections on Race, Democracy, and Revival

From the beginning of European settlement of the North American continent, compelling evidence exists that American society was structured so that the actual and intended beneficiaries of its wealth, status, and power would primarily be affluent White males. Until the end of the Civil War, under the law, Whites exercised unlimited power over 4 million enslaved Blacks. Following the Civil War, significant but incomplete progress has been made to erase the legacy of the pre–Civil War slave regime and the post–Civil War Jim Crow era. It is a historical fact that the color of a person's skin, not individual merit, often determined the benefits of America's apartheid system. This fact is unsettling. What is more unsettling, and difficult for many persons to accept, is that White persons continue to reap advantages from a social system tilted in their favor. Often such individuals do not have a clue—or perhaps refuse to take one.

The truth and reconciliation process confronts yet another adversary: the rise of far right fascist movements in the United States and European nations. The current neo-Nazi revival has an underlying theme that echoes *Dred Scott*: "The Negro has no rights that the white man is bound to respect." The persistent notion that the law can abuse a societal group—Negroes—at will and render members of that group defenseless undergirds twenty-first-century efforts to ensure that other societal scapegoats like persons of color, members of the LGBTQ+ community, Muslims, Jews, and individuals within similar marginalized groups are legally shackled as well as physically intimidated. Legislators, judges, and other policy makers are forging legal chains that would render millions of persons powerless to decide important matters like who and how to love, where to live, when or whether to start a family, and whether or not to believe in a deity. Members of radical right-wing groups have reinforced governmental suppression of the rights of the less privileged. Such private terrorist tactics include death threats both against those who have spoken out in favor of the less privileged as well some public servants like election officials who simply tried to do their jobs and accurately count votes. Governmental and private suppression of individual liberty illuminate a recurrent historical thread (noose?!) brilliantly summed up by Martin Luther King Jr.'s prescient statement in his "Letter from Birmingham Jail": "*Injustice anywhere is a threat to justice everywhere.*"[1]

In America today, the threat to liberty and justice for all is clear, present, and potentially fatal.

Today the people of the United States remain deprived of the right to directly elect their President. Why in 2024 do we still have an Electoral College? In 2000 and 2016, the Founders' minority rule Constitution subverted the will of most Americans who voted for President. The candidates who received less votes from the American people—George W. Bush and Donald J. Trump—became President.

Twenty-first-century vote nullification and similar shenanigans flow from prior American precedents beginning with the 1787 minority rule Constitution. Today's attempts to create a national architecture of political corruption—rigging elections for the politically powerful—draws from the 1787 Constitution. The culture encouraging vote fraud, violence, and impunity flowing from the post-Reconstruction ex-Confederacy still exists—and is intensifying. A salient modern example of such corrupt behavior is the January 6, 2021, attempt to overthrow the government of the United States by force.

The continuing concerted efforts—brazen and incessant—to smother freedom in the United States and install an illegitimate sham democracy may yet succeed. If counterfeit patriots achieve their objectives, the fall of American democracy could portend the demise of liberty in much of the world.

In these circumstances, we must keep our eyes on the primary prize of the twenty-first century—human survival and progress. To achieve it, as Oliver W. Hill said, we must work zealously toward a renaissance in human relations.[2] Put another way: To overcome such threats to liberty and justice, we need a global revival of peace, justice, and love among all human earthlings. A good first step is to follow the Spirit and Jesus' words: "In all things do unto others as you would have them do unto you."

Appendix

# Principal Chief Lewis Downing and the Reconciliation of Cherokee Nation

By Flannery O'Rourke

"OUR PAST HISTORY HAS TAUGHT US that dissentions and party feuds, and *the remembrance of past wrongs* only have a tendency to mar our happiness and retard our civilization."[1] At first blush, Cherokee Nation Principal Chief Lewis Downing's 1868 statement against remembrance appears contrary to philosopher George Santayana's admonition, recited in this book's prologue, that to forget history, is to repeat history.[2] But upon closer inspection, Principal Chief Downing was advocating not for historical amnesia, but for the amnesty necessary for present and future peace both within

[1] Letter of the Secretary of the Interior to the Chairman of the Committee on Indian Affairs, communicating amendments to the Cherokee Treaty concluded July 9, 1868. S. Misc. Doc. No. 148, 41st Cong., 2nd Sess. (1870), available at https://digitalcommons.law.ou.edu/cgi/viewcontent.cgi?article=8978&context=indianserialset [hereinafter Letter of the Secretary]. Principal Chief Downing was responding to the United States' proposed amendments to the Cherokee Treaty of 1866.

[2] The exact quote is: "Those who cannot remember the past are condemned to repeat it." 1 George Santayana, THE LIFE OF REASON: OR THE PHASES OF HUMAN PROGRESS 284 (1905).

Cherokee Nation and between the Nation and the U.S.[3] As a Baptist Minister, Principal Chief Downing believed forgiveness was necessary to heal his divided Cherokee Nation.[4] And heal, he did. Principal Chief Downing is credited with the reconciliation of Cherokee Nation after the Civil War.[5] To better understand Principal Chief Downing's work, a brief history lesson is first necessary. For while Principal Chief Downing did not advocate for historical ignorance, Cherokee Nation's enslavement of Black persons, subsequent role in the Civil War, and relationship with the Freedmen thereafter is oft forgotten. After this background, Principal Chief Downing's personal and political history will be considered. Finally, as epilogue, Cherokee Nation's more recent division is reviewed.

## Black Enslavement in Cherokee Nation

Cherokee Nation, like the other Nations constituting the "Five Civilized Tribes" enslaved Black persons in the nineteenth century.[6] These Nations were so named for their successful conver-

---

[3] Principal Chief Downing advocated for the following language to be added to the 1866 Treaty with the U.S.: "And a general amnesty is hereby agreed upon, and a full pardon granted to all the citizens of the Cherokee nation for all crimes and misdemeanors committed between and among themselves as well as between them and citizens of the United States, up to the date of the ratification of this treaty." Letter of the Secretary, *supra* note 1.

[4] Morris L. Wardell, A POLITICAL HISTORY OF THE CHEROKEE NATION 210 (1938).

[5] Bryan Pollard, *How the US Civil War Divided Indian Nations* History (Nov. 23, 2020), https://www.history.com/news/civil-war-native-american-indian-territory-cherokee-home-guard; Sean Rowley, *Chief Downing Helped Nation Heal After Civil War* Tahlequah Daily Press (Nov. 10, 2017), https://www.tahlequahdailypress.com/news/chief-downing-helped-nation-heal-after-civil-war/article_ecda8870-7c49-58db-89d5-b16345f3bd42.html.

[6] Angie Debo, *And Still the Waters Run: The Betrayal of the Five Civilized Tribes* Loc. 417 (1968 Kindle Edition). The other Nations were the Muscogee (Creek), Chickasaw, Chocktaw, and Seminole Nations.

sion through the United States' "civilization"[7] program with Native Nations.[8] For Cherokee Nation, adoption of the Anglo-American system of property ownership and economic development required abandoning traditional Cherokee beliefs and practices.[9] For example, in Cherokee Nation, roles were gendered.[10] Women were responsible for agricultural work, whereas men were responsible for hunting.[11] However, as the Nation was induced to cede increasing acreage of land required for hunting, men soon were pushed into the agricultural realm.[12] This blurring of the gender lines combined with the U.S. civilization policy pushed Cherokee Nation into adoption of chattel enslavement.

Chattel enslavement, however, was never universally adopted by the Nation.[13] As of 1835, fewer than eight percent of Cherokee households enslaved Black persons.[14] However, nearly a decade earlier, upon passage of the Cherokee Constitution, eleven out of twelve signers of the Constitution were slaveholders.[15] The signers were further distinguished from the rest of Cherokee Nation by their extreme wealth.[16] Given this confluence of characteristics, it is unsurprising that nearly 40% of the laws passed by the General Council after the 1827 Constitution protected property rights.[17] Cherokee Nation rose to the top of the class in the U.S. civilization program through adopting the U.S. approaches to property,

---

7 Theda Perdue, Slavery and the Evolution of Cherokee Society 50 (1979).

8 Debo, *supra* note 6.

9 Perdue, *supra* note 7.

10 *Id.* at 51.

11 *Id.* at 52.

12 *Id.* at 53.

13 *Id.* at 57.

14 *Id.*

15 *Id.*

16 *Id.* at 56.

17 *Id.*

economic development, and governmental structure, down to the oligarchical leadership.

But prior to Removal, chattel enslavement in Cherokee Nation nevertheless remained distinct from the U.S. form.[18] Cherokee Nation laws regarding enslavement generally punished the enslavers, rather than the persons enslaved.[19] Further, contrary to state laws providing more egregious punishments for white women engaging in relationships with Black men, Native women were subjected to lesser punishments for relationships with Black persons than their male counterparts.[20] Thus, Cherokee Nation's initial adoption of chattel enslavement was an "attempt to imitate the plantation society of the white South,"[21] but not a mirror image.

Unsurprisingly, the Cherokee form of chattel enslavement was inextricable from the U.S. racial hierarchy. In 1835, seventy-eight percent of slaveholders in Cherokee Nation had white ancestry.[22] The implementation of plantation slavery split the Nation along economic and cultural lines.[23] The National Party viewed enslavement as an encroachment of white values on Cherokee land.[24] Ironically, the party was led by Principal Chief John Ross, who was a wealthy enslaver.[25] The Treaty Party, led by Stand Watie, advocated for assimilation to white society, including enslavement, as well as renunciation of Cherokee's Nation's uncivilized practices.[26]

Removal only exacerbated the divisions within the Nation. In 1835, in the absence of Principal Chief Ross, Treaty Party member Major Ridge signed the Treaty of New Echota, agreeing to the voluntary removal of the Nation.[27] Cession of Cherokee land was

---

[18] *Id.* at 57.

[19] *Id.*

[20] *Id.* at 57-58.

[21] *Id.* at 58.

[22] *Id.* at 60.

[23] *Id.* at 68.

[24] *Id.* at 69.

[25] *Id.*

[26] *Id.*

[27] Treaty with the Cherokees, 1835, 7 Stat. 478.

a capital offense in the Nation.[28] Thus, after the Trail of Tears in 1838,[29] Major Ridge and his conspirators were promptly executed in 1839.[30]

In the aftermath of Removal, Cherokee Nation was in chaos.[31] Enslaved children were kidnapped.[32] Free Black persons were seized and sold.[33] Yet, ironically, the chaos made Cherokee Nation a haven for runaway slaves from the Southern states.[34] Moreover, some Cherokee citizens who did not engage in enslavement provided refuge for persons who escaped enslavement.[35] Without this aid, the escape of persons enslaved by Cherokee citizens was difficult, as the enslaved persons predominantly spoke Cherokee.[36] Consequently, persons who escaped enslavement within Cherokee Territory, remained in the territory.[37]

For those Black persons trapped within Cherokee Nation's territory, conditions dramatically worsened throughout the post-Removal period.[38] In 1839, the Nation adopted a new constitution spelling out the inferiority of Black persons.[39] In 1841, the Cherokee General Council outlawed the education of Black persons, whether free or enslaved.[40] An 1842 Act subsequently excluded all free Black persons from the Nation, other than those emancipated

---

28 Perdue, *supra* note 7, at 73.

29 Brian Hicks, *The Cherokees vs. Andrew Jackson*, Smithsonian Magazine (Mar. 2011), https://www.smithsonianmag.com/history/the-cherokees-vs-andrew-jackson-277394/.

30 Perdue, *supra* note 7, at 73.

31 *Id.* at 76.

32 *Id.*

33 *Id.*

34 *Id.* at 79.

35 *Id.* at 80.

36 *Id.* at 82.

37 *Id.*

38 *Id.* at 84.

39 *Id.*

40 *Id.* at 88.

by Cherokee citizens.[41] Thus, the U.S. act of removing Cherokee Nation from the last of its ancestral lands led to Cherokee Nation's further entrenchment of the U.S. racial hierarchy. The oppression of Cherokee Nation directly begot the oppression of Black persons.

The increasing harshness in the treatment of Black persons in Cherokee Nation did not indicate a universal acceptance of enslavement by the Nation. While Cherokee citizen's post-Removal enslavement of Black persons was just as egregious as enslavement in the states,[42] most Cherokee citizens did not engage in enslavement. For example, whereas in 1860 only two percent of Cherokee households engaged in enslavement, closer to twenty percent of households in the Southern states enslaved persons.[43] Further, the influence of Baptist missionaries led by Welsh-born Evan Jones, spurred a growing contingency of Cherokee Nation calling for abolition.[44] Thus, in the advent of the U.S. Civil War, Cherokee Nation divided over whether to join the Confederate cause.[45]

Opposing coalitions formed. Stand Watie, formerly of the Treaty party, formed the Knights of the Golden Circle.[46] The group, self-described as half bloods, advocated for slavery and against the neutrality supported by Principal Chief Ross.[47] Thus, the Golden Knights were eager to join the Confederate cause.[48] In contrast, Ross's supporters were made up of members of the Keetoowah

41 *Id.* at 85.

42 Bernard Vincent, *Slaveholding Indians: The Case of Cherokee Nation* 14 DEP (2006).

43 Rick Rouan, *Fact Check: Stat Grossly Misleading About Slave Ownership in 1860*, USA Today (Jul. 16, 2021), https://www.usatoday.com/story/news/factcheck/2021/07/16/fact-check-social-media-post-underrepresents-slave-ownership-1860/7980243002/. The rate was 38% in Georgia, the state from which Cherokee Nation removed. Vincent, *supra* note 42, at 13.

44 Perdue, *supra* note 7, at 123.

45 *Id.* at 129.

46 *Id.*

47 *Id.* at 129-30.

48 *Id.*

Society.[49] The Keetoowah Society was a Baptist organization[50] made up of "full bloods" who advocated for abolition and a return to Cherokee tradition.[51] Lewis Downing was a lead member of the Society. Thus, from here the story of Cherokee Nation, and that of Downing, is inextricably linked.

## Lewis Downing

Lewis Downing was born in Tennessee in 1823.[52] At age 16, he and his family were subjected to the forced westward removal of Cherokee Nation constituting the Trail of Tears.[53] Subsequently, as a disciple of Evan Jones, Downing was ordained as a minister by age 21, and then became a member of the Keetoowah Society.[54] Despite the Keetoowah Society's identification as "full bloods", Downing was only half blood, and bore Cherokee, Irish, and British lineage.[55] This indicates that the Nation used the language of blood quantum to indicate political or cultural preference, rather than ancestry.[56] For example, while the Keetowah Society "full bloods" favored a return to Cherokee culture, the "half bloods" of the Knights of the Golden Circle argued for further assimilation into white society.[57] Downing's support of traditionalism later

---

[49] *Id.* at 130.

[50] Scott Vezeau & Ronald S. Coddington, *Here Among the Chiefs: The Cherokee Nation's Lewis Downing, in Gray and Blue* 64 MI (2018).

[51] Perdue, *supra* note 7, at 130.

[52] John Bartlett Meserve, *Chief Lewis Downing and Chief Charles Thompson (Oochalata)* 317 Chron. of Ok. Vol. 16, No. 3 (Sept. 1938).

[53] Vezeau & Coddington, *supra* note 50, at 63.

[54] *Id.* at 64.

[55] Bethany R. Berger, *"Power Over this Unfortunate Race": Race, Politics and Indian Law in United States v. Rogers*, 45 Wm. & Mary L. Rev. 1957, 2023-25 (2024).

[56] *Id.*

[57] *Id.*

would lead him to serve as Principal Chief Ross's delegate,[58] and even acting replacement.[59]

Downing's political career began a year after becoming pastor of First Baptist Church in 1844.[60] In 1845, he was elected senator of the Goingnake District.[61] He subsequently was elected to Senate in 1851 and again in 1859.[62] He served as a Cherokee Nation delegate to Washington in 1851.[63]

As Downing's political role in the Nation expanded, the Nation's role in the ensuing discord amongst the American states remained unclear. Downing supported Principal Chief John Ross's call for neutrality.[64] However, Principal Chief John Ross's position was not altogether altruistic. Cherokee Nation held dual loyalties.[65] The Nation held allegiance to the U.S. for federal protections.[66] But the Nation also held close ties to the Southern states in which the Nation was assimilated.[67] As an enslaver, Principal Chief Ross also presumed that the U.S. treaty commitments to protect Cherokee Nation property would include human property (enslaved persons).[68] But even as Ross came to renounce slavery, he underestimated the role enslavement played in the economic advancement of citizens of the Nation.[69] Thus, as Stand Watie's Knights of the Golden Circle faction loomed large, and with the abandonment of Union troops from the Cherokee Territory, and simultaneous advancement of Southern troops, Ross caved.[70] By October 1861,

---

58 Vezeau & Coddington, *supra* note 50, at 65.

59 Meserve, *supra* note 52, at 319.

60 *Id.* at 317.

61 *Id.* at 318.

62 *Id.*

63 *Id.*

64 Vezeau & Coddington, *supra* note 50, at 64.

65 Perdue, *supra* note 7, at 127.

66 *Id.*

67 *Id.*

68 *Id.*

69 *Id.* at 129.

70 *Id.* at 131.

Principal Chief Ross signed a treaty aligning Cherokee Nation with the South.[71]

Downing subsequently joined the 1st Cherokee Regiment as Chaplain.[72] The 1st Cherokee Regiment was made up of members of the Keetoowah Society who were Union sympathizers.[73] Downing joined based on the presumption that the Regiment would remain within Cherokee Territory.[74] In contrast with the Union favoring 1st Regiment, the 2nd Cherokee Regiment was led by Colonel Stand Watie, and Confederate sympathizers.[75] While their 1st Regiment Keetoowah counterparts called for unity,[76] members of both regiments had imperfect ideas of equality. For example, early on several 1st Regiment members deserted and sought to harm Watie allies through harming their most valuable property—enslaved persons.[77]

Downing remained in the 1st Cherokee Regiment until 1862.[78] Following the Confederate defeat at the Battle of Pea Ridge, Arkansas in March 1862, Downing led 200 men to join the Union efforts in July 1862.[79] He joined the Union's 3rd Indian Home Guard as lieutenant colonel.[80] Meanwhile, Principal Chief Ross evacuated and established a pro-Union Cherokee government.[81] In opposition, Colonel Watie led the pro-Confederacy Cherokee government.[82] Thus, the U.S. Civil War exacerbated existing fractures within Cherokee Nation, thereby splitting Cherokee Nation in two.

---

71 Brad Agnew, *Our Doom as a Nation Is Sealed: The Five Nations in the Civil War*, in THE CIVIL WAR AND RECONSTRUCTION IN INDIAN TERRITORY 64, 69 (Bradley R. Clampitt ed. 2015).

72 Vezeau & Coddington, *supra* note 50, at 64.

73 *Id.*

74 *Id.*

75 *Id.*

76 *Id.*

77 Perdue, *supra* note 7, at 135.

78 Vezeau & Coddington, *supra* note 50, at 64.

79 *Id.*

80 *Id.*

81 *Id.*

82 *Id.*

Lewis Downing remained in the 3rd Indian Home Guard until 1863.[83] At that point, he was excused to serve as president pro tem over a special meeting of the Cherokee Council.[84] On February 19, 1863, Downing presided over the Council as Cherokee Nation passed its emancipation proclamation.[85] Cherokee Nation was the only Native Nation or state to voluntarily emancipate their enslaved persons during the Civil War.[86]

Notwithstanding the importance of the Cherokee Emancipation Proclamation, it accorded few persons with freedom. Cherokee Nation effectively had two governments.[87] Most slaveholders were allied with Watie's pro-Confederate government.[88] The slaveholding contingent therefore did not recognize the authority of Principal Chief Ross, or his government.[89] Thus, the Cherokee Emancipation Proclamation was meaningless to most enslavers.[90] Further, even where recognized, manumission did not accord persons previously enslaved by the Nation with citizenship.[91] Instead, the newly freed persons were free to stay and work as contract laborers like other non-citizens, else leave.[92]

The citizenship of the Cherokee Freedmen would be at issue in later treaty negotiations with the United States. After signing the Cherokee Emancipation Proclamation, Downing accompanied Principal Chief Ross to treaty negotiations in D.C.[93] Under the Indian Appropriation Act of 1862, Congress declared the U.S. power to break treaties with any Nations that fought for the

---

83 *Id.* at 65.

84 *Id.*

85 William G. McLoughlin, AFTER THE TRAIL OF TEARS 208 (1993).

86 R. Halliburton Jr., RED OVER BLACK: BLACK SLAVERY AMONG THE CHEROKEE INDIANS 132 (1977).

87 McLoughlin, *supra* note 85.

88 *Id.*

89 *Id.*

90 *Id.*

91 *Id.*

92 *Id.*

93 Vezeau & Coddington, *supra* note 50, at 65.

Confederacy.[94] Thus, Cherokee Nation was starting from scratch with the U.S., despite that a significant faction had switched sides and fought for the Union. Further, the division between Cherokee factions were exacerbated by persons like Secretary of the Interior James Harlan, who expressed a willingness to negotiate with the Principal Chief Ross and the Watie coalition as separate entities.[95] Thus, not only was Cherokee Nation wholly disempowered in the negotiations, but the Nation was more fractured than ever.

In the original treaty discussions, the delegates considered what to do with the freed Black persons.[96] Some Cherokee citizens wanted the previously enslaved persons removed.[97] Downing wanted the persons granted land within the Nation for colonization until civil rights were established within the Nation.[98] Downing's plan represented a compromise between the rival factions that took into account the rights of the newly freed Black persons.[99] This commitment to compromise would become characteristic of Downing's later leadership. Yet, the treaty negotiations also foreshadowed challenges Downing would experience in his future leadership role, as Downing's plan was not adopted.

U.S. General John Sanborn, present at negotiations at the behest of Secretary of the Interior James Harlan, called for an extreme alternative.[100] He wanted to reduce land held by the Cherokee Nation.[101] Within the reduced land holding, he called for an area set aside for the newly freed persons to reside.[102] Then, he wanted to further divest Cherokee Nation of land for Railroad Company use and to otherwise be sold by the U.S. government.[103]

---

94 Wardell, *supra* note 4, at 180.

95 *Id.* at 189.

96 *Id.* at 223.

97 *Id.*

98 *Id.* at 224.

99 *Id.*

100 *Id.*

101 *Id.*

102 *Id.*

103 *Id.*

General Sanborn's plan was roughly adopted.[104] Cherokee Freedmen were granted settlements in the southwestern district of Cherokee Reservation called the "Canadian District."[105] Freed persons were granted two years to remove to the area.[106]

Under the Treaty of 1866, persons residing in the Canadian District had all the rights of Cherokee citizens.[107] They could vote, bring suit, and own property.[108] Further, under the Ninth Article, the residents of the Canadian District, as newly freed persons, could obtain full Cherokee citizenship.[109] Consequently, under the Treaty of 1866, the 7,000[110] to 10,000[111] newly freed persons were granted an opportunity to obtain citizenship in Cherokee Nation.[112]

The granting of full Cherokee citizenship to formerly enslaved Black persons was not without issue.[113] The 1866 Treaty gave persons formerly enslaved by the Nation six months to return to the territory to obtain citizenship.[114] Many Cherokee citizens advocated for the opportunity for citizenship to be time limited.[115] The Cherokee position was not exclusively about race. More citizens meant less land and lower per capita payments available to each Cherokee citizen.[116] As noted above, General Sanborn's scheme worked to dispossess the Nation of more land.[117] Further, many Cherokee

---

[104] *Id.* at 225.

[105] *Id.*

[106] *Id.*

[107] *Id.*

[108] *Id.*

[109] *Id.*

[110] Donald A. Grinde Jr. & Quintard Taylor, *Red vs Black: Conflict and Accommodation in the Post Civil War Indian Territory, 1865-1907*, 8 Am. Indian Q. 211, 212 (1984).

[111] McLoughlin, *supra* note 85, at 252.

[112] Wardell, *supra* note 4, at 225.

[113] McLoughlin, *supra* note 85, at 253.

[114] Grinde & Taylor, *supra* note 110, at 212.

[115] McLoughlin, *supra* note 85, at 252.

[116] *Id.*

[117] Wardell, *supra* note 4, at 224.

persons took exception to a contingent of Cherokee Freedmen who supported the Tribe's termination and divvying up of land.[118] There also were some issues with verifying the persons who held rightful claim to Cherokee citizenship.[119] Many persons previously enslaved by white Southerners, rather than Cherokee citizens, came to the Nation seeking citizenship,[120] as Cherokee guarantees of land and rights were actually enforced; U.S. promises to Southern Freedmen were not.[121] Consequently, the issue of the admission of freed persons into Cherokee Nation was both complicated and divisive.

It is around this time that Downing became Principal Chief of the Nation. He initially, albeit briefly, served as acting chief in 1866 after the death of Principal Chief Ross.[122] Months later, the General Council named William Potter Ross (the late Principal Chief Ross's nephew), as Principal Chief.[123] In the subsequent 1867 election, Downing saw an opportunity to demolish the old party lines, through formation of a new party: The Downing Party.[124] In a race against William Ross, Downing actively sought the vote of former adversaries and newly acknowledged citizens.[125] Downing worked to secure the vote of newly naturalized Cherokee Freedmen.[126] They knew him from his prior sermons at their churches.[127] He also sought the support of the Confederate Cherokee citizens, like Stand Watie.[128] Under a platform of unity for all persons in Cherokee Nation, Downing won the election for Principal Chief in

---

118 McLoughlin, *supra* note 85, at 252.

119 *Id.*

120 *Id.*

121 Alaina E. Roberts. *Made Local: Alaina E. Roberts* (Pittsburgh Arts & Lectures, Apr. 22, 2021), available at https://youtu.be/T9TAJzlC5Oo.

122 Meserve, *supra* note 52, at 319.

123 *Id.*

124 Wardell, *supra* note 4, at 209.

125 Meserve, *supra* note 52, at 319.

126 Howard Tyner, THE KEETOOWAH SOCIETY IN CHEROKEE HISTORY 51 (1949).

127 *Id.*

128 Wardell, *supra* note 4, at 210.

1867.[129] So great was the upset of his win that his life was immediately thereafter threatened.[130]

This threat of life reflects that Downing stood at the helm of his Nation during one of its most tumultuous and violent times. The end of the Civil War did not end the division amongst the factions within the Nation.[131] For instance, two years after Downing signed the Cherokee Emancipation Proclamation, Colonel Watie remained at battle for the Confederacy.[132] Further, the Nation had been devastated by the war.[133] As Secretary of the Interior James Harlan wrote in 1865, "The country within the Indian territory has been laid waste, vast amounts of property destroyed, and the inhabitants reduced from a prosperous condition to such extreme destitution that thousands of them must inevitably perish during the present winter, unless timely provisions be made by this [U.S.] government for their relief."[134] Nearly a quarter of all children were orphaned during the War.[135] Further, one third of all women were widowed.[136] Additionally, the Nation was wiped out economically.[137] While the Southern states maintained their economic system based on free, forced, and coerced labor through convict leasing and the crop lien system, in the Indian Territory rights to Black persons were conferred by treaty and honored.[138] Thus, the Nation that had supplanted Cherokee practice and culture with the American plantation system, now needed to adopt a new method to survive.

While Cherokee Nation did not revert to the neoslavery of the South, the situation was still difficult for Cherokee Freedmen. Not all eligible freed persons were granted citizenship. As noted

---

129 Meserve, *supra* note 52, at 320.

130 Wardell, *supra* note 4, at 212.

131 Agnew, *supra* note 71, at 79.

132 *Id.*

133 *Id.* at 78.

134 *Id.*

135 Wardell, *supra* note 4, at 175.

136 *Id.*

137 *Id.* at 175-76.

138 Agnew, *supra* note 71, at 79.

above, the six-month time limit to bring claims for citizenship was impossible for many freed persons to meet.[139] Many persons had scattered great distances during the war.[140] Thus, it was wholly unfeasible for persons to receive notice of the possibility of citizenship and then to return to the Nation within the limited six-month window.[141] This meant that families often returned one by one, with those who did not make it in time classified as intruders and excluded from the Nation.[142] Some persons were even enslaved in the Southern states and could not return to the Nation until some years later.[143]

Downing's efforts to remediate the issue largely failed. Principal Chief Downing introduced a bill to extend the period for citizenship claims, however the bill did not pass.[144] By 1868, only 1,576 freed persons out of 4,000 applicants were granted citizenship.[145] Although an 1869 law allowed the Cherokee Supreme Court to consider the claims of the freedmen, little more than a quarter of persons bringing claims were granted citizenship.[146] Principal Chief Downing asked the General Council to be lenient in reviewing hardship cases, however, again, his request was denied.[147]

Even freed persons granted citizenship faced inequitable conditions.[148] While they were not subjected to terror lynching or prevented from land ownership or employment, as was common in the Southern states, freed persons still faced barriers to equity.[149] For example, they were sent to segregated subpar schools and were not provided orphan services.[150] Principal Chief Downing tried to

---

139 McLoughlin, *supra* note 85, at 253.

140 Wardell, *supra* note 4, at 225.

141 *Id.* at 225-26.

142 *Id.* at 226.

143 *Id.*

144 McLoughlin, *supra* note 85, at 252.

145 *Id.* at 253.

146 Wardell, *supra* note 4, at 226.

147 McLoughlin, *supra* note 85, at 253.

148 *Id.*

149 *Id.*

150 *Id.*

remediate the treatment of the Cherokee Freedmen through introduction of numerous bills throughout his tenure, however all failed to pass.[151] As one Cherokee Freedman, Louis Rough, wrote to U.S. President Ulysses Grant: "The Cherykees says they aint in favour of the black man havin any claim, that they had rather any body else have a rite than us poor blacks .... [Lewis] Downing is for us, . . . and what can [he] doo with so many on the other side?"[152]

Although many of Principal Chief Downing's efforts in support of the Cherokee Freedmen largely failed, he is still credited with the unification of a Nation fraught with internal divisions and external divestment of sovereignty and land.[153] As he stated in his first State of the Union address," Our laws should be uniform, the jurisdiction of our Courts should be the same over every part of our Nation and over every individual citizen."[154] He acted on his words, by reaching out to Stand Watie to end a decades long division so as to strengthen the Nation,[155] and by allowing Confederate Cherokee like Watie to join in delegations to the U.S. government.[156] In doing so, he formed the Downing Party, unifying the interests of Cherokee citizens, regardless of blood quantum, race, or history.[157] Thus, despite his premature departure, dying shortly after he was reelected in 1871, there is much to substantiate historians praise of Principal Chief Downing as the "Cherokee leader who did more for his tribe than any other,"[158] and the lead agent of reconciliation.[159]

## Epilogue

While Principal Chief Downing set the stage for Cherokee Nation's unity and advancement, the U.S. had other plans. In

---

[151] *Id.*

[152] *Id.* at 254.

[153] *Id.* at 253.

[154] Vezeau & Coddington, *supra* note 50, at 65.

[155] Pollard, *supra* note 5.

[156] Wardell, *supra* note 4, at 212.

[157] Meserve, *supra* note 52, at 320.

[158] Rowley, *supra* note 5.

[159] Pollard, *supra* note 5.

1898, Congress passed the Curtis Act bringing allotment to Cherokee Nation.[160] Allotment destroyed the Nation's common ownership of land, by giving each citizen a 40 to 160 acre parcel.[161] Many Cherokee citizens advocated for the Cherokee Freedmen to receive the smaller of the parcels.[162] While inarguably discriminatory, this guaranteed land to the Freedmen lead to a ninety percent Black home ownership rate Cherokee Nation, three times that of Southern Freedmen.[163]

To facilitate the allotment process, the U.S. compiled rolls of Cherokee citizens, with separate lists for persons classified as "Cherokee," "Cherokee by Intermarriage," and "Cherokee Freedmen."[164] The Act also divested the Nation of land and set for the course of action to dissolve the Nation.[165] In 1906, the U.S. dissolved the Nation's sovereignty to the point that Cherokee citizens could no longer choose their Principal Chief.[166] Instead, the leader was chosen by the U.S. president.[167] The U.S. would not honor the inherent sovereignty of the Nation and right to choose its Principal Chief again until 1970.[168] Five years after regaining this right, the

---

160 30 Stat. 495 (1898).

161 Frank Pommersheim, BROKEN LANDSCAPE: INDIANS, INDIAN TRIBES, AND THE CONSTITUTION 129 (2009).

162 Debo, *supra* note 6, at Loc. 939.

163 Melinda C. Miller, *The One Thing Needful: Free Land and Black Mobility* (Nov. 2011), https://economics.yale.edu/sites/default/files/files/Workshops-Seminars/Economic-History/miller-111115.pdf.

164 Nat'l Archives, *Digitized Index to the Final Rolls of Citizens and Freedmen of the Five Civilized Tribes in Indian Territory (Dawes)*, https://www.archives.gov/research/native-americans/rolls/final-rolls.html#cher (last visited Apr. 9, 2021).

165 *Cherokee Nation v. Nash*, 267 F. Supp. 3d 86, 108 (D.D.C. 2017).

166 David E. Wilkins & Shelly Hulse Wilkins, DISMEMBERED: NATIVE DISENROLLMENT AND THE BATTLE FOR HUMAN RIGHTS 131 (2017).

167 *Id.*

168 An Act to authorize each of the Five Civilized Tribes of Oklahoma to select their principal officer, and for other purposes Act 84 Stat. 1091.

Nation would subsequently pass a new Constitution recognizing the citizenship of all descendants of persons listed on the allotment rolls.[169]

However, by 2002, the Nation changed course. The Cherokee Council opted to exclude persons without Cherokee blood, such as persons granted citizenship in the Nation solely due to descendance from the Cherokee Freedmen roll.[170] Consequently, 2,800 descendants of the Cherokee Freedmen were disenrolled, or excluded from citizenship.[171]

Subsequent court challenges did not immediately bring remedy. Lucy Allen, a decedent of the Cherokee Freedmen, brought suit in Cherokee Nation Court.[172] She argued that the Tribal Council's action was violative of the 1975 Cherokee Constitution.[173] The Court agreed, but supplied that if the Nation changed its constitution, Cherokee Freedmen could be legally disenrolled.[174] The Nation subsequently did just that, amending the Constitution by referendum in 2007.[175] The referendum received support of seventy-seven percent of the Nation.[176] A subsequent challenge by descendants of the Cherokee Freedmen, led by Marilyn Vann in the Cherokee Courts ultimately failed.[177]

Marilyn Vann and the other Cherokee Freedmen descendants next pursued remedy in federal court. In *Cherokee Nation v. Nash*, the D.C. District Court held that Cherokee Nation's disenrollment of the descendants of the Cherokee Freedmen violated the 1866 Treaty with the U.S.[178] On remand, the Cherokee Nation Court

---

[169] Wilkins & Wilkins, *supra* note 166.

[170] *Id.*

[171] *Id.*

[172] *Id.*

[173] *Id.*

[174] *Id.* at 131-32.

[175] *Id.* at 132.

[176] *Id.*

[177] *Id.* at 132-33.

[178] *Cherokee Nation v. Nash*, 267 F. Supp. 3d 86, 141 (D.D.C. 2017).

ordered that the Constitution be reverted to its 1975 form.[179] Cherokee Freedmen were subsequently re-enrolled. In 2021, Marilyn Vann became the first descendant of Cherokee Freedmen to serve in a Cherokee government position.[180]

The complicated plight of the Cherokee Freedmen and their descendants both in the decades after Principal Chief Downing's passing and nearly a century later, suggests that the need for reconciliation is perpetual. While Downing's crossing of battle lines, discarding a gray uniform for a blue one, advocating for Cherokee persons, whether full blood, half blood, or Freedmen, were admirable, his plight for unity need not end with him. As Rev. Dr. Martin Luther King, Jr. so amply states: "human progress never rolls in on wheels of inevitability. It comes through the tireless efforts and persistent work of men."[181] Thus, through the work of Marilyn Vann, Lucy Allen, and many others in Cherokee Nation, the persistent work continues, forgiving the past to forge a more unified future.

---

[179] *In re Effect of Cherokee Nation v. Nash and Vann v. Zinke*, Case No. SC-17-07, Cherokee Nation Supreme Ct (Feb. 22, 2021).

[180] Chad Hunter, *First Cherokee of Freedmen Descent Confirmed to Government Position*, Cherokee Phoenix (Sept. 17, 2021).

[181] Martin Luther King Jr., *Letter from Birmingham Jail* (Aug. 1963), available at https://www.csuchico.edu/iege/_assets/documents/susi-letter-from-birmingham-jail.pdf.

# Notes

## Epigraph

1. Richard Delgado, *Affirmative Action as a Majoritarian Device: Or, Do You Really Want to Be a Role Model?*, 89 Mich. L. Rev. 1222, 1225 (1991). *See also* A. LEON HIGGINBOTHAM JR., IN THE MATTER OF COLOR: RACE AND THE AMERICAN LEGAL PROCESS: THE COLONIAL PERIOD (1978).

## Author's Note

1. See Jonathan K. Stubbs, Out of the Boat: Trusting God in the Midst of Life's Storms (Granthouse Publishers and Empire Publishers), 2013.

2. Oliver W. Hill Sr., THE BIG BANG, BROWN V. BOARD OF EDUCATION AND BEYOND: THE AUTOBIOGRAPHY OF OLIVER W. HILL, SR., 100th Birthday Edition 331-32 (Jonathan K. Stubbs ed., 2007).

3. GENNA RAE MCNEIL, GROUNDWORK: CHARLES HAMILTON HOUSTON AND THE STRUGGLE FOR CIVIL RIGHTS, 84 (1983).

4. Okianer Christian Dark, Just My 'Magination, 10 Harv. Black Ltr. J. 21 (1993).

5. Recent scientific studies suggest that there are probably trillions of stars in our expanding universe. The Milky Way Galaxy

where we reside is thought to have over 200 billion stars. And the Milky Way is one of perhaps trillions of galaxies each of which contain hundreds of billions of stars.

## Foreword

1. Author Note: Charles J. Ogletree Jr. wrote this Foreword during the 2013 calendar year.

2. Oliver W. Hill Sr., THE BIG BANG, BROWN V. BOARD OF EDUCATION AND BEYOND: THE AUTOBIOGRAPHY OF OLIVER W. HILL, SR., 100th Birthday Edition 82 (Jonathan K. Stubbs ed., 2007).

3. Genna Rae McNeil, Groundwork: Charles Hamilton Houston and the Struggle for Civil Rights, 79 (1983).

4. *Id.* at 84-85.

5. *Id.* at 76-85; Hill, *supra* note 2 at 79-87.

6. McNeil, *supra* note 3 at 144-45.

7. Hill, *supra* note 2 at 128-29 (Oliver Hill, Thurgood Marshall, Andrew Ranson, William Hastie, and Robert Ming preparing teacher salary litigation in Virginia); Hill, *supra* note 2 at 141-42 (Hill and Houston strategizing on transportation desegregation matters).

8. Alston v. Sch. Bd. of Norfolk, 112 F.2d 992 (4th Cir. 1940), cert. denied, 311 U.S. 693 (1940).

9. Chance v. Lambeth, 186 F.2d 879 (4th Cir. 1951), cert. denied, 341 U.S. 941 (1951).

10. Hill, *supra* note 2 at 153-90.

11. National Park Service, Oliver Hill, https://www.nps.gov/people/oliver-w-hill.htm; Encyclopedia Virginia, Oliver Hill (1907-2007), https://encyclopediavirginia.org/entries/hill-oliver-w-1907-2007/.

12. Hill, *supra* note 2 at xi.

13. C-Span, Brown v. Board (Sept. 23, 2000), https://www.c-span.org/video/?159394-1/brown-v-board-education.

14. Oliver W. Hill Sr., *Reflections on Brown and the Future*, 39 U. Rich. L. Rev. 1 (2004).

## Preface

1. Plessy v. Ferguson, 163 U.S. 537 (1896).
2. Brown v. Board of Education, 347 U.S. 483 (1954).

## Prologue

1. Maggie Masetti, How Many Stars Are in the Milky Way (July 22, 2015), https://asd.gsfc.nasa.gov/blueshift/index.php/2015/07/22/how-many-stars-in-the-milky-way/; Fraser Cain, How Many Stars Are in the Universe (June 3, 2013), https://www.universetoday.com/102630/how-many-stars-are-there-in-the-universe/.

2. *See, e.g.*, "NASA's Webb Takes Star-Filled Portrait of Pillars of Creation," https://www.nasa.gov/feature/goddard/2022/nasa-s-webb-takes-star-filled-portrait-of-pillars-of-creation; Dennis Overbye, "Webb Telescope Captures New View of 'Pillars of Creation'" (Oct. 24, 2022, N.Y. Times).

3. 1 GEORGE SANTAYANA, THE LIFE OF REASON: OR THE PHASES OF HUMAN PROGRESS, 284 (1905).

4. W.E.B. DU BOIS, THE SOULS OF BLACK FOLK, In Three Negro Classics, 207, 209 (Avon Books 1965) (1903) (emphasis added).

5. Rakesh Kochhar & Anthony Cilluffo, How Wealth Inequality Has Changed in the U.S. Since the Great Recession, by Race, Ethnicity and Income, https://www.pewresearch.org/fact-tank/2017/11/01/how-wealth-inequality-has-changed-in-the-u-s-since-the-great-recession-by-race-ethnicity-and-income/.

6. Washington v. Davis, 426 U.S. 229 (1976); Ricci v. DeStefano, 557 U.S. 557 (2009).

7. Adarand Constructors v. Pena, 515 U.S. 200, 245 (1995) (Stevens, dissenting).

8. Students for Fair Admissions v. President and Fellows of Harvard College, 600 U.S. 181 (2023).

9. Students for Fair Admissions v. Univ. of North Carolina. *Id.*

10. Students for Fair Admissions v. Harvard College. *Id.* at 230.

11. *Id.* at 231 (emphasis in original).

12. *Id.* at 359-60 (Sotomayor, dissenting).

13. *See, e.g.*, J. Phillipe Rushton, Race Evolution and Behavior: A Life History Perspective, xiii (Transaction Pub. 1995).

14. *See, e.g.*, Governor DeSantis Announces Legislative Proposal to Stop W.O.K.E. Activism and Critical Race Theory in Schools and Corporations, https://www.flgov.com/2021/12/15/governor-desantis-announces-legislative-proposal-to-stop-w-o-k-e-activism-and-critical-race-theory-in-schools-and-corporations/; *see also* Virginia Governor Glenn Youngkin's first Executive Order: 1 Number One (2022) Ending the Use of Inherently Divisive Concepts, Including Critical Race Theory, and Restoring Excellence in K-12 Public Education

in the Commonwealth, https://www.governor.virginia.gov/media/governorvirginiagov/governor-of-virginia/pdf/eo/EO-1-Ending-the-Use-of-Inherently-Divisive-Concepts.pdf.

15. Marisa Iati, What Is Critical Race Theory, and Why Do Republicans Want to Ban It in Schools? (May 29, 2021 Wash. Post), https://www.washingtonpost.com/education/2021/05/29/critical-race-theory-bans-schools/.

16. *See* Joy Reid, Creator of Term "Critical Race Theory": Kimberlé Crenshaw Explains What It Really Is (June 21, 2021, MSNBC), https://www.msnbc.com/the-reidout/watch/critical-race-theory-explained-as-not-marxist-or-racist-by-its-leading-scholar-kimberle-crenshaw-115226693996.

17. *See* Iati, *supra* note 15; Reid, *supra* note 16.

18. Select Committee to Investigate the January 6th Attack on the United States Capitol, Final Report (117th Congress Second Session, House Report 117-000 Dec. 22, 2022). On the increasing collaboration between neo-Nazis in Europe and the United States, *see*, Mallory Yu, German Far-Right Groups Becoming Increasingly Organized, Says a Historian (NPR Dec. 9, 2022), https://www.npr.org/2022/12/09/1141591204/german-far-right-groups-becoming-increasingly-organized-says-a-historian; Marc Steiner & Bill Fletcher Jr., The Rise of the Far Right Is a Global Phenomenon, Real News Network (Apr. 4, 2022), https://therealnews.com/the-rise-of-the-far-right-is-a-global-phenomenon.

19. Martin Luther King Jr., "I Have A Dream" (Speech Delivered August 28, 1963), Washington, DC, transcript available at https://www.npr.org/2010/01/18/122701268/i-have-a-dream-speech-in-its-entirety.

20. Desmond Mpilo Tutu, No Future Without Forgiveness (Rider Books 1999).

21. *Id.* at 32.

22. *See, e.g.*, Khanyi Mlaba, *Poverty, Inequality and Looting: Everything You Need to Know About South Africa's Protests*, Glob. Citizen (July 13, 2021), https://www.globalcitizen.org/en/content/everything-you-need-to-know-south-africa-protests//; see *also* South Africa Wealth Gap Unchanged Since Apartheid, Says World Inequality Lab, https://time.com/6087699/south-africa-wealth-gap-unchanged-since-apartheid/.

23. Oliver W. Hill Sr., The Big Bang, Brown v. Board of Education and Beyond: The Autobiography of Oliver W. Hill, Sr., 100th Birthday Edition 351 (Jonathan K. Stubbs ed., 2007).

24. Gospel of John 8:32.

25. Richard Delgado, *Affirmative Action as a Majoritarian Device: Or, Do You Really Want to Be a Role Model?*, 89 Mich. L. Rev. 1222, 1225 (1991).

26. Letters from Abigail Adams to John Adams, March 31, 1776, https://founders.archives.gov/documents/Adams/04-01-02-0241.

27. Letter from John Adams to Abigail Adams, April 14, 1776, National Archives, https://founders.archives.gov/documents/Adams/ 04-01-02-0248.

28. Letter from John Adams to James Sullivan (May 26, 1776), National Archives, https://founders.archives.gov/documents/Adams/06-04-02-0091.

29. Joan Gundersen, Independence, Citizenship and the American Revolution, 59, at 65-66 in 13 Signs: Journal of Women in Culture and Society (1987); A. Keyssar, The Right to Vote: The Contested History of Democracy in America, 20 (2000).

30. William Waller Hening, ed., *The Statutes at Large; Being a Collection of All the Laws of Virginia from the First Session of the Legislature, in the Year 1619* (Philadelphia: R. & W. & G. Bartow, 1823), 3:447 at 461 (emphasis added). *And see* An Act Concerning Servants and Slaves (1705), https://encyclopediavirginia.org/entries/an-act-concerning-servants-and-slaves-1705/.

31. Oliver W. Hill Jr., Preface at xviii.

32. Jonathan K. Stubbs, A Demographic History of Federal Judicial Appointments by Sex and Race: 1789-2016, 26 Berkeley La Raza L. J. 92, at 99-100 (2016).

33. United States Census Bureau: Quick Facts, https://www.census.gov/quickfacts/fact/table/US#.

34. *See* https://www.fjc.gov/history/judges/search/advanced-search. To access this material, go the Federal Judicial Center website and click History of the Federal Judiciary, then click Judges, then click Biographical Directory of Article III Judges, 1789-present, then click gender. As of July 29, 2024, there were 1455 sitting federal judges. 482 of the judges were women: 482/1455 = 33%.

35. *See, e.g.*, White male minority rule pervades politics across the United States, research shows available at https://www.theguardian.com/us-news/2021/may/26/white-male-minority-rule-us-politics-research.

36. As of July 29, 2024, there were 1455 federal sitting judges, of which 762 were White men (762/1455 = 52.37%).

37. Elliot Slotnick, Sara Schiavoni & Sheldon Goldman, Obama's Judicial Legacy, J. Law & Courts 365 at 391 (2017).

## Chapter I

1. Peter Carroll & David Noble, The Free and the Unfree: A Progressive History of the United States, 51 (3d ed. 2001). *See also* 2 THEODORE ALLEN, THE INVENTION OF THE WHITE RACE (1997).

2. Pocohontas Revealed (PBS/NOVA Documentary, May 7, 2007).

3. A. LEON HIGGINBOTHAM JR., IN THE MATTER OF COLOR: RACE AND THE AMERICAN LEGAL PROCESS: THE COLONIAL PERIOD, 20 (1978); JOHN HOPE FRANKLIN & ALFRED MOSS JR., FROM SLAVERY TO FREEDOM (7th ed. 1994).

4. William Thorndale, *The Virginia Census of 1619*, 155, 155-56, Virginia Magazine of Genealogy (1995). Some scholars have challenged the argument that the colonists conducted a census in March 1619. They argue that in eighteenth-century England, March was considered the first month of the New Year. These scholars contend that March 1619 census was in fact made in March 1620. However, one resolves the argument, Blacks arrived among the earliest Jamestown settlers.

5. Higginbotham, *supra* note 3 at 20-22. *See also* Cassandra Newby-Alexander, Four Hundredth Anniversary Arrival of Africans in Virginia (C-Span, Aug. 24, 2019), https://www.c-span.org/video/?463584-5/washington-journal-cassandranewby-alexander-discusses-arrival-africans-virginia-1619. *And see* Mallory Noe-Payne, "Honoring the Journey" 400 Years of African-American History at Fort Monroe (NPR Aug. 22, 2019), https://www.wvtf.org/post/honoring-journey-400-years-african-american-history-fort-monroe#stream/0.

6. Cassandra Newby-Alexandra, On Arrival of First Africans in Virginia: 1619 (C-Span Aug. 24, 2019), https://www.c-span.org/video/?463584-5/washington-journal-cassandra-newby-alexander-discusses-arrival-africans-virginia-1619.

7. Ralph Hamor, A TRUE DISCOURSE OF THE PRESENT ESTATE OF VIRGINIA, IN JAMESTOWN NARRATIVES: EYEWITNESS ACCOUNTS OF THE VIRGINIA COLONY—THE FIRST DECADE: 1607-1617 (Edward Wright Haile, ed. 1998) 792, n.1; 2 ALLEN, *supra* note 1 at 54; PETER

CARROLL & DAVID NOBLE, THE FREE AND THE UNFREE: A PROGRESSIVE HISTORY OF THE UNITED STATES, 81 (3d ed. 2001).

8. For a thoughtful overview of British and American Treaty making with Native Americans, *see* JILL ST. GERMAIN, INDIAN TREATY-MAKING POLICY IN THE UNITED STATES AND CANADA, 1867-1877, 3-12 (2001). *See also* FRANCIS P. PRUCHA, AMERICAN INDIAN TREATIES: THE HISTORY OF A POLITICAL ANOMALY (1994); N. BRUCE DUTHU, AMERICAN INDIANS AND THE LAW, 8-15 (2008).

9. JOHN WOOLMAN, THE JOURNAL OF JOHN WOOLMAN, 188-89 (John G. Whittier, Intro., Osgood and Company 1871) (1774).

10. Adrienne Mayor, *The Nessus Shirt in the New World: Smallpox Blankets in History and Legend*, 108 J. Am. Folklore 54, 57-59 (1995). For a general discussion of the devastating impact on indigenous populations of communicable diseases carried by European colonizers, see also Guns, Germs and Steel, https://www.pbs.org/gunsgermssteel/variables/smallpox.html.

11. Cole Harris, *Voices of Disaster: Smallpox Around the Strait of Georgia*, 41 Ethnohistory 591, 591-92 (1994), *Guns, Germs and Steel, Variables*, PBS (2005), https://www.pbs.org/gunsgermssteel/variables/smallpox.html.

12. 1 THEODORE ALLEN, THE INVENTION OF THE WHITE RACE, 27-79 (1994); Hilary McD. Beckles, *A "Riotous and Unruly Lot": Irish Indentured Servants and Freemen in the English West Indies*, 1644-1713, 503, Wm. & Mary Q. (1990).

13. Higginbotham, *supra* note 3 at 22-26.

14. 1 ALLEN, *supra* note 12 at 30.

15. 2 ALLEN, *supra* note 1 at 76; Robert C. Johnson, *The Transport of Vagrant Children from London to Virginia; 1618-22*, 137, 147, *in* EARLY STUART STUDIES (Howard Reinmuth Jr. ed., 1970).

16. 2 ALLEN, *supra* 1 at 119-23. Over 90,000 Europeans came to Maryland and Virginia, the great majority of whom were English indentured servants with few legal rights; Johnson, *supra* note 15.

17. 1 ALLEN, *supra* note 12 at 34-50.

18. JUDITH CARNEY, BLACK RICE: THE AFRICAN ORIGINS OF RICE CULTIVATION IN THE AMERICAS, 85-177 (2001). *See also* Judith A. Carney, *From Hands to Tutors: African Expertise in the South Carolina Rice Economy*, 67 Agricultural History 1 (Summer 1993); Judith A. Carney, *Rice Milling, Gender and Slave Labour in Colonial South Carolina*, 153 Past & Present 124-25 (Nov. 1996); Judith A. Carney, *The Role of African Rice and Slaves in the History of Rice*

*Cultivation in the Americas*, 26 Human Ecology 525-45 (Dec. 1998); Joyce E. Chaplin, *Tidal Rice Cultivation and the Problem of Slavery in South Carolina and Georgia, 1760-1815*, 49 Wm. & Mary Q. Third Series 49 (Jan. 1992); Peter A. Coclanis, *Distant Thunder: The Creation of a World Market in Rice and the Transformations It Wrought*, 98 Am. Hist. R. 1056 (Oct. 1993); Olga F. Linares, *African Rice (Oryza glaberrima): History and Future Potential*, Proc. Nat. Aca. of Sciences (2002).

19. Higginbotham, *supra* note 3 at 28-29.

20. Act CII, "Run-Aways," 2 Henings Statutes at Large, 116-17, https://vagenweb.org/hening/vol02-06.htm.

21. John Stephen Henry, New Commentaries on the Law of England (partially founded on Blackstone) at 263 (1846), https://books.google.com/books?id=-PNKAAAAYAAJ&pg=PA263&lpg=PA263&dq=an+offence+against+public+justice,+as+it+keeps+alive+strife+and+contention,+and+perverts+the+remedial+process+of+the+law+into+an+engine+of+oppression&source=bl&ots=Jp2Iu4Jjib&sig=ACfU3U0G2rbfbYyHWd70SzrV4GIXtYuXZg&hl=en#v=onepage&q=an%20offence%20against%20public%20justice%2C%20as%20it%20keeps%20alive%20strife%20and%20contention%2C%20and%20perverts%20the%20remedial%20process%20of%20the%20law%20into%20an%20engine%20of%20oppression&f=false; *see also* Yick Yick Wo v. Hopkins, 118 U.S. 356, 359 (1886).

22. Steele v. Louisville & N. R. Co., 323 U.S. 192 (1944); Quarles v. Philip Morris, Inc., 271 F. Supp. 842 (E.D. Va. 1967).

23. 323 U.S. 192 (1944); 323 U.S. 210 (1944), respectively.

24. *See* Ricci v. DeStefano, 557 U.S. 557, 610 (2009), Ginsburg, J., dissenting.

25. Higginbotham, *supra* note 3 at 36-37.

26. *Id.* at 24-25.

27. *Id.* at 39. *See also* GEORGE W. WILLIAMS, 1 HISTORY OF THE NEGRO RACE IN AMERICA FROM 1619 TO 1880, 129 (paperback ed., BiblioBazaar 2007) (1883) ("[I]f a slave dared to resist his master while he was correcting him, he could be killed; and the master would be guiltless in the eyes of the law."); PHILLIP J. SCHWARZ, TWICE CONDEMNED SLAVES AND THE CRIMINAL LAWS OF VIRGINIA, 1705-1865, 16 ("Eleven years later, the House of Burgesses reserved for bondspeople the special punishment of thirty lashes should they lift their hands against any Christian"); WILLIAM GOODELL, THE

AMERICAN SLAVE CODE IN THEORY AND PRACTICE: ITS DISTINCTIVE FEATURES SHOWN BY ITS STATUTES, JUDICIAL DECISIONS, AND ILLUSTRATIVE FACTS, 87 Michigan Historical Reprint Series 2006) ("He must never lift a hand in self-defense. He must utter no word of remonstrance. He has no protection and no redress"); *An Act for Preventing Negroes Insurrections* (1680), *reprinted in* 2 The Statutes at Large; Being a Collection of All the Laws of Virginia from the First Session of the Legislature, in the Year 1619 481, 481 (William Waller Hening ed., R. & W. & G. Bartow 1823) ("And it is further enacted by the authority aforesaid that if any negroe or other slave shall presume to lift up his hand in opposition against any Christian, shall for every such offence, upon due proofe made thereof by the oath of the party before a magistrate, have and receive thirty lashes on his bare back well laid on").

28. 2 Allen, *supra* note 1 at 211-16. *See also* Carroll & Noble, *supra* note 7 at 81-84. *And see* 1 SAMUEL ELIOT MORISON, THE OXFORD HISTORY OF THE AMERICAN PEOPLE, 161-66 (Mentor Book 1972), presenting a somewhat more sympathetic view of Bacon.

29. 2 Allen, *supra* note 1 at 203-16.

30. Whereas some doubts have arrisen whether children got by any Englishman upon a negro woman should be slave or free, Be it therefore enacted and declared by this present grand assembly, that all children borne in this country shall be held bond or free only according to the condition of the mother, And that if any christian shall committ ffornication with a negro man or woman, he or she so offending shall pay double the ffines imposed by the former act. Source: *Negro Womens Children to Serve According to the Condition of the Mother*, Hening, ed., The Statutes at Large, vol. 2, p. 170.

31. Higginbotham, *supra* note 3 at 44.

32. And be it further enacted by the authoritie aforesaid, and it is hereby enacted, That if any English woman being free shall have a bastard child by any negro or mulatto, she pay the sume of fifteen pounds sterling, within one moneth after such bastard child be born, to the Church wardens of the parish where she shall be delivered of such child, and in default of such payment she shall be taken into the possession of the said Church wardens and disposed of for five yeares, and the said fine of fifteen pounds, or whatever the woman shall be disposed of for, shall be paid, one third part to their majesties for and towards the support of the government and the contingent charges thereof, and one other third part to the use

of the parish where the offence is committed, and the other third part to the informer, and that such bastard child be bound out as a servant by the said Church wardens untill he or she shall attaine the age of thirty yeares, and in case such English woman that shall have such bastard child be a servant, she shall be sold by the said church wardens, (after her time is expired that she ought by law to serve her master) for five yeares, and the money she shall be sold for divided as is before appointed, and the child to serve as aforesaid. Source: Hening, ed., The Statutes at Large, vol. 3, pp. 86-88.

33. *Id.*

34. Higginbotham, *supra* note 3 at 45.

35. *Id.* at 44.

36. According to the Supreme Court of the United States opinion in Loving v. Virginia, 388 U.S. 1 (1967), in Washington, DC, Richard Loving married Mildred Jeter. Loving was White and Jeter was a Negro. The married couple moved to Caroline County, Virginia, and were arrested. The trial court convicted them of violating Virginia's anti-miscegenation statute. The court sentenced them to one year in prison. The court suspended the sentences on the condition that the couple leave the state and not return for 25 years. The Lovings appealed their conviction and the Supreme Court ruled in their favor unanimously. The Court said that the Virginia statute violated both the Equal Protection and the Due Process Clauses of the Fourteenth Amendment. More recently, controversy has swirled around the question of whether Jeter was a Native American or whether her ancestors were both Native and African. *See* 50 Years Later, the Couple at the Heart of *Loving v. Virginia*, Still Stirs Controversy, June 11, 2017, https://www.wgbh.org/news/2017/06/11/news/50-years-later-couple-heart-loving-v-virginia-still-stirs-controversy.

37. Loving v. Virginia, 388 U.S. 1 (1967).

38. Loving, 388 U.S. at 12.

39. *An Act Concerning Servants and Slaves* (1705), *reprinted in* 3 The Statutes at Large; Being a Collection of All the Laws of Virginia from the First Session of the Legislature, in the Year 1619, at 461 (William Waller Hening ed., R. & W. & G. Bartow 1823) Higginbotham, *supra* note 3 at 56 (emphasis added). *See also* THOMAS D. MORRIS, SOUTHERN SLAVERY AND THE LAW, 1619-1860; Kimberly L. Alderman, *Slave Artists as Powerful Reality Creators: Taking Responsibility and Rejecting Race Consciousness*, 31 T. MARSHALL L. REV. 261 (2008).

40. An Act Concerning Servants and Slaves, William Waller Hening, ed., *The Statutes at Large; Being a Collection of All the Laws of Virginia from the First Session of the Legislature, in the Year 1619* (Philadelphia: R. & W. & G. Bartow, 1823), 3:447 at 460.

41. *Id.*

42. Higginbotham, *supra* note 3 at 58.

43. JOHN WOOLMAN, THE JOURNAL AND MAJOR ESSAYS OF JOHN WOOLMAN 45-46 (Phillips P. Moulton ed., Friends United Press 1971) (1774).

44. THOMAS JEFFERSON, NOTES ON THE STATE OF VIRGINIA, 168-69 (Penguin Books 1999) (1785).

## Chapter II

1. Jean Jacques Rousseau, The Social Contract and Discourses, 13 (G.D.H. Cole ed., J.M. Dent & Sons 1913, originally published 1762).

> So, from whatever aspect we regard the question, the right of slavery is null and void, not only as being illegitimate, but also because it is absurd and meaningless. The words slave and right contradict each other, and are mutually exclusive. It will always be equally foolish for a man to say to a man or to a people: "I make with you a convention wholly at your expense and wholly to my advantage; I shall keep it as long as I like, and you will keep it as long as I like."

2. *Quoted in* A. LEON HIGGINBOTHAM JR., IN THE MATTER OF COLOR: RACE AND THE AMERICAN LEGAL PROCESS: THE COLONIAL PERIOD (1978) at 381.

3. Patrick Henry, Letter to Robert Pleasants, Jan. 18, 1773, https://press-pubs.uchicago.edu/founders/documents/v1ch15s7.html (emphasis added).

4. *See* Oxford English Dictionary, https://www.oed.com/oed2/00139525.

5. David Hume, Esq., "Of the Populousness of Ancient Nations" at 4, in Essays and Treatises on Several Subjects (Amyas Merivale and Peter Millican Hume Texts On Line), https://davidhume.org/texts/empl2/pa.

6. *See also* Africans in America—The Revolutionary War, http://www.pbs.org/wgbh/aia/part2/2narr4.html ("The Governor of Virginia, ... Lord Dunmore ... sought to disrupt the American cause by promising freedom to any slaves owned by Patriot masters who would join the Loyalist forces ... Dunmore officially issued his proclamation in November, 1775, and within a month 300 black men had joined his Ethiopian regiment. Probably no more than 800 eventually succeeded in joining Dunmore's regiment, but his proclamation inspired thousands of runaways to follow behind the British throughout the war"); Lord Dunmore's Ethiopian Regiment, http://www.blackpast.org/?q=aah/lord-dunmore-s-ethiopian-regiment. *See generally* MICHAEL LEE LANNING, AFRICAN AMERICANS IN THE REVOLUTIONARY WAR, 50-59 (2005); BERNARD C. NALTY, STRENGTH FOR THE FIGHT: A HISTORY OF BLACK AMERICANS IN THE MILITARY, 12-13 (The Free Press 1986); NAT'L RESEARCH INSTITUTE, AMERICA BECOMING: RACIAL TRENDS AND THEIR CONSEQUENCES 176 (Neil Smelser, Julius Wilson & Faith Mitchell eds., Comm'n on Behavioral and Soc. Sciences Vol. 2, 2001); Benjamin Quarles, *Lord Dunmore as Liberator*, Wm. & Mary Q. Oct. 1958, at 494-507.

7. Constitution of Virginia (June 29, 1776), http://www.nhinet.org/ccs/docs/va-1776.htm.

8. Virginia Constitution of 1776; *see also* A.E. Dick Howard, Who Belongs: The Constitution of Virginia and the Political Community, 37 J. Law & Politics 99, 104 (2022).

9. Howard, *supra* note 8 at 104.

10. Virginia Museum of History and Culture, 1764-1824, https://virginiahistory.org/learn/story-of-virginia/chapter/causes-revolution; South Carolina Encyclopedia, African Americans in the Revolutionary War, https://www.scencyclopedia.org/sce/entries/african-americans-in-the-revolutionary-war/; GPB, "The American Revolution," https://georgiastudies.gpb.org/c8-s3. *See also* JOHN HOPE FRANKLIN & ALFRED MOSS JR., FROM SLAVERY TO FREEDOM (7th ed. 1994) at 75. BENJAMIN QUARLES, THE NEGRO IN THE AMERICAN REVOLUTION, 119 (1996 North Carolina Press) (1961); ALAN GILBERT, BLACK PATRIOTS AND LOYALISTS, xii (2012).

11. GARY NASH, FORGOTTEN FIFTH: AFRICAN AMERICANS IN THE AGE OF REVOLUTION, 45-52 (2006); Quarles, *supra* note 10 at 167-72; Gilbert, *supra* note 10 at 188-96.

12. PETER CARROLL & DAVID NOBLE, THE FREE AND THE UNFREE: A PROGRESSIVE HISTORY OF THE UNITED STATES, 81, 86-87 (3d ed. 2001); Nash, *supra* note 11 at 78-79.

13. QUARLES, *supra* note 10 at XXVII.

14. Franklin & Moss, *supra* note 10 at 77-78.

15. QUARLES, *supra* note 10 at XXIX; FRANKLIN & MOSS, *supra* note 10 at 76.

16. QUARLES, *supra* note 10 at 58, 184. JACQUELINE JONES, AMERICAN WORK: FOUR CENTURIES OF BLACK AND WHITE LABOR 141 (1998).

17. QUARLES, *supra* note 10 at 173-74.

18. George Liele, *An Account of Several Baptist Churches, Consisting Chiefly of Negro Slaves: Particularly of One at Kingston, in Jamaica: And Another at Savannah in Georgia*, *in* AFRO-AMERICAN RELIGIOUS HISTORY, 43-48 (Milton C. Sernett ed., 2d ed. 1999).

19. FRANKLIN & MOSS, *supra* note 10 at 80-81.

20. PAUL BREST ET AL. PROCESSES OF CONSTITUTIONAL DECISIONMAKING: CASES AND MATERIALS, 18 (7th ed. 2018).

21. *Id.* at 19.

22. RICHARD BROOKHISER, GENTLEMAN REVOLUTIONARY: GOUVERNEUR MORRIS, THE RAKE WHO WROTE THE CONSTITUTION, 91-92 (2003).

23. *Id.* at 81-86.

24. U.S. Const. art. IV, § 2, cl. 3.

25. *Prigg v. Pennsylvania*, 41 U.S. 539 (1842).

26. BREST ET AL., *supra* note 20 at 251, citing Paul Finkelman, *Sorting Out* Prigg v. Pennsylvania, 24 Rutgers L.J. 605 (1993).

27. Finkelman, *supra* note 26 at 609.

28. *Id.* at 612, n.28.

29. *See* Edward Prigg, Maryland State Archives, https://msa.maryland.gov/megafile/msa/speccol/sc5400/sc5496/051200/051268/html/051268bio.html.

30. Prigg, 41 U.S. at 613.

31. *Id.* at 622.

32. MARY FRANCES BERRY, BLACK RESISTANCE WHITE LAW: A HISTORY OF CONSTITUTIONAL RACISM IN AMERICA, 9-10 (2d ed. 1994).

33. Solomon Northup, Twelve Years a Slave (1970 Dover Edition (originally published 1854)).

34. Martin Gruberg, Gag Rule in Congress (discussing Rules adopted in the House of Representatives from 1836 to 1844 that tabled and ignored anti-slavery petitions), https://mtsu.edu/first-amendment/article/1210/gag-rule-in-congress; *see also* Thurman Hart, Abolitionists and Free Speech, https://www.mtsu.edu/first-amendment/article/2/abolitionists-and-free-speech.

35. Berry, *supra* note 32 at 5-13.

36. AKIL REED AMAR, AMERICA'S CONSTITUTION: A BIOGRAPHY, 345-47 (2005); Brookheiser, *supra* note 22 at 85-86; GARRY WILLS, NEGRO PRESIDENT: PRESIDENT JEFFERSON AND THE SLAVE POWER (2003).

37. Willfred Codrington III, "The Electoral College's Racist Origins" (The Brennan Ctr. 2020), https://www.brennancenter.org/our-work/analysis-opinion/electoral-colleges-racist-origins; Wills, *supra* note 36 at 62-63; Amar, *supra* note 36 at 345-47.

38. Thomas Jefferson & Sally Hemings: A Brief Account, https://www.monticello.org/thomas-jefferson/jefferson-slavery/thomas-jefferson-and-sally-hemings-a-brief-account/.

39. *See* Amar, *supra* note 36; Brookheiser, *supra* note 22; Wills, *supra* note 36.

40. JOAN HOFF-WILSON, LAW, GENDER AND INJUSTICE: A LEGAL HISTORY OF U.S. WOMEN, 21-102 (1991); Joan R. Gundersen, *Independence, Citizenship and the American Revolution*, 13 Signs 59, 63-69, 73-77 (1987); A. Keyssar, The Right to Vote: The Contested History of Democracy in America, 6 (2000).

41. *See* Christopher Uggans et al., Locked Out 2022: Estimates of People Denied Voting Rights (Oct. 25, 2022, The Sentencing Project), https://www.sentencingproject.org/reports/locked-out-2022-estimates-of-people-denied-voting-rights/. *See also* New Voting Restrictions in America, Jan. 7, 2019, https://www.brennancenter.org/sites/default/files/legislation/New%20Voting%20Restrictions.pdf; *see also* New Voting Restrictions in America, Oct. 1, 2019, https://www.brennancenter.org/our-work/research-reports/new-voting-restrictions-america.

42. Thomas Jefferson to Jared Sparks (Feb. 4, 1824), http://www.let.rug.nl/usa/presidents/thomas-jefferson/letters-of-thomas-jefferson/jefl276.php.

43. *Id.*

## Chapter III

1. ERIC FONER, FREE SOIL, FREE LABOR, FREE MEN 266-67 (1995). Foner points out that "Democrats did manage to enact a law in 1859, barring anyone with a 'visible admixture' of Negro blood . . ." *Id.* at 286. *See also* NICOLE ETCHESON, BLEEDING KANSAS, 31 (2004), "As migration from the upper South into the lower Midwest had

shown in an earlier period, many whites left the slave states to flee the economic competition of slavery." Etcheson argued that "only a minority of settlers came to Kansas with strong moral positions against slavery; most sought better homes in the west." *Id.* at 49.

2. John Dippel, Race to the Frontier: "White Flight" and Westward Expansion, 222 (2004) (emphasis in original). Dippel also asserted that:

> One way of excluding non-whites was to pass laws making their entry and residence difficult, if not impossible. Although "blacks laws" adopted in Ohio, Illinois and Indiana had not completely stopped the northward stream of ex-slaves, they had reduced it. These discriminatory measures thus provided a model for legally thwarting black migration to the West ... This strategy seemed to work. In 1840, free blacks were virtually non-existent in the trans-Mississippian West.

*Id.* (Arkansas initially required free Blacks to provide a certificate or freedom and a $500 bond in order to settle in its territory. *Id.* at 224).

3. 21 U.S. 543 at 572-73 (1823). The Doctrine of Discovery was derived in part from the May 4, 1493, Demarcation Bull which Pope Alexander VI promulgated. Among other things, Pope Alexander's Bull granted Spain possession of most Lands in the Western Hemisphere (except Brazil, which was being colonized by Portugal).

4. *Id.* at 574.

5. *Id.* at 588-89.

6. *Id.* at 588.

7. *Id.* at 591.

8. *Id.* at 591-92.

9. *Id.*

10. *Id.* at 591.

11. *See* The Smithsonian Institute, "The Different Views of Land" (discussing how Native people in Manhattan, New York, probably believed that they were not selling Manhattan to the Dutch but rather leasing part of the island to them), https://americanindian.si.edu/nk360/manhattan/different-views-land/different-views-land.cshtml; *see also* "Native Americans and the Homestead Act" (National Park Service), https://www.nps.gov/home/learn/history culture/native-americans-and-the-homestead-act.htm.

12. 21 U.S. 543 at 588.

13. Paul Brest et al., Processes of Constitutional Decision Making, 179 (7th ed. 2018); *see also* H. David Williams, Gambling Away the Inheritance: The Cherokee Nation and Georgia's Gold and Land Lotteries of 1832-33, LXXIII Geo. Hist. Qtr. 519 (1989). A sympathetic white judge who had argued for fair treatment of the Cherokees confronted an honorable Georgia pastor with the inconsistency of Christians stealing Native American lands because gold had been discovered. The Georgia parson reluctantly acknowledged the wrongful behavior and nevertheless, concluded: "But then Judge, we want the land." *Id.* at 538.

14. 30 U.S. 1 (1831).

15. 31 U.S. 515 (1832).

16. *Id.* at 559.

17. *Id.*

18. *Id.* at 561.

19. Andrew Jackson, First Annual Message to Congress, Dec. 8, 1829, in II Messages and Papers of the Presidents, 1789-1902, 456-59 (James D. Richardson ed., 1902) (emphasis added). *See also* Williams, Gambling Away the Inheritance, *supra* note 13 at 24-25.

20. For an excellent historical overview of ways in which many members of Western elite circles perceived and reacted to American Indians, *see* ROBERT WILLIAMS, THE AMERICAN INDIAN IN WESTERN LEGAL THOUGHT: THE DISCOURSES OF CONQUEST (1990). *See also* VINE DELORIA JR., THE EVOLUTION OF FEDERAL INDIAN POLICY MAKING, IN AMERICAN INDIAN POLICY IN THE TWENTIETH CENTURY 239-56 (Vine Deloria Jr. ed., 1985) (outlining, among other things, some American government legal responses to Native Americans); DAVID WILKINS & R. TSIANINA LOMAWAIMA, UNEVEN GROUND: AMERICAN INDIAN SOVEREIGNTY AND FEDERAL LAW 19-63 (2001) (presenting a thoughtful historical overview of European and American legal thinking regarding property rights in land which Native Americans had possessed for centuries and which Europeans mysteriously discovered); Carl H. Johnson, *A Comedy of Errors: Why John Baker Is Only a Tentative First Step in the Right Direction*, 18 Ak. L. Rev. 1 (2001) (providing helpful historical information and discussing Alaska Native American courts' jurisdiction versus that of Alaskan state courts); Eric Kades, *The Dark Side of Efficiency:* Johnson v. McIntosh *and the Expropriation of American Indian Lands*, 148 U. Pa. L. Rev. 1065 (2000) (setting forth how American law and policy

was directed toward obtaining Indian lands as cheaply as possible—by fair means or foul).

21. *See* ANN BYERS, THE TRAIL OF TEARS: A PRIMARY SOURCE HISTORY OF THE FORCED RELOCATION OF THE CHEROKEE NATION 45 (2004); *see also* NANCY C. CURTIS, BLACK HERITAGE SITES: AN AFRICAN AMERICAN ODYSSEY AND FINDER'S GUIDE 543 (1995) ("More than 4,000 of the 15,000 Cherokee died on the way to Indian Territory ..."). *See also* THEDA PURDUE, MICHAEL D. GREEN & COLIN G. CALLOWAY, THE CHEROKEE NATION AND THE TRAIL OF TEARS 139 (2007) ("Sociologist Russell Thornton has speculated that removal cost the Cherokees 10,000 individuals between 1835 and 1840, including the children that victims would have produced had they survived"); Tom Donnelly, Note, *Popular Constitutionalism, Civic Education, and the Stories We Tell Our Children*, 118 Yale L.J. 948, 989 (2009) ("[I]n a nightmare journey that the Cherokees called the Trail of Tears, men, women, and children, most on foot, began a 116-day forced march westward.... Roughly 1 out of every 4 Cherokees died of cold or disease, as troops refused to let them pause to rest"); *The Trail of Tears*, http://www.pbs.org/wgbh/aia/part4/4h1567.html ("In 1838 and 1839, as part of Andrew Jackson's Indian removal policy, the Cherokee nation was forced to give up its lands east of the Mississippi River and to migrate to an area in present-day Oklahoma"); according to the National Park Service, the Choctaw walked this long journey from Mississippi to Oklahoma, a harsh trek that killed many along the way. The first American Indian tribe to remove to Oklahoma, the Choctaw suffered greatly. Roughly 70,000 people were forced out of the region and at least 3,000 lost their lives on the march. This forced walk is now commemorated as the Trail of Tears, https://www.nps.gov/natr/learn/historyculture/choctaw.htm. *See also* http://www.choctawnation.com/history/choctaw-nation-. *And see* TIM GARRISON, THE LEGAL IDEOLOGY OF REMOVAL (2002); CHEROKEE REMOVAL: BEFORE AND AFTER (William L. Anderson ed., 1991); SAMUEL CARTER, CHEROKEE SUNSET: A NATION BETRAYED (1976); JOHN EHLE, TRAIL OF TEARS: THE RISE AND FALL OF THE CHEROKEE NATION (1988); GRANT FOREMAN, INDIAN REMOVAL: THE EMIGRATION OF THE FIVE CIVILIZED TRIBES OF INDIANS (1932, 11th printing 1989); 1 FRANCIS PAUL PRUCHA, THE GREAT FATHER: THE UNITED STATES GOVERNMENT AND THE AMERICAN INDIANS, Volume I (1984); ROBERT V. REMINI, ANDREW JACKSON

AND HIS INDIAN WARS (2001); ANTHONY F.C. WALLACE, THE LONG, BITTER TRAIL: ANDREW JACKSON AND THE INDIANS (1993).

22. Byers, *supra* note 21 at 45.

23. 2 SAMUEL ELIOT MORISON, 1789 THROUGH RECONSTRUCTION, THE OXFORD HISTORY OF THE AMERICAN PEOPLE, 188-94 (1972).

24. ROBERT A. WILLIAMS, LINKING ARMS TOGETHER: AMERICAN INDIAN TREATY VISIONS OF LAW AND PEACE, 1600-1800, 14-17 (1997); TIM ALAN GARRISON, THE LEGAL IDEOLOGY OF REMOVAL: THE SOUTHERN JUDICIARY AND THE SOVEREIGNTY OF NATIVE AMERICAN NATIONS, 27-28 (2002).

25. A.S. Dillingham, "What An Indigenous Perspective on U.S. and Mexican History Reveals" (Feb. 10, 2023, Wash. Post).

26. *See* Texas State Historical Society, Consular Services for the Republic of Texas, https://www.tshaonline.org/handbook/entries/consular-service-of-the-republic-of-texas; *see also* Kyle Walker, French Diplomacy with the Republic of Texas (Texas Historical Commission, Oct. 11, 2022) (blog post available at https://www.tshaonline.org/handbook/entries/consular-service-of-the-republic-of-texas).

27. PETER CARROLL & DAVID NOBLE, THE FREE AND THE UNFREE: A PROGRESSIVE HISTORY OF THE UNITED STATES (3d ed. 2001) at 174.

28. 2 Morison, *supra* note 23 at 318; Carroll & Noble, *supra* note 27 at 174. *See also* Justin H. Smith, The Mexican Recognition of Texas, 16 Am. Hist. Rev. 36-55 (1910), "It hardly need be said that from 1836 to 1845, even amid all the inconsistencies that surrounded it, Mexican feeling in regard to Texas and the Texan question was consistently bitter ... The American Union in particular was represented as covetous of its neighbor's territory and even as plotting to extinguish her independence." *See also* Alwyn Barr *Black Texans: A History of African Americans in Texas, 1528-1995* (2d ed. 1996); WILLIAM C. DAVIS, LONE STAR RISING: THE REVOLUTIONARY BIRTH OF THE TEXAS REPUBLIC (2004); STEPHEN L., HARDIN, TEXIAN ILIAD (1994); WALTER LORD, A TIME TO STAND (1978); Martha Manchaca, *Recovering History, Constructing Race: The Indian, Black, and White Roots of Mexican Americans*, The Joe R. and Teresa Lozano Long Series in Latin American and Latino Art and Culture (2001).

29. JEFFERY D. SCHULTZ ET AL., ENCYCLOPEDIA OF MINORITIES IN AMERICAN POLITICS: HISPANIC AMERICANS AND NATIVE

AMERICANS, 489 (2000). "The Mexican War added more than a million square miles of land to the United States, but it also placed the nation on a course toward civil war, as both North and South debated the future of slavery in the new territories." DOUGLAS MEED, THE MEXICAN WAR 1846-1848, 78. Meed states: "The Mexican government was forced to sign the Treaty of Guadalupe Hidalgo on March 10, 1848. Including Texas, the Mexicans had surrendered more than 1,200,000 square miles to the United States. Within a few decades, the vast empty spaces of these rich lands would swarm with peoples from all over the globe." (2003). *See also* OTIS SINGLETARY, THE MEXICAN WAR (1960); JOHN S.D. EISENHOWER, SO FAR FROM GOD: THE U.S. WAR WITH MEXICO, 1846-48 (2000).

30. Karen B. Clay, Property Rights and Institutions Congress and the California Land Act of 1851, 59 J. Econ Hist. 122, 128-29 (1999).

31. *Id.* at 122-29.

32. Cal. Const. Art. II, § 1 (1849).

33. *Id.*

34. 4 Cal. 399 (1854).

35. *Id.* at 404.

36. An Act to create Office of Surveyor-General of the Public Lands in Oregon ... and to make Donations to Settlers of the said Public Lands, ch. LXXVI, sect. 4, 9 Stat. 496, 497 (1850) ("Oregon Land Donation Act" (emphasis added). This provision of the Oregon Land Donation Act also applied to "American half-breed Indians").

37. *Id.* (emphasis added). In *Silver v. Ladd*, 74 U.S. 219 (1868), the Supreme Court held that the Land Donation Act conferred an equitable title in land upon single White women. *Id.* at 227-28.

38. Garrett Epps, To an Unknown God: The Hidden History of *Employment Division v. Smith*, 30 Ariz. St. L.J. 968-69 (1999).

39. 60 U.S. 393 (1857).

40. *Id.* at 407 (emphasis added).

41. *Id.* at 452 (emphasis added).

42. *Id.*

43. *Id.* at 451-52.

44. FREDERICK DOUGLASS, SELECTED SPEECHES AND WRITINGS, 386-87 (edited by Philip S. Foner, abridged and adapted by Yuval Taylor 1999).

45. *Id.* at 387.

46. Thomas Jefferson, Notes on Virginia, 169 (Frank Shuffelton ed., Penguin Books, 1999) (1785).

## Chapter IV

1. *See generally* Douglas Charles Stange, British Unitarians Against American Slavery 1833-1865, 155 (1984) (Following the *Dred Scott* decision, "[t]he Southern oligarchy controlled the entire machinery of the United States government. It had its eyes on Latin America and contemplated the formation of a 'vast Slave-Empire'"); Robert Granville Caldwell, A Short History of the United States 458-59 (1925) ("From 1849 to 1851, Narciso Lopez, a rebellious Spanish general, organized a series of filibustering expeditions against the neighboring island of Cuba, and received recruits and money from those who desired to see another slave state added to the nation as a balance to the newly admitted California. In 1850, he captured, and for a few hours held, the Cuban city of Cardenas, but was compelled to retire on account of the lack of genuine support from the Cubans. In 1851 he landed near Havana with about four hundred young Americans. But military details were mismanaged and the members of the expedition were dispersed and captured by the energy of the ruthless Spanish Captain General Concha. Fifty-one were shot in the public square of Havana, and the rest were sent to a Spanish prison on the coast of Africa."); *see also* The Historic New Orleans Collection, "In the 1850s, Narciso López launched illegal Cuban invasions from New Orleans" (May 21, 2021), https://www.hnoc.org/publications/first-draft/1850s-narciso-lopez-and-fellow-filibusters-launched-cuban-invasions-new; John Ashworth, Slavery, Capitalism, and Politics in the Antebellum Republic Volume 2: The Coming of the American Civil War 1850-1861, 321 (2007) ("In the 1850s there had been a violent attempt to extend slavery into Kansas and a spate of filibustering expeditions into Latin America, some of them with the covert or open support of prominent Democrats. Leading Democrats north and south had sought to obtain Cuba and in 1860 both wings of the democratic party had officially committed themselves to the acquisition of additional territory"); David M. Potter, The Impending Crisis 1848-1861: The New American Nation Series 396 (Henry Steele Commager & Richard B. Morris eds., 1976) (Describing various attempts to get legislatures in southern states to re-implement

the slave trade. "[T]he state legislature in 1857-1859 rejected a series of attempts to bring the issue to a vote, as did the Texas legislature in 1857 … the high tide of the effort to secure legislation came in March 1858, when the Louisiana house of representatives voted 46 to 21 to authorize the importation into Louisiana of 'twenty-five hundred free Africans' as apprentices").

2. The Avalon Project, "Declaration of the Immediate Causes Which Induce and Justify the Secession of South Carolina from the Federal Union" (adopted Dec. 24, 1860), https://avalon.law.yale.edu/19th_century/csa_scarsec.asp; 2 Samuel Eliot Morison, 1789 Through Reconstruction, The Oxford History of the American People, 379 (1972); PETER CARROLL & DAVID NOBLE, THE FREE AND THE UNFREE: A PROGRESSIVE HISTORY OF THE UNITED STATES, 207 (3d ed. 2001).

3. Carroll & Noble, *supra* note 2 at 207; 2 Morison, *supra* note 2 at 380.

4. Carroll & Noble, *supra* note 2 at 208; 2 Morison, *supra* note 2 at 383.

5. Carroll & Noble, *supra* note 2 at 207; 2 Morison, *supra* note 2 at 384.

6. *See* Robert E. Lee resigns from U.S. Army after Virginia Secedes from the Union (A&E Television Networks, originally published Nov. 13, 2009, last updated Apr. 19, 2021), https://www.history.com/this-day-in-history/lee-resigns-from-u-s-army. *See also* William C. Davis, Jefferson Davis & Robert E. Lee: Reluctant "Traitors," in Harold Holzer et al. (ed.), Exploring Lincoln: Great Historians Reappraise Our Greatest President, at 107 (Fordham University Press 2015), https://ebookcentral.proquest.com/lib/richmond/reader.action?docID=3239961&ppg=116.

7. Stanley W. Campbell, *The Slave Catchers: Enforcement of the Fugitive Slave Law, 1850-1860* (1970), Don E. Fehrenbacher, *The Slaveholding Republic: An Account of the United States Government's Relations to Slavery*, 249 (2002); 2 Morison, *supra* note 2 at 381-83.

8. Act to Secure Homesteads to Actual Settlers on the Public Domain, Chap. 75, sec. 1, (1862).

9. 60 U.S. 393 (1857).

10. Martha Menchaca, Chicano Indianism: A Historical Account of Racial Repression in the United States, 20 American Ethnologist 583, 584 (1993).

11. Yugchen Quin, A Century-Old "Puzzle": The Six Companies Role in Chinese Labor Importation in the Nineteenth Century, 12 J. American-East Asian Rel. 225 (2003); Patricia Cloud & David Galenson, Chinese Immigration and Contract Labor in the Late Nineteenth Century, 24 Explorations in Econ. Hist. 22 (1987).

12. *Johnson v. McIntosh*, 21 U.S. 543 (1823); *Dred Scott*, 60 U.S. 393, at 404.

13. *See* 2 Morison, *supra* note 2 at 454 (discussing the scope of land grants under the Act during the Civil War).

14. Ken Drexler, Homestead Act: Primary Documents in American History, Libr. of Cong., https://(guides.loc.gov/homestead-act (December 11, 2020).

15. ERIC FONER, RECONSTRUCTION: AMERICA'S UNFINISHED REVOLUTION: 1863-1877, 1-11 (1988); THE NEGRO IN VIRGINIA (Va. Writers Program of the Works Projects Admin. of the State of Va.) 207-08 (1940); Carroll & Noble, *supra* note 2 at 217.

16. Foner, *supra* note 15 at 34-36.

17. Foner, *supra* note 15 at 36.

18. U.S. Const. Art. III: "Treason against the United States, shall consist only in levying War against them, or in adhering to their Enemies, giving them Aid and Comfort."

19. Foner, *supra* note 15 at 48-49; JOHN HOPE FRANKLIN & ALFRED MOSS JR., FROM SLAVERY TO FREEDOM (7th ed. 1994) at 224; Carroll & Noble, *supra* note 2 at 223.

20. RICHARD D. VALELLY, THE TWO RECONSTRUCTIONS: THE STRUGGLE FOR BLACK ENFRANCHISEMENT, 2 (2004); THE NEGRO IN VIRGINIA, *supra* note 15 at 226.

21. Foner, *supra* 15 at 187-89.

22. Donna Dickerson & David Copeland (eds.), The Reconstruction Era: Primary Documents on the Events 1865-1877, 43-54 (2003); Texas State Library and Archives Commission, The 1890s: Black Codes, https://www.tsl.texas.gov/exhibits/forever/endofanera/page2.html; Foner, *supra* note 15 at 198-204.

23. Foner, *supra* note 15 at 198-204.

24. *Id.* at 199-203.

25. Foner, *supra* note 15 at 119-23.

26. *Id.* at 160-64.

27. *Id.* at 196; CHARLES FLOOD, LEE: LAST YEARS, 116 (Mariner Books 1998) (1981).

28. Foner, *supra* note 15 at 225-26; Flood, *supra* note 27 at 116-24.

29. Foner, *supra* note 15 at 239.

30. Act of April 9, 1866 (Civil Rights Act), Public Law 39-26, 14 STAT 27.

31. Foner, *supra* note 15 at 250; Andrew Johnson, Veto of the Civil Rights Act of 1866 (Mar. 27, 1866) *in* VOL. VI A COMPILATION OF MESSAGES AND PAPERS OF THE PRESIDENTS OF THE UNITED STATES, 405 (James D. Richardson ed., 1902).

32. Foner, *supra* note 15 at 159-61; Valelly, *supra* note 20 at 26-27.

33. Foner, *supra* note 15 at 166-67.

34. *Id.* at 467.

35. McIntosh, 21 U.S. 543 at 588 (1819).

36. Foner, *supra* note 15 at 183-84; Valelly, *supra* note 20 at 27. For a more charitable view of Johnson's actions, *see* 2 Morison, *supra* note 2 at 508-12.

37. U.S. Const. Amd. 14, sect. 1.

38. The rest of Section 1 reads as follows:

> No State shall make or enforce any law which shall abridge the privileges or immunities of citizens of the United States; nor shall any State deprive any person of life, liberty, or property, without due process of law; nor deny to any person within its jurisdiction the equal protection of the laws."

39. The Knights of the White Camellia have recently been described as follows:

> The Knights of the White Camellia, a Texas Klan group led by Charles Lee, along with the Texas chapter of Thom Robb's Knights of the KKK, has been linked to a number of incidents of racial intimidation and harassment in Vidor, Texas. These incidents, which occurred in 1992 and 1993, involved efforts to prevent the desegregation of an all-white Federally assisted housing project in Vidor. Among the reported acts of intimidation was the threat to blow up a housing unit to prevent its integration; residents of the project additionally alleged that the White Camellia Knights carried automatic weapons on a bus they drove through the housing complex and that one Klan member offered white children $50 to beat up African-American children. The Texas Commission on Human Rights has

brought a civil suit against both Klan groups in response to these incidents.

Jewish Virtual Library, Ku Klux Klan, http://www.jewishvirtuallibrary.org/jsource/anti-semitism/KKK.html. *See also* White Supremacy and Terrorism, http://www.pbs.org/tpt/slavery-by-another-name/themes/white-supremacy/. CHARLES LANE, THE DAY FREEDOM DIED: THE COLFAX MASSACRE, THE SUPREME COURT, AND THE BETRAYAL OF RECONSTRUCTION (2009).

40. Foner, *supra* note 15 at 439-44.

41. U.S. Statutes at Large Vol. 17 p. 13 (1871).

42. Foner, *supra* note 15 at 457-58. *See also* Valelly, *supra* note 20 at 116-17.

43. Foner, *supra* note 15 at 457-58.

44. Dickerson & Copeland, *supra* note 22 at 43-45; Foner, *supra* note 15 at 457-58.

45. Foner, *supra* note 15 at 319-20.

46. CAROL FAULKNER, WOMEN'S RADICAL RECONSTRUCTION: THE FREEDMAN'S AID MOVEMENT (2004); THE FREEDMAN'S BUREAU AND RECONSTRUCTION (Paul A. Cimbala & Randall M. Miller eds., 1999); Foner, *supra* note 15 at 25.

47. 83 U.S. 36 at 71 (1873).

48. *Id.* at 76 (1873).

49. *Id.* at 77.

50. 83 U.S. 36 at 71 (1873).

51. *Id.* at 95-96 (Field, J. dissenting).

52. *Id.* at 96.

53. JANE M. FRIEDMAN, AMERICA'S FIRST WOMAN LAWYER: THE BIOGRAPHY OF MYRA BRADWELL (1993); Jill Norgren, Rebels at the Bar: The Fascinating, Forgotten Stories of America's First Women Lawyers, 26-43 (2020); DAWN BRADLEY BERRY, THE 50 MOST INFLUENTIAL WOMEN IN AMERICAN LAW (1996).

54. 83 U.S. 130 at 139 (1873).

55. Minor v. Happersett, 88 U.S. 162 (1874).

56. *Id.* at 164.

57. *Id.* at 177-78.

58. Jonathan K. Stubbs, A Demographic History of Judicial Appointments by Gender and Race, 1789-2016, 26 Berkeley La Raza L.J. 92, 108 (2016).

59. *See* https://www.fjc.gov/history/judges/search/advanced-search. To access this material, go the Federal Judicial Center

website and click History of the Federal Judiciary, then click Judges, then click Biographical Directory of Article III Judges, 1789-present, then click Appointing President, then check Donald J. Trump, then click Personal Characteristics, then click gender, then click male, finally click white. Trump appointed and the Senate confirmed 227 federal judges of which 147 were white males, 147/227 = 64.7%. For an excellent discussion of Trump's attempt to make the federal judiciary look more like that of 1789, see Stacy Hawkins, Trump's Dangerous Judicial Legacy, UCLA L. Rev. (June 13, 2019), https://www.uclalawreview.org/trumps-dangerous-judicial-legacy/.

60. *See* Federal Judicial Center, https://www.fjc.gov/history/judges/search/advanced-search. To access this material, go the Federal Judicial Center website and click History of the Federal Judiciary, then click Judges, then click Biographical Directory of Article III Judges, 1789-present, then click Appointing President, then check Joseph R. Biden, then click Personal Characteristics, then click gender, then click both.

61. *Id.*

62. Foner, *supra* note 15 at 569-75.

63. *Id.* at 429.

64. *Id.* at 503.

65. United States v. Cruikshank, 92 U.S. 542, 548 (1875) (citations omitted).

66. 92 U.S. 542 (1875).

67. *Id.* at 559.

68. *Id.* 554-55.

69. Foner, *supra* note 15 at 575-76.

70. *Id.* at 580.

71. *Id.* at 582-83.

72. *Id.* at 590.

73. Strauder v. West Virginia, 100 U.S. 303 at 307 (1880).

74. *Id.* at 307-08.

75. 109 U.S. at 25.

76. *Id.* at 61-62.

77. *Id.* at 61.

78. 118 U.S. 394 (1886).

79. *Id.*

80. *Id.* at 401.

81. 134 U.S. 418 (1890).

82. *Id.* at 457.

83. *Id.* at 458.

84. PAUL BREST ET AL., PROCESSES OF CONSTITUTIONAL DECISIONMAKING: CASES AND MATERIALS, 460, n.109 (7th ed. 2018).

85. Foner, *supra* note 15 at 467.

86. *Id.* at 467. *See also* Foner, *supra* note 15, 467, n.13.

87. Equal Justice Initiative, Lynching in America: Confronting the Legacy of Racial Terror, 4 (2017); available at https://eji.org/wp-content/uploads/2005/11/lynching-in-america-3d-ed-110121.pdf.

88. Equal Justice Initiative, https://eji.org/racial-justice/. *See also* Timothy V. Kaufman-Osborn, *Capital Punishment as Legal Lynching, in* LYNCH MOBS TO THE KILLING STATE, 50, n.12 (Charles Ogletree Jr. & Austin Sarat eds., 2006); MIA BAY, TO TELL THE TRUTH FREELY: THE LIFE OF IDA B. WELLS, 3 (2009).

89. Nicolas Villanueva, Texas Lynchings of Mexicans in the 1910s, https://www.c-span.org/video/?453206-9/texas-lynchings-mexicans-1910s; Nicolas Villanueva, The Lynching of Mexicans in the Texas Borderlands (2017); History of Lynchings of Mexican Americans Provides Context for Recent Challenges to U.S. Death Penalty, Death Penalty Information Center, https://deathpenaltyinfo.org/search#stq=history%20of%20lynching%20of%20mexican%20americans&stp=1.

90. Edwin T. Arnold, What Virtue There Is in Fire: Cultural Memory and the Lynching of Sam Hose (2009); Reelblack One, W.E.B. Du Bois, A Recorded Autobiography (1961), https://www.youtube.com/watch?v=Ooa-CzT7NWg (Du Bois' discussion of the lynching begins at 24:44 minutes into the oral history.).

91. NAACP, THIRTY YEARS OF LYNCHING IN THE UNITED STATES, 1889-1918 (Arno Press & N.Y. Times 1969) (Apr. 1919), at 13; Bay, *supra* note 88 at 242-44. For graphic photographs of numerous lynchings, see the online resource "Without Sanctuary," https://withoutsanctuary.org/.

92. Reelblack One, Du Bois, A Recorded Autobiography, *supra* note 90.

## Chapter V

1. MICHAEL PERMAN, STRUGGLE FOR MASTERY, DISENFRANCHISEMENT IN THE SOUTH, 1888-1908, 11-22 (2001); A. Keyssar, The Right to Vote: The Contested History of Democracy in America,

106-14 (2000); RICHARD D. VALELLY, THE TWO RECONSTRUCTIONS: THE STRUGGLE FOR BLACK ENFRANCHISEMENT, 121-48 (2004).

2. Perman, *supra* note 1 at 213; Valelly, *supra* note 1 at 124-25.

3. Perman, *supra* note 1 at 213.

4. *Id.* at 193.

5. *Id.*

6. *Id.* at 170-71, footnotes omitted; Valelly, *supra* note 1 at 116-17; Keyssar, *supra* note 1 at 105-07.

7. 170 U.S. 213 (1898).

8. *Id.* at 225.

9. *Id.* at 223 (quoting) Dixon v. The State, Nov. 9, 1896, 20 So. Rep. 839. *See also* Keyssar, *supra* note 1 at 115-16.

10. Perman, *supra* note 1 at 75.

11. *Id.* at 74.

12. *Id.* at 85-90.

13. 2 REPORT OF THE PROCEEDINGS AND DEBATES OF THE CONSTITUTIONAL CONVENTION OF THE STATE OF VIRGINIA 3076-77 (1906). *See also* ANDREW BUNI, THE NEGRO IN VIRGINIA POLITICS: 1902-1965, 17 (1967).

14. Buni, *supra* note 13 at 24.

15. *Id.* at 27; THE NEGRO IN VIRGINIA (Va. Writers Program of the Works Projects Admin. of the State of Va.) 240 (1940).

16. Oliver W. Hill Sr., THE BIG BANG, BROWN V. BOARD OF EDUCATION AND BEYOND: THE AUTOBIOGRAPHY OF OLIVER W. HILL, SR., 100th Birthday Edition xxv (Jonathan K. Stubbs ed., 2007).

17. Lord Acton, *Letter to Bishop Mandell Creighton, 1887, in* 1 LIFE AND LETTERS OF MANDELL CREIGHTON (Louise Creighton ed., 1906) at 371-72.

18. Perman, *supra* note 1 at 213; THE NEGRO IN VIRGINIA, *supra* note 15 at 238-40.

19. 194 U.S. 147 (1904).

20. *Id.* at 148-53; THE NEGRO IN VIRGINIA, *supra* note 15 at 240.

21. Hill, *supra* note 16 at xxv.

22. Wendy R. Weiser & Lawrence Norden, Brennan Center for Justice, Voting Law Changes in 2012, 5 (2012).

23. *Speech: Assistant Attorney General Perez Speaks at the George Washington University Law School Symposium*, U.S. Dep't of Just. Off. of Pub. Aff. (Nov. 16, 2012), https://www.justice.gov/opa/speech/assistant-attorney-general-perez

-speaks-george-washington-university-law-school-symposium; Brentin Mock & Voting Rights Watch, *Voting Rights Haven't Gotten Such Attention Since 1967. What Did We Learn?*, The Nation (Nov. 16, 2012), https://www.thenation.com/article/archive/voting-rights-havent-gotten-such-attention-1965-what-did-we-learn; *Connolly Introduces FAST Voting Act to Improve Election Process*, Congressman Gerry Connolly: In the News (Nov. 16, 2012), https://connolly.house.gov/news/documentsingle.aspx?DocumentID=419; John Fritze, *Push to Speed Voting Process*, Balt. Sun A1 (Nov. 24, 2012)); Mike *Kirby, Opinion, Kirby: Crazy in Florida*, Sun Chr. (Nov. 25, 2012), https://www.thesunchronicle.com/opinion/columns/kirby-crazy-in-florida/article_1b806b9c-6850-5dd7-a5a5-ab88894d8e30.html.

24. Shelby County v. Holder, 570 U.S. 529 (2013).

25. *See* Justice Ginsburg's trenchant dissent, 570 U.S. 529 at 562, quoting 42 U.S.C. § 1973c(a).

26. *Id.* at 540.

27. Thomas Calhoun Walker, The Honey Pod Tree: The Life Story of Thomas Calhoun Walker "Lawyer Walker of Gloucester," 176-78 (John Day Company, 1958).

28. 570 U.S. at 554.

29. *Id.* at 591-92.

30. *See* Election 2016: Restrictive Voting Laws by the Numbers (Brennan Ctr. for Justice, Sept. 28, 2016), https://www.brennancenter.org/our-work/research-reports/election-2016-restrictive-voting-laws-numbers#voterlitigation.

31. James Clapper, Facts and Fears: Hard Truths from a Life in Intelligence, 352-400 (2018).

32. Charles Stewart III, 2016 survey of the Performance of American Elections: Final Report, 22 (2017) (Blacks and Latinos more than twice as likely to be required to show photo identification in order to vote as compared with Whites); Brennan Center, *supra* note 30.

33. *See* Paul Waldman, "Voter Suppression Could Become More Important to the GOP's Election Plans Than Ever," Dec. 18, 2019 (Wash. Post), https://www.washingtonpost.com/opinions/2019/12/18/voter-suppression-could-become-more-important-gops-election-plans-than-ever/; ACLU, Fighting Voter Suppression, https://www.aclu.org/news/by-issue/fighting-voter-suppression; Republicans Escalate Their Efforts at Voter Suppression, Oct. 27,

2019 (Wash. Post), https://www.washingtonpost.com/opinions/republicans-escalate-their-strategy-of-voter-suppression/2019/10/27/69ceef88-f762-11e9-a285-882a8e386a96_story.html.

34. Allen v. Milligan, 599 U.S. 1 (2023).

35. *Id.* at 14 (citations omitted).

36. *Id.* at 25 (citations omitted).

37. *Id.* at 28-29 (citations omitted).

38. *Id.* at 29.

39. Harvey Fireside, Separate and Unequal: Homer Plessy and the Supreme Court Decision That Legalized Racism, 1 (2004).

40. 163 U.S. 537, at 551.

41. *Id.* at 560.

42. 175 U.S. 528 (1899).

43. *Id.* at 542-545.

44. *Id.* at 545.

45. 203 U.S. 1 (1906).

46. *Id.* at 16-17.

47. *Id.* at 29-39.

## Chapter VI

1. General Allotment Act of 1887, 24 Stat. 388 (1887).

2. Marilyn J. Ward Ford, *Twenty-Five Years of the Alaska Native Claims Settlement Act: Self-Determination or Destruction of the Heritage, Culture, and Way of Life of Alaska's Native Americans?* 12 J. Envtl. L. & Litig. 305, 315, and accompanying notes (1997); Juan Perea et al., Race and Races: Cases and Resources for a Diverse America, 221-22 (2d ed. 2007); Peter Carroll & David Noble, The Free and the Unfree: A Progressive History of the United States, 235-37 (3d ed. 2001).

3. United States Dept. Interior, "Native American Ownership and Governance of Natural Resources: General Allotment Act of 1887 (Dawes Act)" (2024), https://revenuedata.doi.gov/how-revenue-works/native-american-ownership-governance/.

4. *Id. See also* Getches, Wilkinson & Williams, Federal Indian Law 168 (3d ed. 1993) *and* references in note 2, *supra*.

5. Emeritus Professor Nelson Valdes of the University of New Mexico has lectured extensively in this area, and in a course dealing

with Land Grants and the U.S. Legal System suggested the following resources:


1. Malcolm Ebright & Rick Hendricks, The Witches of Abiquiu: The Governor, the Priest, the Genízaro Indians and the Devil, UNM Press, 2006.
2. *Malcolm Ebright, Land Grants and Lawsuits in Northern New Mexico*, UNM Press, 1980.
3. Malcolm Ebright, The Tierra Amarilla grant: A history of chicanery, Santa Fe, 1980.
4. Malcolm Ebright, The Embudo Grant: A Case Study of Justice and the Court of Private Land Claims, Journal of the West, July 1980.
5. Malcolm Ebright (Editor), Spanish and Mexican Land Grants and the Law (A Center for Land Grant Studies Book), Santa Fe, 1989.
6. Harold H. Dunham, New Mexico Land Grants with Special Reference to the Title Papers of the Maxwell Grant, 30 N. M. Hist. Rev. 1, 1955.
7. David J. Weber, Foreigners in Their Native Land: Historical Roots of the Mexican Americans, Albuquerque: University of New Mexico, 1973.
8. Victor Westphall, The Public Domain in New Mexico: 1854-1891, Albuquerque: University of New Mexico, 1965.
9. William deBuys, Fractions of Justice, A Legal and Social History of the Las Trampas Land Grant, New Mexico, 56 N.M. Hist. Rev. 71, (1981).
10. Howard Roberts Lamar, The Far Southwest: 1846-1912, New Haven: Yale University Press, 1966.
11. George W. Julian "Land Stealing in New Mexico," 145 N. Am. Rev. 17 (1887).
12. Clark S. Knowlton, "The Town of Las Vegas Community Grant: An Anglo-American Coup D'etat," Journal of the West, Vol. 19, No. 4.


From http://www.unm.edu/~nvaldes/326/lect11.

For additional information on Professor Valdes, *see* http://www.unmalumni.com/valdes.html.

6. Minutes of New Mexico Bar Association at Its Regular Annual Session 26 (Dennis & Co. photo. reprt. 1941) (1904).

7. *Id.*

8. 167 U.S. 278 (1897).

9. *Id.* at 296-98.

10. MALCOLM EBRIGHT, THE GAO REPORT: A WHITEWASH AND A SLAP IN THE FACE, http://www.southwestbooks.org/gaome response.htm.

11. *See* A.S. Dillingham, "What An Indigenous Perspective on U.S. and Mexican History Reveals" (Feb. 10, 2023, Wash. Post).

12. Wilderness Society Action Fund, "New Story Map Details How Last Four Years of Trump Oil and Gas Actions Have Impacted Public Lands and Communities, https://www .wildernessaction.org/new-story-map-details-how-last-four-years-trump-oil-and-gas-actions-have-impacted-public-lands-and-com munities; *see also* Emily Holden, Jimmy Tobias & Alvin Chang, Revealed: The Full Extent of Trump's "Meat Cleaver" Assault on U.S. Wilderness (The Guardian, Oct. 26, 2020), https://www.the guardian.com/environment/ng-interactive/2020/oct/26/revealed -trump-public-lands-oil-drilling.

13. Brian Maffly, New Grand Staircase Plans Green-light Mining on Lands Trump Stripped from Utah Monument, Salt Lake Trib., Aug. 23, 2019, https://www.sltrib.com/news/ environment/2019/08/23/new-grand-staircase-plans/.

14. See references in note 12, *supra*.

## Chapter VII

1. Material from the section comes from Oliver W. Hill Sr., THE BIG BANG, BROWN V. BOARD OF EDUCATION AND BEYOND: THE AUTOBIOGRAPHY OF OLIVER W. HILL, SR., 100th Birthday Edition 78-191 (Jonathan K. Stubbs ed., 2007).

2. *See* Hill, *supra* note 1.

3. *Id.* at 78.

4. *Id.* at 79. *See also* GENNA RAE MCNEIL, GROUNDWORK: CHARLES HAMILTON HOUSTON AND THE STRUGGLE FOR CIVIL RIGHTS (1983).

5. Hill, *supra* note 1 at 79; MCNEIL, *supra* note 4 at 53-55.

6. 271 U.S. 323 (1926).

7. Hill, *supra* note 1 at 79; GILBERT WARE, WILLIAM HASTIE, GRACE UNDER PRESSURE (1984).

8. Jonathan K. Stubbs, A Demographic History of Judicial Appointments by Gender and Race, 1789-2016, 26 Berkeley La Raza L.J. 92, 101 (2016).

9. Hill, *supra* note 1 at 80.

10. 303 U.S. 613 (1938).

11. 309 U.S. 227 (1940).

12. Hill, *supra* note 1 at 157.

13. Ware, *supra* note 7 at 47-53.

14. Hill, *supra* note 1 at 157; Larry S. Gibson, Young Thurgood: The Making of a Supreme Court Justice, 235 (2012).

15. *See e.g.*, RONALD TANAKI, STRANGERS FROM A DIFFERENT SHORE 392-96 (1989) (describing among other matters, the forced internment of many Japanese American citizens and the virtual confiscation of nearly all their material possessions); MALCOLM EBREIGHT, LAND GRANTS AND LAWSUITS IN NORTHERN NEW MEXICO 34-50 (1994) (analyzing American law and policy resulting in Mexican American citizens losing vast tracts of land to the United States government and to their Anglo neighbors); *see U.S. v. Sandoval*, 167 U.S. 278 (1897) (ruling that land held in common by a pueblo under Mexican law passed to the United States under the Treaty of Guadalupe Hidalgo thereby establishing precedent by which millions of acres of land held primarily for the common benefit of Mexican American pueblo residents was transferred to the United States). For a perceptive perspective of how both English and Spanish colonizers unlawfully seized Indigenous Americans' land, see A.S. Dillingham, "What An Indigenous Perspective on U.S. and Mexican History Reveals" (Feb. 10, 2023, Wash. Post).

16. *See* Underwriting Manual, quoted in MELVIN L. OLIVER & THOMAS M. SHAPIRO, BLACK WEALTH/WHITE WEALTH: A NEW PERSPECTIVE ON RACIAL INEQUALITY 18 (1995); John Kimble, Insuring Inequality: The Role of the Federal Housing Administration in the Urban Ghettoization of African Americans, 32 Law D Soc. Inq. 399 (2007), DALTON CONLEY, BEING BLACK, LIVING IN THE RED: RACE, WEALTH AND SOCIAL POLICY IN AMERICA 36-37 (1999).

17. *See* DAVID L. KIRP, JOHN P. DWYER & LARRY ROSENTHAL, OUR TOWN: RACE, HOUSING AND THE SOUL OF SUBURBIA 26 (1997); Kimble, *supra* note 16.

18. Jonathan K. Stubbs, America's Enduring Legacy: Segregated Housing and Segregated Schools, 6 Min. Trial Lawyer 1 (2008).

19. Oliver & Shapiro, *supra* note 16 at 18.

20. National Community Reinvestment Coalition, Income Is No Shield Against Racial Differences in Lending: A comparison of high cost lending in America's metropolitan areas (2007).

21. *See* Oliver & Shapiro, *supra* note 16 at 17-18, 39-41, 136-51 (citations omitted). *See also* Oliver W. Hill Sr., *supra* note 1 at 270; Conley, *supra* note 16; Douglas S. Massey & Nancy A. Denton, American Apartheid, Segregation and the Making of the Underclass 51-55 (1994). *See also* C. Lowell Harris, History and Policies of the Home Owners' Loan Corporation 52-53 (1951) (pointing out that only 1% of applicants for loans in New York region were Negroes, and surmising that this low number reflected the low rate of home ownership among Blacks); Kimble, *supra* note 16.

22. Richard Rothstein, The Color of Law (2017) documents in detail the segregationist policies which federal and state governmental officials pursued in the housing sector of America's economy.

23. *Pearson v. Murray*, 182 A 590 (Md. 1936).

24. 305 U.S. 337 (1938).

25. *Id.* at 351.

26. To Secure These Rights: The Report of the President's Committee on Civil Rights (1947), https://www.trumanlibrary.gov/library/to-secure-these-rights.

27. *Id.* at 151-73.

28. *Sipuel v. Board of Regents of the University of Oklahoma*, 332 U.S. 631 (1948); *McLaurin v. Board of Regents of the University of Oklahoma*, 339 U.S. 637 (1950).

29. *See* Richard Kluger, Simple Justice: The History of Brown v. Board of Education and Black America's Struggle for Equality 256-58 (1976); Anthony M. Platt, The Rise and Fall of Affirmative Action, 11 Notre Dame J. L. Ethics & Pub. Policy 67 (1997); John A. Powell & Marguerite L. Spencer, Remaking the Urban University for the Urban Student: Talking About Race, 30 Conn. L. Rev. 1247, 1262 (1998); F. Michael Higginbotham, Soldiers for Justice: The Role of the Tuskegee Airmen in the Desegregation of the American Armed Forces, 8 Wm. & Mary Bill of Rts. J. 273, 286 n.72 (2000).

30. Platt, *supra* note 29 at 69 (citations omitted)

31. Platt, *supra* note 29 at 69 and accompanying footnotes. *See also* DONALD E. BOLES, MR. JUSTICE REHNQUIST, JUDICIAL ACTIVIST: THE EARLY YEARS 13-14 (1987); WILLIAM H. REHNQUIST, THE SUPREME COURT 3-4 (2001). For a revealing behind-the-scenes perspective of the Rehnquist nomination to the Supreme Court, *see* JOHN W. DEAN, THE REHNQUIST CHOICE: THE UNTOLD STORY OF THE NIXON APPOINTMENT THAT REDEFINED THE SUPREME COURT (2001). *See also* National Archives, "Servicemen's Readjustment 1944," (2024) ("Unfortunately, not all veterans were able to take advantage of the benefits of the G.I. Bill. Black vets were often unable to get bank loans for mortgages in Black neighborhoods, and they faced prejudice and discrimination that overwhelming excluded them from buying homes in 'white' suburban neighborhoods"), https://www.archives.gov/milestone-documents/servicemens-readjustment-act.

32. For discussion of the invidious nature of group-based quotas, particularly as applied to Jews, *see* Marcia Graham Synott, *Anti-Semitism and American Universities: Did Quotas Follow the Jews? in* ANTI-SEMITISM IN AMERICAN HISTORY 233-71 (David A. Gerber ed., 1986); *Grutter v Bollinger*, 288 F.3d at 793-94 (Boggs, J., dissenting); Karen Sacks, *How Did Jews Become White Folks, in* CRITICAL WHITE STUDIES 395-401 (Richard Delgado & Jean Stefanio eds., 1997).

33. Hill, *supra* note 1 at 163. *See McLaurin v. Oklahoma State Regents*, 339 U.S. at 640. *See also* McLaurin v. Oklahoma State Regents, Encyclopedia of the Great Plains, http://plainshumanities.unl.edu/encyclopedia/doc/egp.edu.025; https://www.blackpast.org/african-american-history/mclaurin-george-w-1887-1968/. [White students in class at the University of Oklahoma, and G.W. McLaurin, an African American, seated in anteroom], https://www.loc.gov/item/96515851/.

34. McLaurin v. University of Oklahoma State Regents, 339 U.S. 637, 640 (1950).

35. *Sweatt v. Painter*, 339 U.S. 629 (1950).

36. *Id.* at 633-34.

37. Hill, *supra* note 1 at 153-56.

38. Davis v. County School Board of Prince Edward, 103 F. Supp. 337 (E.D. Va. 1952).

39. Bolling v. Sharpe, 347 U.S. 497 (1954).

40. Bradley v. Sch. Bd. of Richmond, 338 F. Supp 67 (E.D. Va. 1972), *rev'd*, 462 F.2d 1058 (4th Cir. 1973), *aff'd*, 412 U.S. 92 (1973, equally divided Court).

41. Green v. County Sch. Bd. of New Kent County, 391 U.S. 430 (1968); *and see* Danielle Wingfield, "Movement Lawyers: Henry L. Marsh's Long Struggle for Educational Justice" 56 U. Rich. L. Rev. 1339 (2022).

42. Oliver & Shapiro, *supra* note 16 at 151; Conley *supra* note 16 at 43-46.

43. Rakesh Kochar, Pew Hispanic Center, The Wealth of Hispanic Households: 1996-2002, https://www.pewresearch.org/hispanic/2004/10/18/the-wealth-of-hispanic-households/.

44. Rakesh Kochhar, Richard Fry & Paul Taylor, Pew Hispanic Center, Twenty to One: Wealth Gaps Rise to Record Highs Between Whites, Blacks and Hispanics, https://www.pewresearch.org/social-trends/2011/07/26/wealth-gaps-rise-to-record-highs-between-whites-blacks-hispanics/.

45. Thomas Shapiro, Tatjana Meschede & Sam Osoro, The Roots of the Widening Racial Wealth Gap: Explaining the Black-White Economic Divide, Inst. Assets & Soc. Pol'y 6 (Feb. 2013).

46. *Id.* at 6-7.

47. Oliver & Shapiro, *supra* note 16 at 51. *See also* John Creamer et al., U.S. Census Bureau, Current Population Reports No. P60-277, Poverty in the United States: 2021, at 36-45 tbl.A-5 (Sept. 2022), https://www.census.gov/content/dam/Census/library/publications/2022/demo/p60-277.pdf (indicating that for approximately 50 years the rate of poverty for Blacks and Hispanics has been at least two times greater than that of Whites).

48. Oliver & Shapiro, *supra* note 16 at 38; Conley, *supra* note 16 at 135.

49. Oliver & Shapiro, *supra* note 16 at 41-42; Conley, *supra* note 16 at 121-22, 126-32.

50. National Population by Characteristics: 2020-2023, U.S. Bureau of Census, https://www.census.gov/data/datasets/time-series/demo/popest/2020s-national-detail.html (last modified June 20, 2023) (follow "Sex, Race, and Hispanic Origin" hyperlink under "Vintage 2023"; then choose "Males," "Not Hispanic," "One Race," and "One Race: White"). The total of White males (125,624,209) divided by the total population of the United States (333,287,557)

is 29.87%. Id. National Population by Characteristics: 2020-2022, U.S. Census Bureau,

51. GOOD FOR BUSINESS: MAKING FULL USE OF THE NATION'S HUMAN CAPITAL, GLASS CEILING COMMISSION, iii-iv (1995), https://ecommons.cornell.edu/bitstream/handle/1813/79348/GlassCeilingFactFindingEnvironmentalScan.pdf?sequence=1&isAllowed=y. Regarding the composition of CEOs in the top 100 corporations in the United States, 76 are White men; 12 are women, including 2 African American women; and 14% are "diverse," including 6 Asian/Asian Americans, 3 African Americans, 4 Latinos, and 1 Middle Eastern person. *See* Diversity Stagnant Among Fortune 100 Leaders Despite Belief That DE&I Is a Key Contributor to Business Success, Reveals Heidrick & Struggles' Route to the Top 2022 Report (Nov. 17, 2022), https://www.prnewswire.com/news-releases/diversity-stagnant-among-fortune-100-leaders-despite-belief-that-dei-is-a-key-contributor-to-business-success-reveals-heidrick--struggles-route-to-the-top-2022-report-301681143.html.

Lyndon Taylor, regional managing partner of Heidrick & Struggles' CEO & Board of Directors Practice for the Americas and an advisor on diversity, equity, and inclusion strategies has stated:

> Substantial progress is being made in corporate DE&I efforts, but the fact remains that diversity advances among Fortune 100 CEOs is relatively unchanged ... and while the advancements women and other diverse executives have made toward the CEO role are gaining momentum, we still aren't seeing that momentum pivot to notable increases in CEO appointments for these underrepresented groups.

*Id.*

Maxine Waters, "Ranking Member Waters Slams Republican AGs' Attacks on Diversity and Inclusion" Press Release (U.S. House Cmttee. Financial Services, July 28, 2023), https://democrats-financialservices.house.gov/news/documentsingle.aspx?DocumentID=410721. Cathy A. Trower & Richard P. Chait, Faculty Diversity: Too Little for Too Long, Harv. Mag. Mar.-Apr. 2002 at 33-37.

52. As of February 2, 2023, there were 128 women in the House of Representatives. *See* Rebecca Leppert & Drew Disilver, 118th Congress Has Record Number of Women, https://www.pewresearch.org/fact-tank/2023/01/03/118th-congress-has-a-record-number-

of-women/. Twenty-five women currently serve in the United States Senate, *see* https://www.senate.gov/reference/Index/Women.htm.

The Senate has three African American members and 54 African Americans in the House (approximately 12%).

Representation of Hispanics is somewhat complex. Hispanics represent approximately 20% of the U.S. population. Seven Latinos serve in the Senate (7% of Senators); and 45 Latinos serve in the House (approximately 10%). Joseph Marion Hernández, a Cuban American, was the first Hispanic in Congress. He was a Whig Party territorial representative for Florida in 1823. The first to represent a state was Romualdo Pacheco, who represented California in 1877. In 1929, Octaviano Ambrosio Larrazolo became the first Hispanic to be elected to the United States Senate. Ileana Ros-Lehtinen, a Cuban American first elected in 1989, was the first Hispanic woman in Congress.

According to a recent Pew Foundation Report, Asian Americans comprise 4% of House members (14 congresspersons) and about 6% of the national population. *See* U.S. Congress Continues to Grow in Racial, Ethnic Diversity, https://www.pewresearch.org/fact-tank/2023/01/09/u-s-congress-continues-to-grow-in-racial-ethnic-diversity/. There are also two Asian American senators. Dalip Singh Saund was the first South Asian American in Congress. Hiram Fong, who served three decades in the Senate, remains the sole Chinese American member to have ever served in the U.S. Senate. Daniel Inouye was the first Japanese American in the House and later the first in Senate. Patsy Mink was the first Asian American woman in Congress.

In addition, nine Jews serve in the United States Senate (9%) and 33 Jews are members of the House of Representatives (6%). *See* Jeff Diamant, Faith on the Hill: The Religious Composition of the 118th Congress (Pew Foundation, Jan. 3, 2023), https://www.pewresearch.org/religion/2023/01/03/faith-on-the-hill-2023/.

Native Americans comprise approximately 1% of the national population. Population. Four Native Americans serve in the House, and one Native American serves in the Senate.

53. As to the demographic profile of full-time professors, the National Center for Education Statistics states:

Considering full-time faculty only, in fall 2021,

- 73 percent of faculty were White, specifically 35 percent White female and 38 percent White male;
- 12 percent of faculty were Asian, specifically 5 percent Asian female and 7 percent Asian male;
- 6 percent of faculty were Black, specifically 4 percent Black female and 3 percent Black male;
- 6 percent of faculty were Hispanic, specifically 3 percent each Hispanic female and Hispanic male;
- 1 percent were of Two or more races;
- less than one-half of 1 percent were American Indian/ Alaska Native; and
- less than one-half of 1 percent were Pacific Islander.

The racial/ethnic and sex distribution of full-time instructional faculty varied by academic rank at degree-granting postsecondary institutions in fall 2021. Professor and associate professor are higher academic ranks, which are usually tenured, meaning that they cannot be terminated without just cause. Assistant professor is typically an entry-level position, which can lead to higher ranks. Instructor and lecturer are typically lower ranks with no potential for tenure. In 2021, White male and Asian male faculty made up higher percentages of faculty in the higher ranks (tenure-track) than they did in the lower ranks (non-tenure-track). Specifically, 40 percent of tenure-track faculty were White males and 8 percent were Asian males. Meanwhile, 34 percent of non-tenure-track faculty were White males and 5 percent were Asian males. Other groups made up similar or lower percentages of faculty in the higher ranks than in the lower ranks. For example, Hispanic females made up 2 percent of faculty in tenure-track ranks and 4 percent in non-tenure-track ranks. (footnotes omitted)

*See* Fast Facts: Race, Ethnicity of College Faculty, https://nces.ed.gov/fastfacts/display.asp?id=61.

54. *See* Jonathan K. Stubbs, *Why America Still Needs Affirmative Action*, 57 Va. Lawyer 18 (2008); George Stephanopulis &

Christopher Edley Jr., Report on the Review of Federal Affirmative Action Programs, July 19, 1995, https://clintonwhitehouse4.archives.gov/WH/EOP/OP/html/aa/aa-lett.html.

55. *A Disparity Study for the Commonwealth of Virginia Commonwealth* (July 11, 2011) at 5-3–5-11 (Exhibits 5-1, 5-3, 5-4, 5-6, respectively).

56. *Id.* at 5-12–5-13 (Exhibit 5-7).

57. *Adarand Constructors v. Pena*, 515 U.S. 200, 208 (1995); Stephanopoulus & Edley, *supra* note 54.

58. 515 U.S. at 208.

59. *See* John Creamer et al., *supra* note 47; Annual Estimates of the Resident Population by Sex, Race, and Hispanic Origin for the United States: April 1, 2020-July 1, 2021, U.S. Bureau of Census, https://www.census.gov/data/datasets/time-series/demo/popest/2020s-national-detail.htm. In addition, the Act allowed third persons to furnish evidence to rebut the presumption of disadvantage claimed by individual members of gender and so-called racial groups. 515 U.S. at 208.

60. 515 U.S. 200 (1995).

61. *Id.* at 227 (emphasis in the original, citations omitted).

62. *Id.* at 245.

63. *Grutter v. Bollinger*, 539 U.S. 306 (2003).

64. *Id.* at 336-37.

65. *Id.* at 327 (citations omitted).

66. *Id.* at 336-37 (citations omitted).

67. *Id.* at 338-39 (citations omitted). The *Grutter* Court endorsed Justice Lewis Powell's view expressed in *Bakke v. Board of Regents* that race could be considered in the admission process provided that each individual received individualized attention, and race was given appropriate weight. Powell specifically noted that race could be used as a plus factor but did not elaborate on precisely how one would determine how much of a plus a specific individual's application should receive based on the racial diversity of a candidate. 438 U.S. 265 at 317-18 (1978).

68. 539 U.S. at 329.

69. *Id.* Of course, not only is the individual freedom of humans enhanced in such circumstances, but also to the extent that an institution is an individual under the First Amendment, the university can enjoy its right to promote freedom of thought.

70. *Id.*

71. *Id.* at 342 (quoting brief of respondents Bollinger).

72. *Id.* at 343.

73. *Id.* at 346 (Ginsburg, J. concurring.).

74. 136 S. Ct. 2198 (2016).

75. *Id.* at 2207.

76. Sweatt v. Painter, 339 U.S. 634 (1950) (emphasis added).

77. Fisher v. Texas, 579 U.S. 365, 375 (2016).

78. U.S. v. Singer, No. 1:19-cr-10078 (E.D. Mass. 2019) (a vast criminal conspiracy involving hundreds of parents, their children, and about a dozen well-regarded colleges and universities, including Yale, Georgetown, and University of Southern California); *see* Press Release, U.S. Att'y's Off., Dist. of Mass., Arrests Made in Nationwide College Admissions Scam: Alleged Exam Cheating & Athletic Recruiting Scheme (Mar. 12, 2019), https://www.justice.gov/usao-ma/pr/arrests-made-nationwide-college-admissions-scam-alleged-examcheating-athletic [https://perma.cc/P4XZ-RKBH]. Rick Smith, an alleged mastermind of the conspiracy, received a jail sentence of 42 months. Tovia Smith & Jaclyn Diaz, "Rick Singer, Head of the College Admissions Bribery Scandal, Gets 42 Months in Prison" (NPR: All Things Considered, Jan. 4, 2023), https://www.npr.org/2023/01/04/1146837418/rick-singer-sentenced-varsity-blues-college-admissions-bribery-scandal.

79. 600 U.S. 181, 206-07 (2023) (citations omitted).

80. *Id.* at 214 (citations omitted).

81. *Id.*

82. *Id.* at 216.

83. *Id.* at 218.

84. *Id.* at 230.

85. *Id.* at 347 (Sotomayer, J. dissenting) (citations omitted).

86. *Id.* at 347-48 (citations omitted).

87. *Id.* at 349, n.28 (citations omitted). Sotomayor said that the trial court's found that UNC "rewards different kinds of diversity, and evaluates a candidate within the context of their lived experience" [567 F. Supp. at 658] and that "The parties stipulated, and the evidence shows, that readers evaluate applicants by taking into consideration dozens of criteria" [567 F. Supp. 3d at 659.]. At trial, Sotomayor noted that "even SFFA's expert 'concede[d] that the University's admissions process is individualized and holistic.'" 567 F. Supp. 3d at 662 (finding that UNC "rewards different kinds of

diversity, and evaluates a candidate within the context of their lived experience"); *id.* at 659.

88. *Id.* at 349, n.28 (citations omitted).

89. *Id.* at 353.

90. *Id.* at 386-89, Jackson dissenting.

91. *Id.*

92. *Id.* at 391 (footnotes omitted).

93. *Id.* at 392 (footnote omitted).

94. *Id.* at 393-94 (footnotes omitted).

95. *Id.* at 409-10.

96. Richard Delgado, Affirmative Action as a Majoritarian Device: Or, Do You Really Want to Be a Role Model?, 89 Mich. L. Rev. 1222, 1225 (1991).

97. Kimberly J. Robinson, *How a Federal Right to Education Might Play Out*, Dec. 10, 2019, https://www.youtube.com/watch?v=N1DrbffZ2Yg&t=98s. *See also* Robinson's path-breaking book, "A Federal Right to Education: Fundamental Questions for Our Democracy," which she edited for NYU Press in 2019.

98. Danielle Wingfield, The Resurgence of Massive Resistance, 82 Wash. & Lee L. Rev. (2025 forthcoming).

99. A Disparity Study for the Commonwealth of Virginia Commonwealth, *supra* note 55.

100. United States v. Carolene Products Co., 304 U.S. 144, 152, n.4 (1938).

101. Lester Thurow, *Affirmative Action in a Zero Sum Society, in From Different Shores: Perspectives on Race and Ethnicity in America* 235, 240 (Ronald Takaki ed., 2d ed. Oxford University Press 1994).

102. Hill, *supra* note 1 at 188-89.

## Chapter VIII

1. *See* The Robert E. Lee Mural, USA Civ. War Website, https://www.usa-civil-war.com/Opinions/lee.shtml; *See also* Jonathan I. Lieb, Robert E. Lee "Race," Representation and Redevelopment Along Richmond, Virginia's Canal Walk, 44 Southeastern Geographer, 236-62 (2004).

2. *See* Harry Kollatz Jr., A display along the floodwall in the late '90s resulted in fire and ire, Richmond Magazine (Aug. 18,

2022) available at https://richmondmagazine.com/news/richmond-history/banner-days/.

3. *See* The Robert E. Lee Mural, *supra* note 1, https://www.usa-civil-war.com/Opinions/lee.shtml.

4. Jonathan I. Lieb, Robert E. Lee "Race," Representation and Redevelopment Along Richmond, Virginia's Canal Walk, 44 Southeastern Geographer, 236, at 253 (2004).

5. *See* Scott Tong et al., Five Years After Her Daughter's Death at the Unite the Right Rally, Mother of Heather Heyer Reflects (Here and Now, WBUR, Aug. 12, 2022), https://www.wbur.org/hereandnow/2022/08/12/heather-heyer-mother-charlottesville.

6. *See* Hannah Gais & Michael Edison Hayden, White Nationalists, Other Republicans Brace for "Total War" (Southern Poverty Law Center, Dec. 11, 2022), https://www.splcenter.org/hatewatch/2022/12/11/white-nationalists-other-republicans-brace-total-war; Elizabeth Yates, Domestic Extremism in America: Examining White Supremacist Violence in Light of Recent Attacks, Testimony before U.S. Senate Cmtte. on Homeland Security and Gov't Affairs (June 9, 2022), https://humanrightsfirst.org/library/domestic-extremism-in-america-examining-white-supremacist-violence-in-the-wake-of-recent-attacks/.

7. *See* Max Burns, Republicans Just Can't Stop Calling for Civil War (The Hill: Sept. 6, 2023), https://thehill.com/opinion/campaign/4187490-republicans-just-cant-stop-calling-for-civil-war/; *see also* White Nationalists, Other Republicans Brace for "Total War," *supra* note 6. *See also* the comments of Ohio State Senator George Lang, who issued this warning regarding his view of the consequences if former President Trump lost the election:

> I'm afraid if we lose this one, it's going to take a civil war to save the country, and it will be saved. It's the greatest experiment in the history of mankind, and if we come down to a civil war, I'm glad we got people like ... Bikers for Trump on our side.

*See* Sarah Fortinsky, GOP official at JD Vance rally 'afraid' civil war needed if Trump loses, later recants (The Hill, July 22, 2024).

8. *See* Thomas C. Walker, *The Honey-Pod Tree: The Life Story of Thomas Calhoun Walker "Lawyer Walker of Gloucester"* (John Day Company: 1958); *and see* George Washington Fields, Esq., *Come on Children: The Autobiography of George Washington*

*Fields Born a Slave in Hanover County, Virginia*, 1-65 (Kevin M. Clermont, ed. 2024). In a similar vein, see Rev. Peter Rudolph, *Sketches of a Slave's Life: Or The Peculiar Institution*.

9. A well-known example involving "children of the plantation" is the decades long extraordinarily intimate relationship between the third United States president, Thomas Jefferson, and his enslaved lover, Sally Hemings. *See Thomas Jefferson and Sally Hemings: A Brief Account*, Monticello, https://www.monticello.org/thomas-jefferson/jefferson-slavery/thomas-jefferson-and-sally-hemings-a-brief-account; *see also* Traci Wilson-Kleekamp, Esoteric Clues: It's No Secret That Slaveholders Fathered Children with Their Slaves, Christine Sleeter (Jan. 14, 2019), https://www.christinesleeter.org/esoteric-clues. *See* THULANI DAVIS, MY CONFEDERATE KINFOLK: A TWENTY FIRST CENTURY FREEDWOMAN DISCOVERS HER ROOTS, 95-157 (2006); *see also* Davis' fascinating Family Tree.

10. Harry Kollatz Jr., Banner Days: A Display Along the Flood Walls in the '90s Result in Fire and Ire (Richmond Magazine, Aug. 18, 2022), https://richmondmagazine.com/news/richmond-history/banner-days/.

11. Oliver W. Hill Sr., THE BIG BANG, BROWN V. BOARD OF EDUCATION AND BEYOND: THE AUTOBIOGRAPHY OF OLIVER W. HILL, SR., 100th Birthday Edition xxiv (Jonathan K. Stubbs ed., 2007); ANDREW BUNI, THE NEGRO IN VIRGINIA POLITICS: 1902-1965, 17 (1967).

12. Hill, *supra* note 11 at xxv; THE NEGRO IN VIRGINIA (Va. Writers Program of the Works Projects Admin. of the State of Va.) 239 (1940).

13. Douglas Ramseur, Esq., Motion to Conduct Trial in a Courtroom That Does Not Contain Confederate Symbols, Memorials, and Iconography, October 15, 2018, 16th Judicial Circuit, Louisa County, Virginia.

14. *Id.* at 8.

15. *Id.* at 8-11.

16. Order on Motion regarding removal of Robert E. Lee portrait, p. 2, Nos. CR16000204-01 to -05, CR 16000239-01 to -02 and CR17000054-00 (Louisa Cnty. Ct., 16th Cir. Ct. of Va. Nov. 15, 2019), https://nccred.org/resources/judge-order-on-motion-to-conduct-trial-in-a-courtroom-that-does-not-contain-confederate-symbols

-memorials-and-iconography (letter opinion issued by J. Timothy K. Sanner), on file with author.

17. *Id.*

18. *Id.*

19. *Id.*

20. *Id.*

21. *Id.* at 3.

22. Letter Regarding Renewed Mot. to Conduct Trial in a Courtroom That Does Not Contain Confederate Symbols, Memorials and Iconography at 2-3, *Commonwealth v. Murphy*, Nos. CR16000204-01 to -05, CR 16000239-01 to -02, and CR17000054-00 (Louisa Cnty. Ct., 16th Cir. Ct. of Va. Sept. 10, 2020), https://valawyersweekly.com/wp-content/blogs.dir/1/files/2020/09/020-8-098.pdf (letter opinion and order issued by J. Timothy K. Sanner).

23. *Id.*

24. U.S. Const. Art. III, Sect. 3: "Treason against the United States, shall consist only in levying War against them, or in adhering to their Enemies, giving them Aid and Comfort."

25. David J. Eicher, Robert E. Lee: A Life Portrait, 69-70 (2002), https://ebookcentral.proquest.com/lib/richmond/reader.action?docID=1078713&ppg=49; Brian C. Melton, Robert E. Lee, a Biography, 42-44 (2012), https://ebookcentral.proquest.com/lib/richmond/reader.action?docID=946727&ppg=16. Alan T. Nolan, Lee Considered, 38-46 (1991).

26. Eicher, *supra* note 25 at 73; Melton, *supra* note 25 at 43; Nolan, *supra* note 25 at 38-46.

27. Eicher, *supra* note 25 at 77; Nolan, *supra* note 25 at 38-46.

28. Charles Flood, Lee: Last Years, 51 (Mariner Books 1998) (1981); David J. Eicher, Robert E. Lee: A Life Portrait, 236 (2002), https://ebookcentral.proquest.com/lib/richmond/reader.action?docID=1078713&ppg=236.

29. Melton, *supra* note 25 at 135; Eicher, *supra* note 25 at 235.

30. *See* History of the Law School, https://law.wlu.edu/about-wandl-law/leadership/history; *see also* Charles Bracelen Flood, Lee: The Last Years, p. 204 (First Mariner Books ed. 1998, originally published 1981).

31. Melton, *supra* note 25 at 141-42.

32. Flood, *supra* note 28 at 65-66; The Negro in Virginia, *supra* note 12 at 248; Melton, *supra* note 25 at 136.

33. Flood, *supra* note 28 at 136.

34. Abraham Lincoln, The Gettysburg Address, Nov. 19, 1863.

35. John M. Langston, From the Virginia Plantation to the National Capital: An Autobiography at 299-317 (1894).

36. *Id.* at 347-49.

37. *Id.* at 409-12.

38. *Id.* at 479-80.

39. *Id.* at 474-504.

40. *Id.* at 512.

41. *See* Luis Alejandro Dinnella-Borrego, From the Ashes of the Old Dominion: Accommodation, Immediacy and Progressive Pragmatism in John Mercer Langston's Virginia, 117 Va. Mag. Hist. & Biog, 215, 236-39 (2009).

42. *See* The Brennan Center For Justice, "Voting Laws Roundup: June 2023 https://www.brennancenter.org/our-work/research-reports/voting-laws-roundup-june-2023.

43. John Elrod, Lee as Educator Sought to Heal Wounds, Richmond Times Dispatch, June 9, 1999, at A-17.

44. DESMOND MPILO TUTU, NO FUTURE WITHOUT FORGIVENESS 35 (Rider, imprint of Ebury Press Random House, 1999).

45. Brendan Wolfe, Battle of the Crater, Encyclopedia of Virginia, https://encyclopediavirginia.org/entries/crater-battle-of-the/; No Quarter Expected, No Quarter Given: The Brutal Experience of Black Virginians in Blue in the Battle of the Crater and Beyond (John L. Nau III Center for Civil War History, University of Virginia), https://naucenter.as.virginia.edu/blog-page/916.

46. Battle of the Crater, *supra* note 45.

47. Nelson Blake, William Mahone of Virginia, Soldier and Political Insurgent 72 (1935).

48. *Id.* at 73.

49. *Id.* at 74.

50. *See* Abraham Lincoln, "Proclamation of Amnesty and Reconstruction" (Dec. 8, 1863), https://avalon.law.yale.edu/19th_century/john_chap_01.asp.

51. Blake, *supra* note 47 at 103-09.

52. *Id.* at 106-10.

53. *Id.* at 144-45, n.65.

54. James Tice Moore, Two Paths to the New South, 36-37 (University of Kentucky Press 2014).

55. *Id.* at 22; *See also* John Fabian Chappo, William H. Mahone of Virginia: An Intellectual Biography: 1830-1890, at 181-92 (PhD

Dissertation, 2008). *See also* the prescient insights of Professor Danielle Wingfield in The Resurgence of Massive Resistance, 82 Wash. & Lee L. Rev. (forthcoming 2025).

56. Chappo, *supra* note 55 at 191-92.

57. Virginia State University, About Virginia State University History, https://www.vsu.edu/about/history/. The Negro in Virginia, *supra* note 12 at 234; Luther P. Jackson, Negro Office Holders in Virginia 1865-1895, at 20 (1945); Moore, *supra* note 54 at 89.

58. The Negro in Virginia, *supra* note 12 at 234; Jackson, *supra* note 57 at 20; Blake, *supra* note 47 at 188-90.

59. Edward Ayers, The Promise of the New South: Life After Reconstruction, 46-47 (2007).

60. Chappo, *supra* note 55 at 210.

61. James Tice Moore, Two Paths to the New South, at 103 (University of Kentucky Press 2014).

62. Moore, *supra* note 54 at 103-06.

63. Chappo, *supra* note 55 at 203-206.

64. Langston, *supra* note 35 at 445-501.

65. Chappo, *supra* note 55 at 209; Blake, *supra* note 47 at 232.

66. Flannery O'Rourke, Esq. (University of Richmond School of Law Class of 2022) provided invaluable research for this section: her excellent manuscript helped to frame this section. *See* Flannery O'Rourke, Principal Chief Lewis Downing and the Reconciliation of Cherokee Nation (see the Appendix of this book).

67. Theda Perdue, Slavery and the Evolution of Cherokee Society, 57-58 (1979).

68. *Id.* at 55-59.

69. Scott Vezeau & Ronald Coddington, Here Among the Chiefs: The Cherokee Nations' Lewis Downing, in Gray and Blue, 36 Mil. Images 62, at 64 (2018). *See also* John Bartlett Meserve, Chief Lewis Downing and Chief Charles Thompson, 16 Chronicles of Okla. 315 at 317-18 (1938), http://keetoowahsociety.org/meserve.htm.

70. Vezeau & Ronald, *supra* note 69 at 64.

71. *Id.*; Sean Rowley, Chief Downing Helped Nation Heal After Civil War (Tahlequah Daily Press, Nov. 15, 2017), https://www.tahlequahdailypress.com/news/chief-downing-helped-nation-heal-after-civil-war/article_ecda8870-7c49-58db-89d5-b16345f3bd42.html.

72. 1866 Treaty with the Cherokees, 74 Stat. 799 (Ratified July 27, 1866), https://treaties.okstate.edu/treaties/treaty-with-the-cherokee-1866-0942.

73. Rowley, *supra* note 71; Vezeau & Coddington, *supra* note 69 at 65.

74. Vezeau & Coddington, *supra* note 69 at 65.

## Epilogue

1. Martin Luther King Jr., A Letter from a Birmingham Jail p. 290 (1963) in A Testament of Hope (James Washington ed., 1986) (emphasis added).

2. Oliver W. Hill Sr., THE BIG BANG, BROWN V. BOARD OF EDUCATION AND BEYOND: THE AUTOBIOGRAPHY OF OLIVER W. HILL, SR., 100th Birthday Edition 351 (Jonathan K. Stubbs ed., 2007).

# Selected Bibliography

## Articles


Kimberly L. Alderman, *Slave Artists as Powerful Reality Creators: Taking Responsibility and Rejecting Race Consciousness*, 31 T. MARSHALL L. REV. 261 (2008).

Hilary McD. Beckles, *A "Riotous and Unruly Lot": Irish Indentured Servants and Freemen in the English West Indies, 1644-1713*, 503, Wm. & Mary Q. (1990).

Judith A. Carney, *From Hands to Tutors: African Expertise in the South Carolina Rice Economy*, 67 Agricultural History 1 (Summer 1993).

Judith A. Carney, *Rice Milling, Gender and Slave Labour in Colonial South Carolina*, 153 Past & Present 108 (Nov. 1996).

Judith A. Carney, *The Role of African Rice and Slaves in the History of Rice Cultivation in the Americas*, 26 Human Ecology 525 (Dec. 1998).

Joyce E. Chaplin, *Tidal Rice Cultivation and the Problem of Slavery in South Carolina and Georgia, 1760-1815*, 49 Wm. & Mary Q. Third Series 49 (Jan. 1992).

Karen B. Clay, *Property Rights and Institutions Congress and the California Land Act of 1851*, 59 J. Econ Hist. 122 (1999).

Patricia Cloud & David Galenson, Chinese Immigration and Contract Labor in the Late Nineteenth Century, 24 Explorations in Econ. Hist. 22 (1987).

Peter A. Coclanis, *Distant Thunder: The Creation of a World Market in Rice and the Transformations It Wrought*, 98 Am. Hist. R. 1056 (Oct. 1993).

Okianer Christian Dark, Just My 'Magination, 10 Harv. Black Ltr. J. 21 (1993).

William deBuys, Fractions of Justice, A Legal and Social History of the Las Trampas Land Grant, New Mexico, 56 N.M. Hist. Rev. 71 (1981).

Richard Delgado, *Affirmative Action as a Majoritarian Device: Or, Do You Really Want to Be a Role Model?*, 89 Mich. L. Rev. 1222 (1991).

Jeff Diamant, Faith on the Hill: The Religious Composition of the 118th Congress (Pew Foundation, Jan. 3, 2023), https://www.pewresearch.org/religion/2023/01/03/faith-on-the-hill-2023/.

Luis Alejandro Dinnella-Borrigo, From the Ashes of the Old Dominion: Accommodation, Immediacy and Progressive Pragmatism in John Mercer Langston's Virginia, 117 Va. Mag. Hist. & Biog. 215 (2009).

Diversity Stagnant Among Fortune 100 Leaders Despite Belief That DE&I Is a Key Contributor to Business Success, Reveals Heidrick & Struggles' Route to the Top 2022 Report (Nov. 17, 2022), https://www.prnewswire.com/news-releases/diversity-stagnant-among-fortune-100-leaders-despite-belief-that-dei-is-a-key-contributor-to-business-success-reveals-heidrick--struggles-route-to-the-top-2022-report-301681143.html.

Tom Donnelly, Note, *Popular Constitutionalism, Civic Education, and the Stories We Tell Our Children*, 118 Yale L.J. 948 (2009).

Harold H. Dunham, New Mexico Land Grants with Special Reference to the Title Papers of the Maxwell Grant, 30 N. M. Hist. Rev. 1, 1955.

Malcolm Ebright, The GAO Report: A Whitewash and a Slap in the Face, http://www.southwestbooks.org/gaomeresponse.htm.

Garrett Epps, *To an Unknown God: The Hidden History of Employment Division v. Smith*, 30 Ariz. St. L.J. 953 (1999).

Marilyn J. Ward Ford, *Twenty-Five Years of the Alaska Native Claims Settlement Act: Self Determination or Destruction of the Heritage, Culture, and Way of Life of Alaska's Native Americans?*, 12 J. Envtl. L. & Litig. 305 (1997).

Joan Gundersen, Independence, Citizenship and the American Revolution, 59, in 13 Signs: Journal of Women in Culture and Society (1987).

Cole Harris, *Voices of Disaster: Smallpox Around the Strait of Georgia*, 41 Ethnohistory 591 (1994).

Stacy Hawkins, Trump's Dangerous Judicial Legacy, UCLA L. Rev. (June 13, 2019), https://www.uclalawreview.org/trumps-dangerous-judicial-legacy/ (An excellent discussion of Trump's attempt to make the federal judiciary look more like that of 1789).

F. Michael Higginbotham, *Soldiers for Justice: The Role of the Tuskegee Airmen in the Desegregation of the American Armed Forces*, 8 WM. & MARY BILL OF RTS. J. 273 (2000).

Oliver W. Hill Sr., Reflections on Brown and the Future, 39 U. Rich. L. Rev. 1 (2004).

A.E. Dick Howard, Who Belongs: The Constitution of Virginia and the Political Community, 37 J. Law & Politics 99 (2022).

Carl H. Johnson, *A Comity of Errors: Why John Baker is Only a Tentative First Step in the Right Direction*, 18 Ak. L. Rev. 1 (2001) (providing helpful historical information and discussing Alaska Native American courts' jurisdiction versus that of Alaskan state courts).

George W. Julian "Land Stealing in New Mexico," 145 N. Am. Rev. 17 (1887).

Eric Kades, *The Dark Side of Efficiency:* Johnson v. McIntosh *and the Expropriation of American Indian Lands*, 148 U. Pa. L. Rev. 1065 (2000) (setting forth how American law and policy was directed toward obtaining Indian lands as cheaply as possible–by fair means or foul).

John Kimble, *Insuring Inequality: The Role of the Federal housing Administration in the Urban Ghettoization of African Americans*, 32 LAW D SOC. INQ. 399 (2007).

Clark S. Knowlton, "The Town of Las Vegas Community Grant: An Anglo-American Coup D'etat," Journal of the West, Vol. 19, No. 4.

Rakesh Kochar, Pew Hispanic Center, The Wealth of Hispanic Households: 1996-2002, https://www.pewresearch.org/hispanic/2004/10/18/the-wealth-of-hispanic-households/.

Rakesh Kochhar, Richard Fry & Paul Taylor, Pew Hispanic Center, Twenty to One: Wealth Gaps rise to Record Highs Between Whites, Blacks and Hispanics, https://www.pewresearch.org/social-trends/2011/07/26/wealth-gaps-rise-to-record-highs-between-whites-blacks-hispanics/.

Rebecca Leppert & Drew Disilver, 118th Congress Has Record Number of Women, https://www.pewresearch.org/fact-tank/2023/01/03/118th-congress-has-a-record-number-of-women/.

Jonathan I. Lieb, Robert E. Lee "Race," Representation and Redevelopment Along Richmond, Virginia's Canal Walk, 44 Southeastern Geographer, 236 (2004).

Olga F. Linares, *African Rice (Oryza glaberrima): History and Future Potential*, Proc. Nat. Aca. of Sciences (2002).

Adrienne Mayor, *The Nessus Shirt in the New World: Smallpox Blankets in History and Legend*, 108 J. AM. FOLKLORE 54 (1995).

Martha Menchaca, *Chicano Indianism: A Historical Account of Racial Repression in the United States*, 20 AMERICAN ETHNOLOGIST 583 (1993).

Anthony M. Platt, *The Rise and Fall of Affirmative Action*, 11 NOTRE DAME J. L. ETHICS & PUB. POLICY 67 (1997).

John A. Powell & Marguerite L. Spencer, *Remaking the Urban University for the Urban Student: Talking About Race*, 30 CONN. L. REV. 1247 (1998).

Benjamin Quarles, *Lord Dunmore as Liberator*, WM. & MARY Q. Oct. 1958, at 494.

Yugchen Quin, *A Century-Old "Puzzle": The Six Companies Role in Chinese Labor Importation in the Nineteenth Century*, 12 J. AMERICAN-EAST ASIAN REL. 225 (2003).

Thomas Shapiro, Tatjana Meschede, & Sam Osoro, *The Roots of the Widening Racial Wealth Gap: Explaining the Black-White Economic Divide*, INST. ASSETS & SOC. POL'Y 6 (Feb. 2013).

Elliot Slotnick, Sara Schiavoni, & Sheldon Goldman, *Obama Judicial Legacy*, J. LAW & COURTS 365 (2017).
Justin H. Smith, *The Mexican Recognition of Texas*, 16 AM. HIST. REV. 36 (1910).
NAT'L RESEARCH INSTITUTE, AMERICA BECOMING: RACIAL TRENDS AND THEIR CONSEQUENCES 176 (Neil Smelser, Julius Wilson & Faith Mitchell, eds., Comm'n on Behavioral and Soc. Sciences Vol. 2 2001).
Jonathan K. Stubbs, *A Demographic History of Judicial Appointments by Gender and Race, 1789-2016*, 26 BERKELEY LA RAZA L.J. 92 (2016).
Jonathan K. Stubbs, *America's Enduring Legacy: Segregated Housing and Segregated Schools*, 6 MIN. TRIAL LAWYER 1 (2008).
William Thorndale, *The Virginia Census of 1619*, 155 VIRGINIA MAGAZINE OF GENEALOGY (1995).
Cathy A. Trower & Richard P. Chait, *Faculty Diversity: Too Little For Too Long*, HARV. MAG. Mar.-Apr. 2002 at 33-37.
Maxine Waters, Not Only Should Affirmative Action be Preserved, It Should be Expanded to Eliminate Discrimination, Roll Call (Dec. 8, 1997).
Wendy R. Weiser & Lawrence Norden, Brennan Center for Justice, Voting Law Changes in 2012 (2012).

## Books

1 THEODORE ALLEN, THE INVENTION OF THE WHITE RACE (1994).
2 THEODORE ALLEN, THE INVENTION OF THE WHITE RACE (1997).
AKIL REED AMAR, AMERICA'S CONSTITUTION: A BIOGRAPHY (2005).
CHEROKEE REMOVAL: BEFORE AND AFTER (William L. Anderson, ed. 1991).
Edwin T. Arnold, What Virtue There is in Fire: Cultural Memory and the Lynching of Sam Hose (2009).
JOHN ASHWORTH, SLAVERY, CAPITALISM, AND POLITICS IN THE ANTEBELLUM REPUBLIC VOLUME 2: THE COMING OF THE AMERICAN CIVIL WAR 1850–1861 (2007).
Edward Ayers, The Promise of the New South: Life After Reconstruction (2007).

Alwyn Barr, *Black Texans: A History of African Americans in Texas, 1528–1995* (2d ed. 1996).
DAWN BRADLEY BERRY, THE 50 MOST INFLUENTIAL WOMEN IN AMERICAN LAW (1996).
MIA BAY, TO TELL THE TRUTH FREELY: THE LIFE OF IDA B. WELLS (2009).
MARY FRANCES BERRY, BLACK RESISTANCE WHITE LAW: A HISTORY OF CONSTITUTIONAL RACISM IN AMERICA (2d ed. 1994).
Nelson Blake, William Mahone of Virginia: Soldier and Political Insurgent (1935).
DONALD E. BOLES, MR. JUSTICE REHNQUIST, JUDICIAL ACTIVIST: THE EARLY YEARS (1987).
PAUL BREST ET AL., PROCESSES OF CONSTITUTIONAL DECISIONMAKING: CASES AND MATERIALS (7th ed. 2018).
RICHARD BROOKHISER, GENTLEMAN REVOLUTIONARY: GOUVERNOR MORRIS, THE RAKE WHO WROTE THE CONSTITUTION (2003).
ANDREW BUNI, THE NEGRO IN VIRGINIA POLITICS: 1902-1965 (1967).
ANN BYERS, THE TRAIL OF TEARS: A PRIMARY SOURCE HISTORY OF THE FORCED RELOCATION OF THE CHEROKEE NATION (2003).
Stanley W. Campbell, *The Slave Catchers: Enforcement of the Fugitive Slave Law, 1850-1860* (1970).
JUDITH CARNEY, BLACK RICE: THE AFRICAN ORIGINS OF RICE CULTIVATION IN THE AMERICAS (2001).
PETER CARROLL & DAVID NOBLE, THE FREE AND THE UNFREE: A PROGRESSIVE HISTORY OF THE UNITED STATES (3d ed. 2001).
Samuel Carter, Cherokee Sunset: A Nation Betrayed (1976).
John Fabian Chappo, William H. Mahone of Virginia: An Intellectual Biography: 1830-1890 (PhD Dissertation, 2008).
THE FREEDMAN'S BUREAU AND RECONSTRUCTION (Paul A. Cimbala & Randall M. Miller, eds. 1999).
JAMES CLAPPER, FACTS AND FEARS: HARD TRUTHS FROM A LIFE IN INTELLIGENCE (2018).
DALTON CONLEY, BEING BLACK, LIVING IN THE RED: RACE, WEALTH AND SOCIAL POLICY IN AMERICA (1999).
NANCY C. CURTIS, BLACK HERITAGE SITES: AN AFRICAN AMERICAN ODYSSEY AND FINDER'S GUIDE (1995).
WILLIAM C. DAVIS, LONE STAR RISING: THE REVOLUTIONARY BIRTH OF THE TEXAS REPUBLIC (2004).
William C. Davis, Jefferson Davis and Robert E. Lee: Reluctant "Traitors," in Harold Holzer et al. (ed.), Exploring Lincoln: Great

Historians Reappraise our Greatest President, at 107 (Fordham University Press 2015), https://ebookcentral.proquest.com/lib/richmond/reader.action?docID=3239961&ppg=116.

JOHN W. DEAN, THE REHNQUIST CHOICE: THE UNTOLD STORY OF THE NIXON APPOINTMENT THAT REDEFINED THE SUPREME COURT (2001).

Karen Sacks, *How Did Jews Become White Folks, in* CRITICAL WHITE STUDIES 395-401 (Richard Delgado & Jean Stefanio, eds. 1997).

VINE DELORIA JR., THE EVOLUTION OF FEDERAL INDIAN POLICY MAKING, IN AMERICAN INDIAN POLICY IN THE TWENTIETH CENTURY 239-56 (Vine Deloria Jr., ed., 1985).

Donna Dickerson & David Copeland (eds.), The Reconstruction Era: Primary Documents on the Events 1865-1877 (2003).

JOHN DIPPEL, RACE TO THE FRONTIER: "WHITE FLIGHT" AND WESTWARD EXPANSION (2004).

A Disparity Study for the Commonwealth of Virginia Commonwealth (July 11, 2011).

W.E.B. DU BOIS, THE SOULS OF BLACK FOLK, In Three Negro Classics (Avon Books 1965) (1903).

N. BRUCE DUTHU, AMERICAN INDIANS AND THE LAW (2008).

Malcolm Ebright & Rick Hendricks, The Witches of Abiquiu: The Governor, the Priest, the Genízaro Indians and the Devil, UNM Press, 2006.

Malcolm Ebright, *Land Grants and Lawsuits in Northern New Mexico,* UNM Press (1980).

MALCOLM EBRIGHT, LAND GRANTS AND LAWSUITS IN NORTHERN NEW MEXICO (1994).

Malcolm Ebright, The Tierra Amarilla Grant: A History of Chicanery, Santa Fe, 1980.

Malcolm Ebright, The Embudo Grant: A Case Study of Justice and the Court of Private Land Claims, Journal of the West, July 1980.

Malcolm Ebright (Editor), Spanish and Mexican Land Grants and the Law (A Center for Land Grant Studies Book) (1989).

John Ehle, Trail of Tears: The Rise and Fall of the Cherokee Nation (1988).

David J. Eicher, Robert E. Lee: A Life Portrait (2002), https://ebookcentral.proquest.com/lib/richmond/reader.action?docID=1078713&ppg=49.

John S.D. Eisenhower, So Far from God: the U.S. War with Mexico, 1846-48 (2000).

Nicole Etcheson, Bleeding Kansas: Contested Liberty in the Civil War Era (2004).

Carol Faulkner, Women's Radical Reconstruction: The Freedman's Aid Movement (2004).

Don E. Fehrenbacher, *The Slaveholding Republic : An Account of the United States Government's Relations to Slavery* (2002).

Harvey Fireside, Separate and Unequal: Homer Plessy and the Supreme Court Decision that Legalized Racism (2004).

Colonial American History (Kirsten Fischer & Eric Hinderaker eds., paperback, ed., Blackwell Publishers 2002).

Charles Flood, Lee: Last Years (Mariner Books 1998) (1981).

Eric Foner, Free Soil, Free Labor, Free Men (1995).

Eric Foner, Reconstruction: America's Unfinished Revolution: 1863-1877 (1988).

Grant Foreman, Indian Removal: The Emigration of the Five Civilized Tribes of Indians (1932, 11th printing 1989).

John Hope Franklin & Alfred Moss Jr., From Slavery to Freedom (7th ed. 1994).

Jane M. Friedman, America's First Woman Lawyer: The Biography of Myra Bradwell (1993).

Tim Alan Garrison, The Legal Ideology of Removal: The Southern Judiciary and the Sovereignty of Native American Nations (2002).

Marcia Graham Synott, *Anti-Semitism and American Universities: Did Quotas Following the Jews, in* Anti-Semitism in American History 233-71 (David A. Gerber, ed. 1986).

Getches, Wilkinson and Williams, Federal Indian Law (3d ed. 1993).

Larry S. Gibson, Young Thurgood: The Making of a Supreme Court Justice (2012).

Alan Gilbert, Black Patriots and Loyalists (2012).

Good for Business: Making Full Use of the Nation's Human Capital, Glass Ceiling Commission (1995).

William Goodell, The American Slave Code in Theory and Practice: Its Distinctive Features Shown by its Statutes, Judicial Decisions, and Illustrative Facts (Michigan Historical Reprint Series, 2006).

Stephen L., Hardin, Texian Iliad (1994).

C. Lowell Harris, History and Policies of the Home Owners' Loan Corporation (1951), https://babel.hathitrust.org/cgi/pt?id=uc1.$b37493&seq=41.

John Stephen Henry, New Commentaries on the Law of England (partially founded on Blackstone) at p. 263 (1846), https://books.google.com/books?id=-PNKAAAAYAA-J&pg=PA263&lpg=PA263&dq=an+offence+against+-public+justice,+as+it+keeps+alive+strife+and+conten-tion,+and+perverts+the+remedial+process+of+the+law+in-to+an+engine+of+oppression&source=bl&ots=-Jp2Iu4Jjib&sig=ACfU3UoG2rbfbYyHWd70SzrV4GIX-tYuXZg&hl=en#v=onepage&q=an%20offence%20against%20public%20justice%2C%20as%20it%20keeps%20alive%20strife%20and%20contention%2C%20and%20per-verts%20the%20remedial%20process%20of%20the%20law%20into%20an%20engine%20of%20oppression&f=false.

A. Leon Higginbotham Jr., In the Matter of Color: Race and the American Legal Process: The Colonial Period (1978).

Oliver W. Hill Sr. The Big Bang, Brown v. Board of Education and Beyond: The Autobiography of Oliver W. Hill, Sr., 100th Birthday Edition (Jonathan K. Stubbs, ed. 2007).

Andrew Jackson, First Annual Message to Congress, Dec. 8, 1829, in II Messages and Papers of the Presidents, 1789-1902, 456-9 (James D. Richardson, ed. 1902).

Luther P. Jackson, Negro Office Holders in Virginia 1865-1895 (1945).

Thomas Jefferson, Notes on Virginia (Frank Shuffelton, ed., Penguin Books, 1999) (1785).

Robert C. Johnson, *The Transport of Vagrant Children from London to Virginia; 1618-22*, 137 *in* Early Stuart Studies (Howard Reinmuth Jr., ed. 1970).

Jacqueline Jones, American Work: Four Centuries of Black and White Labor (1998).

Alexander Keyssar, The Right to Vote: The Contested History of Democracy in America (2000).

David L. Kirp, John P. Dwyer & Larry Rosenthal, Our Town: Race, Housing and the Soul of Suburbia (1995).

Richard Kluger, Simple Justice: The History of Brown v. Board of Education and Black America's Struggle for Equality (1976).

Howard Roberts Lamar, The Far Southwest: 1846-1912, New Haven: Yale University Press, 1966.

CHARLES LANE, THE DAY FREEDOM DIED: THE COLFAX MASSACRE, THE SUPREME COURT, AND THE BETRAYAL OF RECONSTRUCTION (2009).

John M. Langston, From the Virginia Plantation to the National Capital: An Autobiography (1894).

MICHAEL LEE LANNING, AFRICAN AMERICANS IN THE REVOLUTIONARY WAR ( 2005).

Kurt T. Lash, THE RECONSTRUCTION AMENDMENTS: THE ESSENTIAL DOCUMENTS (Kurt T. Lash, ed. 2021).

Walter Lord, A Time to Stand (1978).

Martha Manchaca, *Recovering History, Constructing Race: The Indian, Black, and White Roots of Mexican Americans*, The Joe R. and Teresa Lozano Long Series in Latin American and Latino Art and Culture (2001).

DOUGLAS S. MASSEY & NANCY A. DENTON, AMERICAN APARTHEID, SEGREGATION AND THE MAKING OF THE UNDERCLASS (1994).

GENNA RAE MCNEIL, GROUNDWORK: CHARLES HAMILTON HOUSTON AND THE STRUGGLE FOR CIVIL RIGHTS (1983).

DOUGLAS MEED, THE MEXICAN WAR 1846-1848 (2003), https://web-p-ebscohost-com.newman.richmond.edu/ehost/ebookviewer/ebook?sid=891a907a-fb1c-4929-aa51-827f5f3d82d3%40redis&vid=0&format=EB.

Brian C. Melton, Robert E. Lee, a Biography (2012), https://ebookcentral.proquest.com/lib/richmond/reader.action?docID=946727&ppg=16.

Minutes of New Mexico Bar Association, 26 (Jan 6, 1904).

James Tice Moore, Two Paths to the New South (Univ. Kentucky Press 2014).

1 SAMUEL ELIOT MORISON, THE OXFORD HISTORY OF THE AMERICAN PEOPLE (Mentor Book 1972).

2 SAMUEL ELIOT MORISON, 1789 THROUGH RECONSTRUCTION, THE OXFORD HISTORY OF THE AMERICAN PEOPLE (1972).

Thomas D. Morris, Southern Slavery and the Law, 1619–1860.

NAACP, THIRTY YEARS OF LYNCHING IN THE UNITED STATES, 1889-1918 (Arno Press & N.Y. Times 1969) (Apr.1919).

BERNARD C. NALTY, STRENGTH FOR THE FIGHT: A HISTORY OF BLACK AMERICANS IN THE MILITARY (The Free Press 1986).

GARY NASH, FORGOTTEN FIFTH: AFRICAN AMERICANS IN THE AGE OF REVOLUTION (2006).

NATIONAL COMMUNITY REINVESTMENT COALITION, INCOME IS NO SHIELD AGAINST RACIAL DIFFERENCES IN LENDING: A COMPARISON OF HIGH COST LENDING IN AMERICA'S METROPOLITAN AREAS (2007).

Alan T. Nolan, Lee Considered (University of North Carolina Press 1991).

Solomon Northup, Twelve Years a Slave: Narrative of Solomon Northup: A Citizen of New-York, Kidnapped in Washington City in 1841, and Rescued in 1853, From a Cotton Plantation Near the Red River, in Louisiana (2013 Penguin Books Edition) (originally published 1854).

Timothy V. Kaufman-Osborn, *Capital Punishment as Legal Lynching*, *in* LYNCH MOBS TO THE KILLING STATE (Charles Ogletree Jr. & Austin Sarat, eds. 2006).

Theda Perdue, Slavery and the Evolution of Cherokee Society (1979).

JUAN PEREA ET AL., RACE AND RACES: CASES AND RESOURCES FOR A DIVERSE AMERICA (2d ed. 2007).

MICHAEL PERMAN, STRUGGLE FOR MASTERY, DISENFRANCHISEMENT IN THE SOUTH, 1888-1908 (2001).

DAVID M. POTTER, THE IMPENDING CRISIS 1848–1861: THE NEW AMERICAN NATION SERIES (Henry Steele Commager & Richard B. Morris eds., 1976).

FRANCIS P. PRUCHA, AMERICAN INDIAN TREATIES: THE HISTORY OF A POLITICAL ANOMALY (1994).

FRANCIS PAUL PRUCHA, THE GREAT FATHER: THE UNITED STATES GOVERNMENT AND THE AMERICAN INDIANS. VOLUME I (1984).

THEDA PURDUE, MICHAEL D. GREEN & COLIN G. CALLOWAY, THE CHEROKEE NATION AND THE TRAIL OF TEARS (2007).

BENJAMIN QUARLES, THE NEGRO IN THE AMERICAN REVOLUTION (1996 North Carolina Press) (1961).

WILLIAM H. REHNQUIST, THE SUPREME COURT (2001).

Robert V. Remini, Andrew Jackson and his Indian Wars (2001).

2 REPORT OF THE PROCEEDINGS AND DEBATES OF THE CONSTITUTIONAL CONVENTION OF THE STATE OF VIRGINIA 3076-77 (1906).

Richard Rothstein, The Color of Law (2017).

J. Phillipe Rushton, Race Evolution and Behavior (Transaction Pub. 1995).

GEORGE SANTAYANA, THE LIFE OF REASON: OR THE PHASES OF HUMAN PROGRESS (1905).

JEFFERY D. SCHULTZ ET AL., ENCYCLOPEDIA OF MINORITIES IN AMERICAN POLITICS: HISPANIC AMERICANS AND NATIVE AMERICANS, 489 (2000).

George Liele, *An Account of Several Baptist Churches, Consisting Chiefly of Negro Slaves: Particularly of One at Kingston, in Jamaica: And Another at Savannah in Georgia, in* AFRO-AMERICAN RELIGIOUS HISTORY, 43-48 (Milton C. Sernett ed., 2d ed. 1999).

JILL ST. GERMAIN, INDIAN TREATY-MAKING POLICY IN THE UNITED STATES AND CANADA, 1867-1877 (2001).

Phillip J. Schwarz, Twice Condemned Slaves and the Criminal Laws of Virginia, 1705–1865.

OTIS SINGLETARY, THE MEXICAN WAR (1960).

DOUGLAS CHARLES STANGE, BRITISH UNITARIANS AGAINST AMERICAN SLAVERY 1833–1865 (1984).

George Stephanopulis & Christopher Edley Jr., Report on the Review of Federal Affirmative Action Programs, July 19, 1995, https://clintonwhitehouse4.archives.gov/WH/EOP/OP/html/aa/aa-lett.html.

Charles Stewart III, 2016 survey of the Performance of American Elections: Final Report, 22 (2017), Harvard Dataverse, https://dataverse.harvard.edu/file.xhtml?persistentId=doi:10.7910/DVN/Y38VIQ/2NJDL9&version=1.0.

RONALD TANAKI, STRANGERS FROM A DIFFERENT SHORE 392-96 (1989).

Lester Thurow, *Affirmative Action in a Zero Sum Society, in From Different Shores: Perspectives on Race and Ethnicity in America* 235, 240 (Ronald Takaki, ed., 2d ed. Oxford U. Press 1994).

TO SECURE THESE RIGHTS: THE REPORT OF THE PRESIDENT'S COMMITTEE ON CIVIL RIGHTS (1947).

DESMOND MPILO TUTU, NO FUTURE WITHOUT FORGIVENESS (1999).

Underwriting Manual, quoted in MELVIN L. OLIVER AND THOMAS M. SHAPIRO, BLACK WEALTH/WHITE WEALTH: A NEW PERSPECTIVE ON RACIAL INEQUALITY (1995).

Richard D. Valelly, The Two Reconstructions: The Struggle for Black Enfranchisement (2004).
Nicolas Villanueva, The Lynching of Mexicans in the Texas Borderlands (2017).
THE NEGRO IN VIRGINIA (Va. Writers Program of the Works Projects Admin. of the State of Va.) (1940).
Thomas Calhoun Walker, The Honey Pod Tree: The Life Story of Thomas Calhoun Walker "Lawyer Walker of Gloucester" (John Day Company, 1958).
Anthony F.C. Wallace, The Long, Bitter Trail: Andrew Jackson and the Indians (1993).
GILBERT WARE, WILLIAM HASTIE, GRACE UNDER PRESSURE (1984).
David J. Weber, Foreigners in Their Native Land, Albuquerque: University of New Mexico, 1973.
Victor Westphall, The Public Domain in New Mexico: 1854-1891, Albuquerque: University of New Mexico, 1965.
DAVID WILKINS & R. TSIANINA LOMAWAIMA, UNEVEN GROUND: AMERICAN INDIAN SOVEREIGNTY AND FEDERAL LAW (2001).
GEORGE W. WILLIAMS, 1 HISTORY OF THE NEGRO RACE IN AMERICA FROM 1619 TO 1880 (paperback ed., BiblioBazaar 2007) (1883).
ROBERT WILLIAMS, THE AMERICAN INDIAN IN WESTERN LEGAL THOUGHT: THE DISCOURSES OF CONQUEST (1990).
ROBERT A. WILLIAMS, LINKING ARMS TOGETHER: AMERICAN INDIAN TREATY VISIONS OF LAW AND PEACE, 1600-1800 (1997).
GARRY WILLS, NEGRO PRESIDENT: PRESIDENT JEFFERSON AND THE SLAVE POWER (2003).
JOAN HOFF-WILSON, LAW, GENDER AND INJUSTICE: A LEGAL HISTORY OF U.S. WOMEN (1991).
JOHN WOOLMAN, THE JOURNAL OF JOHN WOOLMAN (John G. Whittier, Intro., Osgood and Company 1871) (1774).

## Cases

*Adarand Constructors v. Pena*, 515 U.S. 200 (1995).
*Bakke v. Board of Regents*, 438 U.S. 265 (1978).
*Bolling v. Sharpe*, 347 U.S. 497 (1954).
*Bradley v. Sch. Bd. of Richmond*, 338 F. Supp. 67 (E.D. Va. 1972), *rev'd*, 462 F.2d 1058 (4th Cir. 1973), *aff'd*, 412 U.S. 92 (1973, equally divided Court).

*Brown v. Board of Education*, 347 U.S. 483 (1954).
*Davis v. County School Board of Prince Edward*, 103 F. Supp. 337 (E.D. Va. 1952).
*Dixon v. The State*, Nov. 9, 1896, 20 So. Rep. 839.
*Fisher v. Texas*, 576 U.S. 216 (2016)
*Grutter v. Bollinger*, 539 U.S. 306 (2003).
*Johnson v. McIntosh*, 21 U.S. 543 (1823).
*Loving v. Virginia*, 388 U.S. 1 (1967).
*McLaurin v. Oklahoma State Regents*, 339 U.S. 637 (1950).
*Plessy v. Ferguson*, 163 U.S. 537 (1896).
*Quarles v. Philip Morris, Inc.*, 271 F. Supp. 842 (E.D. Va.1967).
*Prigg v. Pennsylvania*, 41 U.S. 539 (1842).
*Ricci v. DeStefano*, 557 U.S. 557 (2009).
*United States v. Sandoval*, 167 U.S. 278 (1897).
*Dred Scott*, 60 U.S. 393 (1857).
*Shelby County v. Holder*, 133 S. Ct. 2612 (2013).
*Silver v. Ladd*, 74 U.S. 219 (1868).
*Sipuel v. Board of Regents*, 332 U.S. 631 (1948).
*Santa Clara County v. Southern Pacific Railroad Co.*, 118 U.S. 394 (1886).
*Steele v. Louisville & N. R. Co.*, 323 U.S. 192 (1944).
*Students for Fair Admissions, Inc. v. President & Fellows of Harvard Coll. (SFFA)*, 397 F. Supp. 3d 126 (D. Mass. 2019).
*Students for Fair Admissions v. Harvard et al.*, 143 S. Ct. 2141 (2023).
*Sweatt v. Painter*, 339 U.S. at 629 (1950).
*United States v. Carolene Products Co.*, 304 U.S. 144, 152, n.4 (1938).
*United States v. Cruikshank*, 92 U.S. 542 (1876).
*Washington v. Davis*, 426 U.S. 229 (1976).
*Yick Yick Wo v. Hopkins*, 118 U.S. 356 (1886).

## Weblinks

ACLU, Fighting Voter Suppression, https://www.aclu.org/news/by-issue/fighting-voter-suppression.
John Bartlett Meserve, Chief Lewis Downing and Chief Charles Thompson, 16 Chronicles of Okla. 315 (1938), http://keetoowahsociety.org/meserve.htm.

Scott Vezeau & Ronald Coddington, Here Among the Chiefs: The Cherokee Nations' Lewis Downing, *in* Gray and Blue, 36 Mil. Images 64 (2018).

Maggie Masetti, How Many Stars Are in the Milky Way, https://asd.gsfc.nasa.gov/blueshift/index.php/2015/07/22/how-many-stars-in-the-milky-way/.

Peter Cain, How Many Stars Are in the Universe, https://www.universetoday.com/102630/how-many-stars-are-there-in-the-universe/.

John Creamer et al., U.S. Census Bureau, Current Population Reports No. P60-277, Poverty in the United States: 2021, at 36-45 tbl.A-5 (Sept. 2022), https://www.census.gov/content/dam/Census/library/publications/2022/demo/p60-277.pdf.

Reelblack One, *W.E.B. Du Bois: A Recorded Autobiography (1961)*, YouTube (Mar. 4, 2021), https://www.youtube.com/watch?v=Ooa-CzT7NWg.

Fast Facts: Race, Ethnicity of College Faculty, https://nces.ed.gov/fastfacts/display.asp?id=61.

Federal Judicial Center, https://www.fjc.gov/history/judges/search/advanced-search.

"NASA's Webb Takes Star-Filled Portrait of Pillars of Creation," https://www.nasa.gov/feature/goddard/2022/nasa-s-webb-takes-star-filled-portrait-of-pillars-of-creation.

Rakesh Kochhar & Anthony Cilluffo, How Wealth Inequality Has Changed in the U.S. Since the Great Recession, by Race, Ethnicity and Income, https://www.pewresearch.org/fact-tank/2017/11/01/how-wealth-inequality-has-changed-in-the-u-s-since-the-great-recession-by-race-ethnicity-and-income/.

Governor DeSantis Announces Legislative Proposal to Stop W.O.K.E. Activism and Critical Race Theory in Schools and Corporations, https://www.flgov.com/2021/12/15/governor-desantis-announces-legislative-proposal-to-stop-w-o-k-e-activism-and-critical-race-theory-in-schools-and-corporations/.

Virginia Governor Glenn Youngkin Executive Order: 1 Number One (2022), Ending the Use of Inherently Divisive Concepts, Including Critical Race Theory, and Restoring Excellence in K-12 Public Education in the Commonwealth, https://www.governor.virginia.gov/media/governorvirginiagov/

governor-of-virginia/pdf/eo/EO-1-Ending-the-Use-of-Inherently-Divisive-Concepts.pdf.

Marisa Iati, What is critical race theory, and why do Republicans want to ban it in schools?, (May 29, 2021 Wash. Post), https://www.washingtonpost.com/education/2021/05/29/critical-race-theory-bans-schools/.

Joy Reid, Creator of term 'Critical Race Theory' Kimberlé Crenshaw explains what it really is (June 21, 2021, MSNBC), https://www.msnbc.com/the-reidout/watch/%20critical-race-theory-explained-as-not-marxist-or-racist-by-its-leading-scholar-kimberle-crenshaw-115226693996.

Mallory Yu, German far-right groups becoming increasingly organized, says a historian (NPR Dec. 9, 2022), https://www.npr.org/2022/12/09/1141591204/german-far-right-groups-becoming-increasingly-organized-says-a-historian.

Marc Steiner and Bill Fletcher, Jr., The Rise of the Far Right Is a Global Phenomenon (April 4, 2022), https://therealnews.com/the-rise-of-the-far-right-is-a-global-phenomenon.

Choctaw Nation of Oklahoma, http://www.choctawnation.com/history/choctaw-nation-

https://www.globalcitizen.org/en/content/everything-you-need-to-know-south-africa-protests//.

https://time.com/6087699/south-africa-wealth-gap-unchanged-since-apartheid/.

United States Census Bureau: Quick Facts, https://www.census.gov/quickfacts/fact/table/US#.

Federal Judicial Center (Resource for information on the Federal Judiciary), https://www.fjc.gov/history/judges/search/advanced-search.

White male minority rule pervades politics across the US, research shows available at https://www.theguardian.com/us-news/2021/may/26/white-male-minority-rule-us-politics-research.

Election 2016: Restrictive Voting Laws by the Numbers (Brennan Ctr. for Justice, Sept. 28, 2016), https://www.brennancenter.org/our-work/research-reports/election-2016-restrictive-voting-laws-numbers#voterlitigation.

*Thomas Jefferson and Sally Hemings: A Brief Account*, Monticello, https://www.monticello.org/thomas-jefferson/jefferson

-slavery/thomas-jefferson-and-sally-hemings-a-brief-account/.

Robert E. Lee resigns from U.S. Army after Virginia Secedes from the Union (A&E Television Networks, originally published Nov. 13, 2009, last updated Apr. 19, 2021), https://www.history.com/this-day-in-history/lee-resigns-from-u-s-army.

Cassandra Newby-Alexander, Four Hundredth Anniversary Arrival of Africans in Virginia, C-SPAN, Aug. 24, 2019, https://www.c-span.org/video/?463584-5/washington-journal-cassandra-newby-alexander-discusses-arrival-africans-virginia-1619.

Mallory Noe-Payne, 'Honoring the Journey' 400 Years of African-American History at Fort Monroe, NPR Aug. 22, 2019, https://www.wvtf.org/post/honoring-journey-400-years-african-american-history-fort-monroe#stream/0.

"Native Americans and the Homestead Act" (National Park Service), https://www.nps.gov/home/learn/historyculture/native-americans-and-the-homestead-act.htm.

Pocohontas Revealed (PBS/NOVA Documentary, May 7, 2007), https://www.pbs.org/wgbh/nova/pocahontas/.

Edward Prigg, Maryland State Archives, https://msa.maryland.gov/megafile/msa/speccol/sc5400/sc5496/051200/051268/html/051268bio.html.

Guns, Germs and Steel, https://www.pbs.org/gunsgermssteel/variables/smallpox.html.

Africans in America—The Revolutionary War, http://www.pbs.org/wgbh/aia/part2/2narr4.html.

Lord Dunmore's Ethiopian Regiment, http://www.blackpast.org/?q=aah/lord-dunmore-s-ethiopian-regiment.

Battle of the Crater, Encyclopedia of Virginia, https://encyclopediavirginia.org/entries/crater-battle-of-the/.

No Quarter Expected, No Quarter Given: The Bitter Experience of Black Virginians in Blue in the Battle of the Crater and Beyond (John L. Nau III Center for Civil War History, University of Virginia), https://naucenter.as.virginia.edu/blog-page/916.

Thomas Jefferson and Sally Hemings: A Brief Account, https://www.monticello.org/thomas-jefferson/jefferson-slavery/thomas-jefferson-and-sally-hemings-a-brief-account/.

Jewish Virtual Library, Ku Klux Klan, http://www.jewishvirtuallibrary.org/jsource/anti-semitism/KKK.html.

Traci Wilson-Kleekamp, Esoteric Clues: It's No Secret that Slaveholders Fathered Children with Their Slaves, Christine Sleeter (Jan. 14, 2019), https://www.christinesleeter.org/esoteric-clues#.

Harry Kollatz Jr., Banner Days: A Display Along the Flood Walls in the '90's Result in Fire and Ire (Richmond Magazine, Aug. 18, 2022), https://richmondmagazine.com/news/richmond-history/banner-days/.

McLaurin v. Oklahoma State Regents, http://plainshumanities.unl.edu/encyclopedia/doc/egp.edu.025.

George W. McLaurin (1887-1968), https://www.blackpast.org/african-american-history/mclaurin-george-w-1887-1968/.

http://www.archives.gov/education/lessons/desegregation/oklahoma.html.

National Park Service, https://www.nps.gov/natr/learn/history culture/choctaw.htm.

New Voting Restrictions in America, Jan. 7, 2019, https://www.brennancenter.org/sites/default/files/legislation/New%20Voting%20Restrictions.pdf.

New Voting Restrictions in America, Oct. 1, 2019, https://www.brennancenter.org/our-work/research-reports/new-voting-restrictions-america.

Sean Rowley, Chief Downing Helped Nation Heal After Civil War (Tahlequah Daily Press, Nov. 15, 2017), https://www.tahlequahdailypress.com/news/chief-downing-helped-nation-heal-after-civil-war/article_ecda8870-7c49-58db-89d5-b16345f3bd42.html.

The Smithsonian Institute, "The Different Views of Land," https://americanindian.si.edu/nk360/manhattan/different-views-land/different-views-land.cshtml.

*The Trail of Tears*, http://www.pbs.org/wgbh/aia/part4/4h1567.html.

Texas State Historical Society, Consular Services for the Republic of Texas, https://www.tshaonline.org/handbook/entries/consular-service-of-the-republic-of-texas.

Texas State Library and Archives Commission, The 1890s: Black Codes, https://www.tsl.texas.gov/exhibits/forever/endofanera/page2.html.

Christopher Uggans et al., Locked Out 2022: Estimates of People Denied Voting Rights (Oct. 25, 2022 The Sentencing Project), https://www.sentencingproject.org/reports/locked-out-2022-estimates-of-people-denied-voting-rights/.

United States Senate: "Women in the Senate," https://www.senate.gov/reference/Index/Women.htm (number of women serving as United States Senators).

USA Civil War Website, https://www.usa-civil-war.com/Opinions/lee.shtml.

U.S. Congress Continues to Grow in Racial, Ethnic Diversity, https://www.pewresearch.org/fact-tank/2023/01/09/u-s-congress-continues-to-grow-in-racial-ethnic-diversity/.

Nicolas Villanueva, Texas Lynchings of Mexicans in the 1910s, https://www.c-span.org/video/?453206-9/texas-lynchings-mexicans-1910s.

History of Lynchings of Mexican Americans Provides Context for Recent Challenges to U.S. Death Penalty, Death Penalty Information Center, https://deathpenaltyinfo.org/search#stq=history%20of%20lynching%20of%20mexican%20americans&stp=1.

Kyle Walker, French Diplomacy With the Republic of Texas (Texas Historical Commission, Oct. 11, 2022), blog post available at https://www.tshaonline.org/handbook/entries/consular-service-of-the-republic-of-texas.

White Supremacy and Terrorism, http://www.pbs.org/tpt/slavery-by-another-name/themes/white-supremacy/.

Wilderness Society Action Fund, "New Story Map Details How Last Four Years of Trump Oil and Gas Actions Have Impacted Public Lands and Communities, https://www.wildernessaction.org/new-story-map-details-how-last-four-years-trump-oil-and-gas-actions-have-impacted-public-lands-and-communities.

"Without Sanctuary," https://withoutsanctuary.org.

## Popular Media Articles and Reports

Margaret Alexander, Trump Administration Sides Against Harvard in Asian American Affirmative Action Case, (Daily Telegraph, Aug. 30, 2018), https://www.telegraph.co.uk/news/2018/08/30/trump-administration-sides-against-harvard-asian-american-affirmative/.

*Speech: Assistant Attorney General Perez Speaks at the George Washington University Law School Symposium*, U.S. Dep't of Just. Off. of Pub. Aff. (Nov. 16, 2012), https://www.justice.gov/opa/speech/assistant-attorney-general-perez-speaks-george-washington-university-law-school-symposium.

Brentin Mock & Voting Rights Watch, *Voting Rights Haven't Gotten Such Attention Since 1967. What Did We Learn?*, The Nation (Nov. 16, 2012), https://www.thenation.com/article/archive/voting-rights-havent-gotten-such-attention-1965-what-did-we-learn.

*Connolly Introduces FAST Voting Act to Improve Election Process*, Congressman Gerry Connolly: In the News (Nov. 16, 2012), https://connolly.house.gov/news/documentsingle.aspx?DocumentID=419; John Fritze, *Push to Speed Voting Process*.

John Elrod, Lee as Educator sought to Heal Wounds, Richmond Times Dispatch, June 9, 1999 at A-17.

Mike Kirby, Opinion, *Kirby: Crazy in Florida*, Sun Chr. (Nov. 25, 2012), https://www.thesunchronicle.com/opinion/columns/kirby-crazy-in-florida/article_1b806b9c-6850-5dd7-a5a5-ab88894d8e30.html.

John Fritze, *Push to Speed Voting Process*, Balt. Sun A1 (Nov. 24, 2012).

Emily Holden, Jimmy Tobias & Alvin Chang, "Revealed: The Full Extent of Trump's "Meat Cleaver" Assault on U.S. Wilderness (The Guardian, Oct. 26, 2020), https://www.theguardian.com/environment/ng-interactive/2020/oct/26/revealed-trump-public-lands-oil-drilling.

Brian Maffly, New Grand Staircase Plans Greenlight Mining on Lands Trump Stripped from Utah Monument, Salt Lake Trib., Aug. 23, 2019, https://www.sltrib.com/news/environment/2019/08/23/new-grand-staircase-plans/.

Evan Osnos, Tim Kaine's Radical Optimism (The New Yorker Mag., Oct. 17, 2016), https://www.newyorker.com/magazine/2016/10/24/tim-kaines-radical-optimism.

Dennis Overbye, "Webb Telescope Captures New View of 'Pillars of Creation'" (Oct. 24, 2022, N.Y. Times).

Republicans Escalate Their Efforts at Voter Suppression, Oct. 23, 2019 (Wash. Post), https://www.washingtonpost.com/opinions/republicans-escalate-their-strategy-of-voter-sup

pression/2019/10/27/69ceef88-f762-11e9-a285-882a8e386a96_story.html.

50 Years Later, the Couple at the Heart of Loving v. Virginia, Still Stirs Controversy, June 11, 2017, https://www.wgbh.org/news/2017/06/11/news/50-years-later-couple-heart-loving-v-virginia-still-stirs-controversy.

Scott Tong et al., Five Years After Her Daughter's Death at the Unite the Right Rally, Mother of Heather Heyer Reflects (Here and Now, WBUR, Aug. 12, 2022), https://www.wbur.org/hereandnow/2022/08/12/heather-heyer-mother-charlottesville.

Trump Administration Backs Asian Americans in Harvard Affirmative Action Case (NPR News Hour, August 30, 2018), https://www.pbs.org/newshour/nation/trump-administration-backs-asian-americans-in-harvard-case.

Paul Waldman, Voter suppression could become more important to the GOP's election plans than ever," Dec. 18, 2019 (Wash. Post), https://www.washingtonpost.com/opinions/2019/12/18/voter-suppression-could-become-more-important-gops-election-plans-than-ever/.

White Nationalists, Other Republicans Brace for "Total War" (Southern Poverty Law Center, Dec. 11, 2022), https://www.splcenter.org/hatewatch/2022/12/11/white-nationalists-other-republicans-brace-total-war.

Elizabeth Yates, Domestic Extremism in America: Examining White Supremacist Violence in Light of Recent Attacks (Testimony before U.S. Senate Cmtte. On Homeland Security and Gov't Affairs (June 9, 2022), https://humanrightsfirst.org/library/domestic-extremism-in-america-examining-white-supremacist-violence-in-the-wake-of-recent-attacks/.

## Legislative Reports and Statutes

Select Committee to Investigate the January 6th Attack on the United States Capitol, Final Report (117th Congress Second Session, House Report 117-000 December 22, 2022).

William Waller Hening, ed., *The Statutes at Large; Being a Collection of All the Laws of Virginia from the First Session of the Legislature, in the Year 1619* (Philadelphia: R. & W. & G. Bartow, 1823).

Acts of the Commonwealth of Virginia 1642 and 1680, http://www.pbs.org/wnet/slavery/experience/responses/docs1.html.

An Act Concerning Servants and Slaves (1705), https://encyclopediavirginia.org/entries/an-act-concerning-servants-and-slaves-1705/.

1866 Treaty with the Cherokees, 74 Stat. 799 (Ratified July 27, 1866), https://treaties.okstate.edu/treaties/treaty-with-the-cherokee-1866-0942.

An Act to create Office of Surveyor-General of the Public Lands in Oregon . . . and to make Donations to Settlers of the said Public Lands, ch. LXXVI, sect. 4, 9 Stat. 496, 497 (1850) ("Oregon Land Donation Act").

Act to Secure Homesteads to Actual Settlers on the Public Domain, Chap. 75, sec. 1 (1862).

Library of Congress, Homestead Act, https://www.loc.gov/rr/program/bib/ourdocs/homestead.html.

General Allotment Act of 1887, 24 Stat. 388 (1887).

## Presidential Speeches, Vetoes, and Other Actions

Andrew Jackson, First Annual Message to Congress, Dec. 8, 1829, in II Messages and Papers of the Presidents, 1789-1902, 456-9 (James D. Richardson, ed. 1902).

Andrew Johnson, Veto of the Civil Rights Act of 1866 (March 27, 1866), *in* VOL. VI A COMPILATION OF MESSAGES AND PAPERS OF THE PRESIDENTS OF THE UNITED STATES, 405 (James D. Richardson, ed. 1902).

Abraham Lincoln, Gettysburg Address, Nov. 19, 1863.

Abraham Lincoln, "Proclamation of Amnesty and Reconstruction" (Dec. 8, 1863), https://avalon.law.yale.edu/19th_century/john_chap_01.asp.

## Constitutions

The Constitution of the United States.

Constitution of Virginia (June 29, 1776), http://www.nhinet.org/ccs/docs/va-1776.htm.

## Speeches

Martin Luther King Jr., "I Have A Dream" (Speech Delivered August 28, 1963), Washington, DC, transcript available at https://www.npr.org/2010/01/18/122701268/i-have-a-dream-speech-in-its-entirety.

## Biblical Texts

Gospel of John 8:32.

## Letters

Lord Acton, *Letter to Bishop Mandell Creighton, 1887*, in 1 LIFE AND LETTERS OF MANDELL CREIGHTON (Louise Creighton, ed. 1906).

Letter from Abigail Adams to John Adams (Mar. 31, 1776), Nat'l Archives: Founders Online, https://founders.archives.gov/documents/Adams/04-01-02-0241.

John Adams to Abigail Adams, April 14, 1776, National Archives, https://founders.archives.gov/documents/Adams/04-01-02-0248.

John Adams to James Sullivan (May 26, 1776), National Archives, https://founders.archives.gov/documents/Adams/06-04-02-0091.

Patrick Henry, Letter to Robert Pleasants, Jan. 18, 1773, https://press-pubs.uchicago.edu/founders/documents/v1ch15s7.html.

Thomas Jefferson to Jared Sparks, Feb. 4, 1824, http://www.let.rug.nl/usa/presidents/thomas-jefferson/letters-of-thomas-jefferson/jefl276.php.

Martin Luther King Jr., A Letter from a Birmingham Jail p. 290 (1963), in A Testament of Hope (James Washington, ed. 1986).

## Miscellaneous Court Orders and Letter Opinions

Douglas Ramseur, Esq., Def.'s Mot. to Conduct Trial in a Courtroom That Does Not Contain Confederate Symbols, Memorials and

Iconography at 7, Commonwealth v. Murphy, Nos. CR16000 204-01 to -05, CR 16000239-01 to -02, and CR17000054-00 (Louisa Cnty. Ct., 16th Cir. Ct. of Va. Oct. 15, 2018), https://nccred.org/resources/motion-to-conduct-trial-in-a-court room-that-does-not-contain-confederate-symbols-memo rials-and-iconography (filed by Douglas A. Ramseur, Esq., Capital Defender).

Louisa County Circuit Court Letter Opinion regarding removal of Robert E. Lee portrait (Nov. 15, 2019).

Letter Regarding Renewed Mot. to Conduct Trial in a Courtroom That Does Not Contain Confederate Symbols, Memorials and Iconography at 2-3, Commonwealth v. Murphy, Nos. CR16000204-01 to -05, CR 16000239-01 to -02, and CR17000054-00 (Louisa Cnty. Ct., 16th Cir. Ct. of Va. Sept. 10, 2020), https://valawyersweekly.com/wp-content/blogs .dir/1/files/2020/09/020-8-098.pdf (letter opinion and order issued by J. Timothy K. Sanner).

Order on Mot. Regarding Removal of Robert E. Lee Portrait at 2, Commonwealth v. Murphy, Nos. CR16000204-01 to -05, CR 16000239-01 to -02, and CR17000054-00 (Louisa Cnty. Ct., 16th Cir. Ct. of Va. Nov. 15, 2019), https://nccred.org/resources/judge-order-on-motion-to-conduct-trial-in-a -courtroom-that-does-not-contain-confederate-symbols-me morials-and-iconography (letter opinion issued by J. Timothy K. Sanner) (on file with author).

# Index